Rememberin

Remembering John Adams

The Second President in History, Memory and Popular Culture

Marianne Holdzkom

McFarland & Company, Inc., Publishers
Jefferson, North Carolina

This book has undergone peer review.

Library of Congress Cataloguing-in-Publication Data

Names: Holdzkom, Marianne, 1962– author.
Title: Remembering John Adams : the second president in history, memory and popular culture / Marianne Holdzkom.
Description: Jefferson, North Carolina : McFarland & Company, Inc., Publishers, 2023. | Includes bibliographical references and index.
Identifiers: LCCN 2023001745 | ISBN 9781476683430 (paperback : acid free paper) ∞ ISBN 9781476649207 (ebook)
Subjects: LCSH: Adams, John, 1735–1826—Influence. | Adams, John, 1735–1826—In mass media. | Adams, John, 1735–1826—In literature. | Presidents—United States—Historiography. | Memory—United States.
Classification: LCC E322 .H654 2023 | DDC 973.4/4092 [B]—dc23/eng/20230201
LC record available at https://lccn.loc.gov/2023001745

British Library cataloguing data are available

ISBN (print) 978-1-4766-8343-0
ISBN (ebook) 978-1-4766-4920-7

Front cover image: John Adams, circa 1800/1815, oil on canvas:
73.7 × 61 cm (29 × 24 in.), Gilbert Stuart (painter)
American, 1755–1828 (Gift of Mrs. Robert Homans,
image courtesy National Gallery of Art. Public Domain)

Printed in the United States of America

*McFarland & Company, Inc., Publishers
Box 611, Jefferson, North Carolina 28640
www.mcfarlandpub.com*

Dedicated to the memory of KELLY COBBLE (1962–2022),
curator at the Adams National Historical Park,
and to my husband, ALBERT J. CHURELLA

Table of Contents

Preface
and Acknowledgments

I first became interested in John Adams in the summer of 1976. The Bicentennial celebration was in full swing and one of the networks broadcast the film version of *1776*. I had never seen the show and did not know what to expect, but I was instantly intrigued by the John Adams (played with flair by William Daniels) I saw coming alive. I had heard of John Adams in my schooling and knew that he had served on the Declaration committee, for I was one of those lucky students who had an excellent history teacher in middle school. I still remember him telling us the story of the Declaration. Yet beyond that, I knew little about Adams. After seeing him characterized in *1776*, I wanted to know more. I often say that William Daniels's portrayal of Adams is the reason I eventually pursued history as my profession.

From that moment to this, I have never been able to fully escape John Adams. In college, my "fun reading" consisted of books on John Adams. I started with Catherine Drinker Bowen's *John Adams and the American Revolution*, then progressed to Page Smith's two-volume biography. I did not ignore the primary sources, either, devouring *The Book of Abigail and John: Selected Letters of the Adams Family, 1762–1784* edited by L.H. Butterfield. Even though I was pursuing a drama degree at that point in my career, John Adams was always with me. I will admit, I developed a soft spot for him.

When I decided to pursue graduate degrees in history, I wrote my master's thesis on John and Samuel Adams, concentrating on their different approaches to the coming of the American Revolution. My original plan was to expand this work and examine how these two cousins, who had worked so well together, came to disagree on the vision for the new nation. However, as I worked toward my Ph.D. and needed a dissertation topic, I decided that I needed to try something more in line with the trends of the 1990s. That work was on the developing of historical memory,

1

although John Adams was not a part of the research. He was never far from my mind, however.

Now, after some twenty-five years, I have returned to him to do the work I have always wanted to do. Because of my fascination with and love for *1776*, I wanted to see how many other ways John Adams has been remembered in popular culture. When I began my research, I had no idea how often he appears! I would be happy to report to Mr. Adams that, for a man who thought he would not be remembered, he has not been forgotten by any means. Yet just how has he been remembered by historians and creative artists? Would he be pleased? That is a difficult question to answer. It is safe to say that he would not be surprised by his various depictions, nor would he be shocked to learn that there is still no monument to him in Washington, D.C. Despite this fact, various people in numerous ways have found him worth remembering. That fact is the subject of the following pages. Thank you, William Daniels—and John Adams—for bringing me here.

The decision to write this book was my own, but to paraphrase a famous saying, it takes a village to write a manuscript. I never could have completed this work without the following people and organizations.

I have given several conference papers on John Adams over the years, and I am grateful to the panel chairs who gave me those opportunities. I am especially grateful to Dr. Tiffany Knoll for accepting two of these papers and indulging my interest in such an unlikely Founding Father. In addition, Tiffany wrote a letter of support for my application to the Tenured Faculty Enhancement Program at KSU. Thanks for the boosts, Tiffany!

This work was made possible in part with the support of the Center for Excellence in Teaching and Learning at Kennesaw State University. Their Tenured Faculty Enhancement Program gave me the freedom to complete my research and writing on this manuscript. I am also indebted to the Department of History and Philosophy for numerous travel grants and to Dr. Alice Pate, Dr. David Parker, and Dr. Bryan McGovern for their encouragement and support. I am also grateful to Rene Westland and other members of the staff in our department for making my life easier at every turn.

Digitized collections are an invaluable tool and—especially during a pandemic—a gift beyond measure. I relied heavily on the digital edition of the Adams Family Papers, courtesy of the Massachusetts Historical Society, as well as Founders Online provided by the National Archives. I am grateful to the countless souls who made these collections possible.

Dealing with artistic works can sometimes be tricky. Getting permissions to quote certain pieces is vital to a book of this nature. I am grateful to Maarten Kooij, Senior Vice-President for Business Affairs at ICM Partners, for *1776* guidance and to Dennis Aspland, Acting Agent for the Estate of William Gibson, Aspland Management, for permission to quote from *American Primitive*. I would also like to thank actor James Beaman for allowing me to quote from his blog, "Becoming John Adams." I wish I could have seen his performance.

Several people have read portions of this manuscript, checking for typos and grammatical errors as well as comprehension. I am grateful to Dr. Mark Stevens for reading the Ezra Pound section of the literature chapter. He sensed my unease with this poet and graciously stepped in to reassure me on the content. Former students Mary Baldwin and Miranda Clody offered invaluable proofreading services on several chapters, Miranda taking on the two historiography chapters in particular.

I am indebted to Dr. Julie Newell who, in addition to always believing in my abilities, volunteered to read the entire rough draft, and offered invaluable suggestions on organization and content before my initial submission to my publisher. She made the manuscript stronger, and I am grateful.

Janelle Runge read the first version of the *1776* chapter and other portions of the book. More than that, she has been my biggest cheerleader. She more than anyone, understands what this project means to me. Aside from me, she has lived with it the longest (how many times have we watched *1776* together?). Thanks for coming on the journey with me from college to now! Susan Webb also provided proofreading services, but in addition to that, she accompanied me on my research trip to Quincy, Massachusetts, and served as my unofficial assistant there. She took notes, asked questions, snapped pictures, and trudged through the Adams history with good humor and grace. I would have been a wreck without her presence and can never thank her enough!

Doing research and traveling during a pandemic is challenging to say the least. Fortunately, I have had the help of several people in Quincy, Massachusetts—both in person and remotely—with my research. I am deeply indebted to Bill Westland at First United Parish Church for providing me with any number of historical vignettes about the church and the final resting places of John and Abigail. Not only is he a font of information, but ever since I first contacted Bill concerning the wreath-laying ceremonies, he has also been a great correspondent and a fantastic cheerleader. I am also grateful to Dr. Edward Fitzgerald, executive director of the Quincy Historical Society, for his time and expertise. Thanks also to Alexandra Elliot, curator of the Quincy Historical Society, and Corinne Waite also of the Quincy Historical Society for their assistance in tracking down information about various statues in town.

I am grateful to several staff members at the Adams National Historical Park for their assistance and enthusiasm for my project. Superintendent Marianne Peak has been supportive throughout my research, writing, and revision process. She offered valuable insight and suggestions for my chapter on the park. I am also grateful to Alison M. Kiernan and Richard Shaner for talking with me about John Adams and providing their own perspectives. Their quotes in this book are golden!

Since 2019, I have had the wonderful support of McFarland. They, too, have expressed enthusiasm for this book from my first contact with them. I am grateful to Adam Phillips, sales manager, who discussed my sketchy outline at the Organization of American Historians meeting in 2019 and said, "A project like this is our bread and butter!" From then on, I have had a great experience with McFarland. I am especially grateful to Layla Milholen, Managing Editor, Operations, whose reassurance and understanding through the challenges of Covid-19 have been invaluable. My thanks also goes to the two anonymous readers of my rough draft who offered helpful suggestions to make the book stronger. Everyone associated with McFarland has been wonderful and I thank them all!

Writing this book could not have happened without the love and support of my family and friends. They have served as advocates who helped to keep me going on this project. For all of you who have asked "when will the book be out?" and "where can I buy a copy?" I am so grateful. I am especially indebted to my big brother, Stephen P. Holdzkom, for being the best sibling a sister could want and for providing me with my very own portrait of John Adams to keep me motivated, one I am happy to have. Finally, I could not have made this journey without some much-needed distraction. For this, I especially want to thank Bryan F. Black, conductor, and members of the Georgia Symphony Orchestra Chorus for cheering me on and helping to feed my soul. Making music with all of you has been a wonderful diversion from the work!

The assistance of a supportive home has also been invaluable to me and part of that has come from a lovable Lab-Pit mix named Lindsey. She always knows when I've worked enough and gives me joy every single day. Even when the writing was not going well, she looked at me with love and provided much-needed snuggles.

Last, but certainly not least, this book is dedicated to two people: first, to the memory of Kelly Cobble (1962–2022), Curator at the Adams National Historical Park. From our first conversation, as I was planning my initial trip to Quincy, Kelly was helpful and enthusiastic about my project. Her passion for her job and her professionalism as well as her humor made her a joy to work with. She has left a huge hole at the park she loved. I am grateful that I had a chance to work with her, if only briefly. I could not have finished this manuscript without her help. I only wish that she could have seen the book in print. Rest in peace, Kelly.

Finally, I dedicate this book also to my husband, Dr. Albert J. Churella. I do not have the words to express what his love and support has meant to me as I have struggled through the years with this project. I have also been inspired by his example and his work ethic. In addition, he has made sure that I take breaks when I need to and has kept me well fed! To paraphrase John Adams, I am, with love that can only end with my life, and I hope not then, your wife and friend. Thank you for everything!

Introduction

In 1774, two men, both lawyers and brilliant in their own ways, stand on a hill overlooking Casco Bay in present-day Maine. They have come to a crossroads in their long friendship. One is firmly on the side of the crown in its dispute with its North American colonists. The other is squarely on the side of the colonials and their rights as Englishmen. He is so committed, in fact, that he will be attending an historic continental meeting to discuss the imperial crisis. One man begs the other, his dear friend, not to attend the meeting. He warns that the colonies cannot win against the might of England. The other man, displaying a passion that will define his career, tells his friend that he must attend the Congress, that "Swim or sink, live or die, survive or perish, [I am] with my country...."

This was a heartbreaking moment for both men, for it will be the last time they see each other until the 1780s. By this time, the first friend is a forgotten man, living as best he can in England. The other has been a major mover in the American Revolution and now represents the new United States at the Court of St. James's.[1] No stage or screen drama has included this dramatic moment between friends—Jonathan Sewall and John Adams—even though it is mentioned in many biographies of Adams. Scholars have correctly seen it as a moment that defined John Adams and his commitment to the cause of American liberty. It also demonstrated a trait that is lost in many depictions of John Adams: his deep love for and loyalty to his friends.

Why this scene between friends does not appear in popular culture treatments of John Adams is baffling, given the drama of the moment. Yet it could be that such an episode does not fit into the crusty persona these formats always emphasize. While there are moments in the depictions of John Adams that show his human side, for the most part, his love for his friends and the pain over losing them rarely, if ever, appears—even though one of the more fascinating aspects of his life for many people was his remarkable friendship with Thomas Jefferson.

Few of our founders were easy people to know or love. They were all flawed and often did not work and play well with each other. Yet some have always stood out as elegant, sophisticated, and charming. Others are known for overcoming nearly impossible obstacles to be found worthy of monuments and places on currency. John Adams does not fit into any of these categories.

Very few people doubt John Adams's contributions to the founding of the United States. However, he is often best remembered for his awkward manner, his lack of tact, his poor judgment as president, and as "obnoxious and disliked," to quote the running joke in the musical *1776*. While the last is a paraphrase of a famous self-description, it is easy to see why he is so often overlooked in the pantheon of the founders.

John Adams has, however, been fascinating to historians and creative artists. There are countless biographies of him. He has been the subject of a miniseries based upon one of those works. He—like Alexander Hamilton—is the subject of a Broadway musical, later made into a film. Although the show's title does not bear his name, he is clearly the star from the beginning of the show to the end. In addition, he has appeared in novels, plays, and television shows from time to time. There is something about the man that draws and keeps our attention.

The intention of this work is not to write yet another biography of John Adams. Many scholars have done this to varying degrees of success. Rather, it will examine how John Adams has been *remembered*, not just by historians, but also by creative artists who found him worthy of their attention and by the National Park Service. Scholars and journalists alike have observed that the Founders have reentered the spotlight since the early 2000s. Evan Thomas of *Newsweek* put a name to the phenomenon: "Founders Chic." Interestingly enough, Thomas used this phrase in an article in which he discussed, among other works, David McCullough's blockbuster biography of none other than John Adams.[2] Historian Gregory H. Nobles noted that the term coined by Evans has been embraced by scholars as well and there are any number of articles that use the phrase when discussing the success of the Broadway musical, *Hamilton*.[3]

What has emerged in the early 21st century is a renewed interest in the Founders. Given that 2026 marks the 250th anniversary of the Declaration of Independence, it is easy to understand why scholars and the public alike are reassessing the American Revolution once again. Understanding how the nation has remembered the Founding generation to date is key to exploring the ways in which the nature of the American Revolution is redefined in different eras. For this reason, studying both history and the memory of it is vital.

The concept of history and memory has become increasingly popular amongst scholars. It also takes on many different names and definitions.

Some schools of thought use the term "adaptation" to include memory studies. Others discuss "representation." In other words, defining what we mean by "history and memory" can be muddy. Catharine R. Stimpson, Chair of the New York Council for the Humanities in 1986, summed up the problem this way: "Some people think that interpretation is the shore over which the waves of history gather, fall, and wash," she suggested. "Others think that history is the shore over which the waves of interpretation gather, fall, and wash." She continued, "Both schools of thought are right. For history and our interpretations of it, the actions of the past and our perceptions of those actions in the present, constantly collide, and then, like sand and water, intermingle."[4] This is why commemoration studies are tricky. Still, the study of memory offers us a new perspective on the historical events that have shaped us and on the people who participated in those events. Studying *how* we remember a person or event reveals a great deal about the ways in which the United States sees itself in the present day. It also demonstrates that historical accuracy is not always a priority. Artistic license allows for playing fast and loose with the facts. In many cases, writers will rearrange, omit, conflate, or create to add drama. Rarely is this done with any agenda in mind, although there are exceptions. What is interesting in doing memory studies is that historical accuracy is only one part of the equation.

Placing a piece in its proper context, understanding the time in which it was created, and seeing messages for the present in the re-telling of the past are all equally important aspects of the field of history and memory. Scholars have studied these various aspects over decades. In fact, academics have often cited a concept that was iterated as early as 1918 when Van Wyck Brooks coined the term "usable past." Brooks was a literary historian and wrote about the state of literature in the United States during his time. He argued, "The present is a void, and the American writer floats in that void because the past that survives in the common mind of the present is a past without living value." That being the case, Brooks asked if this was the only past to which writers could look. If, in fact, another past is needed, is it possible to create one? "Discover, invent a usable past we certainly can," he concluded.[5]

Given Brooks' attention to the past and the reconstruction of it, it is not surprising that scholars in other fields would find his concept intriguing. Historians concerned with memory studies have borrowed Brooks' term on several occasions, finding it compelling in contemplating the ways in which past events are remembered.[6] Even without using Brooks' term, scholars have often discussed how the past is reconstructed for the present. Film historian Peter C. Rollins, for example, emphasized the role of Hollywood in creating ideas about the past. "Not satisfied with merely depicting the past," Rollins argued, "Hollywood has often attempted to influence history by turning out films consciously designed to change public attitudes toward matters of social or political importance."[7] Other examples include the works of historians Thomas L. Connelly and William Garrett Piston who studied the images of Civil War generals Robert E. Lee and James Longstreet respectively in order to understand their places and influences on southern history and American society.[8]

Scholars interested in the American Revolution have often focused on this idea of a usable past and have discussed the ways in which this pivotal event has been molded to meet the needs of the present. Historian Michael Kammen, in his influential work *A Season of Youth: The American Revolution and the Historical Imagination*, studied what he termed "the problem of tradition" and noted, "I simply have in view the comparative lack of shared historical interest in the United States or the weakness with which *national* tradition … has been felt, perceived and perpetuated." Kammen also argued for the value of examining popular culture by stating, "We can never fully know the intricacies through which a society weaves a knowledge of its origins and development; but we are likely to learn more from the gossip of popular culture than from the gospel of academe."[9] Kammen offered a model on how to study the creation of a usable past by examining paintings, iconography, and historical novels concerning the American Revolution.

In the 21st century, scholars have considered the analysis of memory and the United States' founding moment in interesting and creative ways. In 2006, for example, historian François Furstenberg published *In the Name of the Father: Washington's Legacy, Slavery, and the Making of a Nation*. His book studied the creation of the idea of the "Founding Fathers" alongside the existence of slavery and the rise of American nationalism.[10] Historian Andrew M. Schocket explored the use of the American Revolution in the nation's culture, politics, and society. Schocket hoped to "untangle the ways that battles over the contemporary memory of the American Revolution serve as proxies for America's contemporary ideological divide."[11] Michael D. Hattem, was interested in how colonists used British history to advance the cause of their revolution. He argued that in order to "understand the creation of the United States as a nation it is necessary to understand the ways in which colonists shed their previously shared British past and created a newly shared American past." Hattem posited that shared histories are created and that "uncovering how shared pasts were constructed by revolutionary Americans will tell us much about how they understood the revolutionary moment in which they were living and why they navigated as they did the twists and turns along the way."[12] Finally, an interesting addition to the historiography of the American

Revolution in memory came from historian Keith Beutler who examined the many ways Americans in the 19th century used historical relics such as locks of George Washington's hair to create a usable past.[13]

In addition to George Washington, historians have examined other figures from the revolutionary period and how they have been remembered. Abigail Adams was the subject of an historiographical essay called "The Abigail Industry" in 1988. Written by Edith B. Gelles, an expert on Mrs. Adams, the article focused on the many biographies that had been written about her and the ways in which she had been manipulated to fit a certain image for a particular time. While Gelles briefly mentioned *Those Who Love*, the biographical novel by Irving Stone, her main interest was the agenda of scholars who had depicted Abigail in various ways.[14]

Historian Alfred F. Young examined the memory of the Boston Tea Party by writing a study of one of the lesser known participants. While analyzing the life of George Robert Twelves Hewes and how he remembered the Boston Tea Party, Young became intrigued with which characters from the Revolution are remembered and why. He wished to investigate "who decides whose heroes and heroines school children learn about, what statues and monuments are erected, what historic buildings are saved, and what events are commemorated."[15] Most recently, historian Mitch Kachun investigated the ways in which various groups and people have used the memory of Chrispus Attucks. Since the facts surrounding Attucks's life are scant, Kechun called him "a virtual blank slate upon which different groups and individuals have inscribed diverse meanings to suit a wide range of political and cultural agendas."[16]

These works, and many like them, emphasize the importance of representation, adaptation, and revisionism in understanding how people remember and how they create a usable past. Whether examining a large event or the individuals involved in it, scholars have gained valuable insight into the perceptions of the past. In order to add to this scholarship, the present study will focus on the various ways in which John Adams has been depicted in history and culture, examining the different approaches by which he has been remembered in the usable past of the American Revolution and the early nation. In addition, it will argue that along with a usable past, the many ways in which Adams has been remembered constitute the creation of a "usable John Adams."[17] Whether he is touted as a model for certain generations of Americans or as a counter to more congenial founders, Adams has always served a purpose in the many genres in which he appears.

Because of the nature of this work, the events of John Adams's life, as interesting as they may be, are not the culmination of his story. While the book discusses historical accuracy in the works considered, what is more important here is that a man who was sure he would be forgotten by his country, *has*, in fact been remembered and in many different genres. The ways in which artists have done this and the aspects of his personality that they chose to emphasize give us a new way of understanding him and the memory surrounding the American Revolution. Even when Adams does not fit neatly into the constructed past created by later generations of Americans, he is present in histories and popular culture, offering an intriguing counterpoint to Washington, Jefferson, or other members of the founding generation. In order to understand Adams's place in historical memory, this book will focus on several different genres.

The first part of this study is a brief narrative of Adams's life and then turns to the historians' and biographers' views of the man. The vast array of biographies and the focuses they take is an essential element, for scholars, too, create depictions of historical characters. Working with the same facts, they come to many different conclusions or choose to emphasize certain elements of a person's life. For some Adams biographers, his Puritan ancestry and New England background provide the center of their studies. For others, his brilliant political mind captivates them. Still others create in Adams a model of a certain philosophy or ideology. Some are fascinated with his personality, his mental health, or his physical ailments. Whatever the scholar's focus, the result is inevitably a sketch or representation of the man. While there are some common elements that run through all these scholarly biographies, the thesis of each work creates a different representation of the Founder. These works provide excellent context for the many ways in which John Adams has been depicted in popular culture.

With the scholarly backdrop in place, the focus will turn to culture and popular culture, with an analysis of poetry, novels, plays, films, and television shows in which Adams has been portrayed. Two of these works—the musical *1776* and the HBO miniseries based upon David McCullough's biography—receive special attention herein. The musical and the miniseries placed Adams center stage and have had the most impact on his memory.

In the last two chapters, the book turns to Adams's hometown: Quincy, Massachusetts. This city exudes the Adams legacy and has come to embrace it with pride. At the center of the town's remembrance is the Adams National Historical Park. This National Park Service site preserves the birthplace of John Adams, the small saltbox house in which he and Abigail lived upon their marriage (the birthplace of John Quincy Adams), and the home that Adams shared with Abigail after his return from his European diplomatic missions—a house that he named Peacefield. While the site is dedicated to the entire Adams family, John Adams is considered the founder of that dynasty. The John Adams narrative, as told through public history at this park, provides yet another perspective on his life and legacy. The book also discusses Adams's burial place at United First Parish Church—a part of the Adams park.

Finally, no study of John Adams in public history would be complete without discussing the one large way that the second president has *not* been remembered. There is no monument to John Adams in Washington, D.C. The reasons for this vary. He is not considered by many to have been one of our better presidents and he is saddled with the legacy of the Alien and Sedition Acts, his signing of which demonstrated an unfortunate lapse of judgment during his presidential administration. Still, there have been efforts to create a monument to him that, as of yet, have been unsuccessful. Interestingly enough, Adams predicted that there would be no monuments to him. He was not altogether correct in this, but if one is looking in Washington, D.C., his prediction, thus far, has been accurate. Whether or not this changes in the future, it is still important in a history and memory study to discuss the ways in which an historical character has not been commemorated.

As the events of the American Revolution unfolded, John Adams understood the importance of the times in which he lived. He often expressed his awe and his anxiety to his family and friends. He was also keenly aware of the importance of posterity, as were most of the Founders, and his vision never strayed far from what future generations would think of the actions he took. This explains, in part, his oft-repeated lament that the country would not remember him. "Mausoleums, statues, and monuments will never be erected to me," he wrote and added—not altogether convincingly—"I wish them not."[18] While he protested he did not want monuments, the idea that there would be none stung. Whether or not he would be happy with the attention he has received from scholars and artists, it is safe to say that he has, in fact, been remembered. One of the recurring themes in Adams biographies is his neglect. Over and over, scholars lament the lack of attention paid to Adams and try to convince their readers that he deserves their notice. Upon studying the many biographies and fictional depictions of John Adams, this refrain does not ring true. While John Adams may have disappeared for a time from the historical narrative of the American Revolution, he has come roaring back as a key player.

The issue in John Adams remembrance is no longer one of neglect, but rather the scrutiny given to Adams that the other Founders have escaped. The depiction of John Adams's personality that has emerged over the years—a rather one-dimensional caricature of the man—is not entirely satisfying. This is not to say that there is a certain way in which Adams *should* be remembered. However, as with every other human being who has ever lived, John Adams was multi-layered. He was crusty but warm, intelligent but volatile, awkward but effective, blunt but easily wounded by the words and actions of others. He loved—and hated—deeply. No representation of Adams has failed to observe his flaws. What is sometimes missing is the depth of his private character. He could act boldly and that is apparent, but he could also embrace warmly. He could forgive and did so often in his later years. He was not a pessimist, but a realist. Even though he had great hopes for the future of the nation he helped to create, his pragmatic view of human nature ran counter to the more idealistic attitudes of Thomas Jefferson and others like him. As a result, he does not always fit into either the usable past created around the American Revolution or the idea of American Exceptionalism.

Rarely does any one piece of scholarly work or popular culture capture all the nuances of John Adams's character. The question is this: Is that even possible? Robert Rosenstone, in his 2006 study on film and history, addressed the question of the possible. In his introduction to his work, he asked, "How do you tell the past? How do you render that vanished world of events and people in the present? How can we (try to) understand the human generations who came before us?" He argued that even the works of historians are simply "words on the page."[19] Yet in studying all the different approaches to John Adams, it is feasible to gain some understanding of who he was. Beyond this, examining the many different aspects of John Adams's representations, both scholarly and popular, offers an opportunity to better understand the times in which he lived as well as the usable past created by future generations. While he may be best remembered as being "obnoxious and disliked," Adams is certainly not forgotten. The following pages examine the many ways in which he lives on in historical memory.

In studying John Adams in history and memory, utilizing his own writing was vital. Adams—and many of his correspondents—did not follow modern rules of spelling or capitalization. In order to avoid the distracting "[sic]" to indicate what is original to these 18th-century texts, this manuscript has retained the original grammatical practices, unique spellings, and creative capitalization in all places where he or his family and colleagues are quoted directly. The book will also retain original spellings and grammatical practices evident in 19th-, 20th-, and 21st-century writings that are quoted directly.

ONE

John Adams: A Brief Life Summary[1]

In 1965, Wendell D. Garrett, associate editor of *The Adams Papers,* made the kind of discovery all historians wish they could experience. He found, in the Royall Tyler Collection at the Vermont Historical Society, a diary segment written by John Adams, dating from 1753, while he was still at Harvard. This predated what scholars had considered his first diary, begun in 1755.[2] Knowing the life of John Adams as many do, this earliest of diaries was an exciting find. Yet the first entry offered no foreshadowing concerning the life this man would build. It reads, "At colledge. A Clowdy, Dull morning, and so continued till about 5 a Clock, when it began to rain moderately But continued not long, But remained Clowdy all night in which night I watched with Powers."[3]

This is not exactly earth shattering. At least the diary he started in 1755 began with his observation of an earthquake, a more fitting prediction of the life to come. Still, to catch a glimpse of the young Adams in his college years is gold to the people who study him. It is not hard to imagine the young man, finally the scholar that his father had wanted him to be, ready to learn all he could. Like every other young person in similar circumstances, he could not foresee what lay ahead of him. As the reader approaches this early diary with 20-20 hindsight, it is easy to smile at this simple entry. Yet what John Adams began on that day was a practice that he continued off and on through most of his life.

At the other end of his career, as he wrote his autobiography, he made no mention of this cloudy, rainy, cloudy again day at school. He had other things on his mind. During the early years of his retirement, John Adams was restless. After a life of active participation, he found himself with plenty to do, but also a racing mind. He was disappointed at the outcome of the 1800 Presidential election. He felt rejected by the people he had served for most of his life. He returned to his farming but was wrestling with demons from his past. His wife, Abigail, saw this, as did his eldest son, John Quincy. Therefore, according to one Adams biographer, John Quincy urged his father to write his autobiography. The older Adams resisted the idea at first, but on October 5, 1802, he sat down to begin. He would not finish the work and what he did complete is sporadic and sketchy. Yet in it, the reader catches a glimpse of Adams's attitudes toward such works. Once Adams had explained his justification for writing his life story—replete with the bitterness he was feeling in the moment—he began his narrative. Here Adams gave his readers insights into his early life—skipping the weather.[4]

John Adams was born on October 19 (old style; October 30, new style),[5] 1735 in the small village of Braintree, Massachusetts. He was the eldest son of John and Susanna (Boylston) Adams. Adams provided a genealogy of his family to the point of his birth in the first few pages of his autobiography. His roots ran to the early days of Massachusetts Bay, his earliest ancestor arriving in 1638, a mere eight years after the colony's founding. His grandfather, Joseph had five sons and five daughters. One of those sons was Adams's father. While the majority of his genealogy is dedicated to his father's line, he was also proud to mention his mother's important family tree. He made a point to mention that Zabiel Boylston, his great-uncle on his mother's side of the family, "first introduced into the British Empire the practice of Inocculation for the Small Pox."[6] By all accounts, Adams had a happy childhood. His father was both fond of reading and a great believer in education. Since Adams was the eldest son, he was always slated for college. His father's hope was that his son would enter the ministry, but this required a college education and the only choice worth considering in Massachusetts was Harvard College.

Adams's road to Harvard was not an easy one. In his early years, he was not a keen student. He preferred the outdoor life to the dreary classroom and did not care for all his teachers. While he loved the school run by a Mrs. Belcher, he outgrew this institution and was required to begin study at the Latin School run then by Joseph Cleverly. According to Adams, Cleverly was not interested in what is called today student engagement. "His [Cleverly's] inattention to his Schollars was such as gave me a disgust to Schools, to books and to study...."[7] Adams's father noticed his son's inattention to his studies and became concerned.

Adams confessed to his father that he did not wish to go to college. When he told his father that he preferred farming, the senior Adams was determined to demonstrate to his son what a difficult life that could be. After a full day of farming duties designed to break the back of even the most experienced man, his father asked Adams how he liked farming now. Adams replied that he liked it very well, but his father would not be deterred. He told his son in no uncertain terms that he would, in fact, go to Harvard. A more likeable tutor came into Adams's life at this point and suddenly he discovered the joy of learning. John Adams did attend Harvard and did well there, but he never lost his love for farming.

Even at this early age, one can see Adams's stubbornness. He was never a person to back away from a challenge although his diary is full of self-doubt and recrimination. He was driven by duty, by ambition, and by a puritanical work ethic. All of these qualities are evident in his early years.

By the time Adams had graduated from Harvard, he already had doubts about a career in the ministry. While he was a devout man, he had witnessed firsthand the kind of theological debates that could destroy the reputation of a minister. His own parish clergyman was accused of having Arminian sympathies and of being less than ministerial in his conduct. While this controversy simmered to a boil in his church, Adams related he saw "such a Spirit of Dogmatism and Bigotry in Clergy and Laity" that he had very strong doubts about entering the ministry himself.[8] Yet what were his alternatives?

Like many college graduates then and now, John Adams came out of Harvard not knowing what he wanted to do with his life. He was increasingly sure that he did not want to be a minister, despite his parents' hopes for that. Adams did what many young people do. He took a job that would allow him to make his way in the world while he decided on a career. Adams was offered the position of schoolmaster in Worcester, Massachusetts. He was not an enthusiastic teacher although he wrote one delightful diary entry in which he imagined himself "as some Dictator at the head of a commonwealth." He went on to describe all the citizens in wonderful detail.[9] Still, Adams knew that being a schoolmaster was not what he wished to do. After a good deal of thought and agonizing, he settled on the law as his profession. He announced this decision with little fanfare in his diary. The entire entry reads, "Came to Mr. Putnams and began Law. And studied not very closely this Week."[10] Adams worked with Putnam for two years and, after pleading his case with prominent lawyers in Boston, was sworn to the bar. By this time, he had moved home to Braintree and would begin his law practice there—where he promptly lost his first case.[11] Soon, however, he was gaining more clients, riding the law circuit around New England, and making a name for himself as a good lawyer. In addition, he continued to read and study as much as he could, a lifelong habit.

John Adams first met Abigail Smith in the summer of 1759. It was not love at first sight for either of them. Abigail was still a teenager and John's attentions still lay with Hannah Quincy, whom he courted for a time. Yet John's legal business with Abigail's father, the Reverend William Smith, and the fact that John's good friend Richard Cranch was courting Abigail's older sister meant that John was in the Smith household several times over the next three years. At some point in this period, Abigail caught his eye. He realized that she was an attractive young woman, but also that she had an amazing intellect and a love for books that he shared. John was always drawn to intelligent women. This, too, would be a quality that continued throughout his life. Once John and Abigail noticed one another, their courtship began in earnest and as historian Joseph Ellis noted, the first of their remarkable letters to one another appeared in 1761. After some delays—one so that John could get inoculated against smallpox—the couple were married on October 25, 1764. The remarkable partnership had begun.[12]

Most biographies note the changes that Abigail brought to John's life and personality. Historians agree that she was a stabilizing force for him and that he relied on her counsel more than on anyone else's. One sad aspect of their marriage is that they spent so much time apart from one another, but as a result of this, scholars have their letters to one another, encompassing the years of the American Revolution and beyond. Through their correspondence, the reader sees a marriage, sometimes tense, but always loving. Their mutual respect and affection for one another was evident. They would have six children together, four who survived to adulthood, and they both watched with pride as their eldest son, John Quincy, served the new nation that his father and mother had helped to create.

John Adams married an extraordinary woman. Any number of biographers have studied her life with respect and appreciation. John, too, understood the prize he had in Abigail. While this is evident in their letters, their most famous exchange does not reflect his admiration of her. Abigail, however, had no qualms about bringing up a subject near and dear to her heart.

In March of 1776, Abigail wrote to John, voicing her opinion to him about the progress of the Congress toward independency.

> I long to hear that you have declared an independency—and by the way in the new Code of Laws which I suppose it will be necessary for you to make I desire you would Remember the Ladies, and be more generous and favourable to them than your ancestors. Do not put such unlimited power into the hands of the Husbands. Remember all Men would be tyrants if they could. If perticuliar care and attention is not paid to the Ladies we are determined to foment a Rebelion, and will not hold ourselves bound by any Laws in which we have no voice, or Representation. That your Sex are Naturally Tyrannical is a Truth so thoroughly established as to admit of no dispute, but such of you as wish to be happy willingly give up the harsh title of Master for the more tender and endearing one of Friend.[13]

Adams's response to this letter is dismissive, despite the fact that he did see Abigail as a partner and trusted advisor:

As to your extraordinary Code of Laws, I cannot but laugh. We have been told that our Struggle has loosened the bands of Government every where. That Children and Apprentices were disobedient—that schools and Colledges were grown turbulent—that Indians slighted their Guardians and Negroes grew insolent to their Masters. But your Letter was the first Intimation that another Tribe more numerous and powerfull than all the rest were grown discontented.—This is rather too coarse a Compliment but you are so saucy, I wont blot it out.

Depend upon it, We know better than to repeal our Masculine systems. Altho they are in full Force, you know they are little more than Theory. We dare not exert our Power in its full Latitude. We are obliged to go fair, and softly, and in Practice you know We are the subjects. We have only the Name of Masters, and rather than give up this, which would completely subject Us to the Despotism of the Peticoat I hope General Washington, and all our brave Heroes would fight.[14]

Abigail could not be called a feminist in the modern sense. Yet she was in a wonderful position to remind her husband that women had an important role to play in this new country he wished to create. Throughout their marriage, she continued to advise him in all things.[15]

Beginning in 1765, John Adams became embroiled in the growing crisis between England and her North American colonies. His initial work for the cause of the colonies involved writing more than debating. He wrote against the Stamp Act of 1765 and authored *A Dissertation on the Canon and Feudal Law* in which he outlined the rights of the colonists in great detail. While John Adams was a member of the Sons of Liberty, he was not the firebrand that his older cousin, Samuel, was. He hated mob violence and was adamant that colonial resistance should respect law and order. He took his place in the resistance by arguing for colonial rights within the parameters of the British Constitution. In the midst of the Stamp Act Crisis of 1765, he argued for the opening of the courts without the use of stamped paper. In 1768, he defended John Hancock against the charges of smuggling, arguing that Hancock's rights as an Englishman had been violated by the seizure of one of his ships, aptly named the *Liberty*. Most famously, he defended the British soldiers accused of murder following the so-called Boston Massacre. Despite his allegiance to the colonial cause, Adams believed these soldiers deserved a fair trial and that the mob violence evident in Boston should be separated from the reputation of the city. Through the 1760s and into the 1770s, Adams clearly sided with his fellow colonials who argued that their rights were being violated by Parliament, but he was never a fan of violence and anarchy.

In 1774, John Adams was chosen as one of the Massachusetts delegates to the First Continental Congress in Philadelphia. His selection to attend, and his commitment to the meeting, led to one of the more painful moments in his personal life. Adams would sacrifice his long-time friendship with Jonathan Sewall (1728–1796) for the sake of the colonial cause.

There have not been many scholarly studies of the role of friendship in shaping history or the loss of camaraderie because of historic events. One recent work which addressed this issue centered on the relationship between John Adams and Jonathan Sewall. Colin Nicolson (Senior Lecturer in History at the University of Stirling) and Owen Dudley Edwards (Irish historian and former Reader in Commonwealth and American History at the University of Edinburgh, Scotland) examined the friendship of these two men in light of their disagreements on British policy. Yet before these two lawyers became enemies because of their chosen loyalties, they were friends. In examining their relationship, Nicolson and Edwards first analyzed friendship, calling it "easier to experience than to explain across time and space." According to these two historians, both Adams and Sewall "idealized their friendship as heroic historical drama: adversarial, playful, cerebral, mysterious."[16] The fact that the friendship could not survive the American Revolution was heartbreaking for both of them.

As part of their study of this friendship, Nicolson and Edwards discussed the 1774–1775 newspaper debate that Adams believed he was conducting with Sewall. He was mistaken. The man writing the essays in favor of British policy and using the pseudonym *Massachusettensis* was Daniel Leonard. However, in 1774 when the essays appeared, Adams felt certain that they were Sewall's work. Responding to each essay, using the pseudonym *Novanglus*, Adams answered his friend point by point, and he did so with Sewall in mind. For Nicolson and Edwards, Adams's belief that he was debating his long-time friend made his work personal as well as political.[17] Beyond this newspaper debate, however, was a long-time relationship begun when both men were starting their law careers.

Jonathan Sewall was one of John Adams's dearest friends. From the time the two men were struggling lawyers in the 1750s, through the 1760s and early 1770s, they had remained close despite their disagreements over British policy. Sewall often voiced deep admiration for his friend and when tensions were brewing between England and her colonies, Sewall attempted to save Adams from what he saw as a dangerous path. In 1768, Sewall came to Adams with an offer from the royal governor of Massachusetts. Sewall had recommended Adams for the post of Advocate General of the Court of Admiralty, and he wanted his friend to accept the post. As Adams biographer Page Smith related the story, Sewall saw this offer as a "last effort to retrieve his companion from a course which, Sewall felt, could lead only to disaster, to resistance to the Crown and finally proscription as a traitor." In Sewall's mind, he was "wrestling with the Devil for the soul of his friend."[18] This is just one instance that demonstrated the depth of friendship between these two men. The pain they both felt at their parting is another example.

As Nicolson and Edwards observed, there is no extant recollection of the moment from Sewall and the words he spoke to Adams came from Adams's retelling of the moment. Yet the historians do not doubt Sewall's intent. They argued that while Sewall was "a colder man than Adams, he probably meant exactly what he said and implied: that among his motives was a genuine fear for Adams and an anxiety to save him from destruction."[19] Yet Adams was determined to do what he thought was right. Sewall could not dissuade him. As a result, the two men parted company before the First Continental Congress convened and would not see each other again until the Revolution was over.

Before 1774, Adams had never travelled outside New England, nor did he feel he was up to the important task that lay ahead of him. By this point in the crisis with England, few colonial leaders were prepared to discuss the idea of independence. The Massachusetts delegates were split on the issue and not all scholars agree that Adams was quite ready for the break with England. In the early days of the Congressional meeting, Adams's diary entries are replete with character sketches of the men he was meeting for the first time. "This [Edward] Rutledge is young—sprightly but not deep. He has the most indistinct, inarticulate Way of Speaking." "Cæsar Rodney is the oddest looking Man in the World. He is tall—thin and slender as a Reed—pale—his Face is not bigger than a large Apple. Yet there is Sense and Fire, Spirit, Wit and Humour in his Countenance." His diary for this time period is full of such descriptions as well as notes on the proceedings of the Congress.[20] The reader finds a man who was enjoying himself at first, delighting in Philadelphia and the people he was meeting. As the weeks wore on, however, his enthusiasm and patience waned. "The Deliberations of the Congress, are spun out to an immeasurable Length. There is so much Wit, Sense, Learning, Acuteness, Subtilty, Eloquence, &c. among fifty Gentlemen … that an immensity of Time, is spent unnecessarily."[21] Adams began to demonstrate the impatience that would stay with him through the rest of 1774, into 1775 and 1776.

When he returned to Philadelphia for the Second Continental Congress in May of 1775, the battles at Lexington and Concord were fresh in his mind. From that time forward, he became a strong advocate for independence and demanded that the Congress adopt the army in Massachusetts. He was responsible for nominating George Washington to lead that army, feeling the necessity of promoting someone from outside New England to emphasize the importance of Continental participation in the war with England. Biographers have often noted his tireless work in the Congress. He served on a number of important committees in addition to being a strong debater in meetings. His conviction made him obnoxious to some who wished for reconciliation with England. By early 1776, Adams was encouraging the states to write constitutions, preparing themselves for the departure of English government officials. He understood the importance of courting the countries of Europe and asking for their aid and recognition of the colonies as independent from England. He was on the committee responsible for drafting the Declaration of Independence. One of the more famous stories of how Thomas Jefferson came to write the Declaration was related by Adams himself and has been repeated often in his biographies. There is some question concerning his memory of events, but his version has been accepted as true despite the fact that Jefferson did not remember things in quite the same way.[22]

Adams continued to serve in the Congress until 1777, but his duties soon shifted to diplomacy. In 1778, he travelled to France with his young son, John Quincy, to help negotiate a treaty with France. He described in great detail his Atlantic crossing in the winter of 1778. While he felt it his duty to go to France, he did express regret at one point that he had brought John Quincy. He was glad of his company, but worried about exposing him to the danger of the crossing in wartime. However, he noted, "Mr. Johnnys Behaviour gave me a Satisfaction that I cannot express—fully sensible of our Danger, he was constantly endeavouring to bear it with a manly Patience, very attentive to me and his Thoughts constantly running in a serious Strain."[23]

Adams also related his feelings when he helped attend the ship's doctor who had to amputate the leg of one of the sailors. The officer, named by Adams as Mr. Barron, begged Adams to see to his family should he die. In a footnote in the diary the editor, Lyman H. Butterfield, noted that Barron died after the amputation and that "[t]here is evidence that JA kept his pledge to write on behalf of Barron's family" and that "JA endeavored to do something on behalf of Barron's orphaned children during his brief return to Massachusetts in 1779."[24]

By the time he arrived in France, his colleague Benjamin Franklin had already achieved the goal of a treaty with that country, thanks to the surrender of British General John Burgoyne at Saratoga, New York. Adams found himself adrift with nothing to do, although he put himself to work organizing the records and budgets for the delegation. He also found himself in the middle of a feud between Benjamin Franklin and one other man on the commission, Arthur Lee. It was apparent to Adams that the delegation had split into factions which he described in his diary.[25] He also made his frustration about the disorganization of the delegation clear: "The public Business has never been methodically conducted. There never was before I came, a minute Book, a Letter Book or an Account Book—and it is not possible to obtain a clear Idea of our Affairs."[26] While he attempted to be useful in France, he felt dissatisfied with his role and was relieved to return home for a brief period in 1779.

United with the rest of his family, Adams was home for a short time when he was elected to serve as a delegate to the convention that would write the new Massachusetts State Constitution. Adams served on the drafting committee, and as was often the case with him, was the principal writer of the text. Aside from a few amendments, his document is still the Constitution for Massachusetts today. It is touted as "the world's oldest functioning constitution" and as a model for the Federal constitution written in 1787.[27] Soon, however, Adams was asked to return to France to begin the peace negotiations that would end the Revolutionary War. This time he would be in Europe much longer and would find himself once again frustrated with his role.

On this trip to Europe, Adams brought both John Quincy and his younger son, Charles, feeling that the experience was essential to both boys' education. Charles, although he did fine while his older brother was with him, when John Quincy left for Russia to serve as secretary to Francis Dana, Charles's homesickness was acute. John was concerned for him and eventually sent him home in the care of a man returning to Boston. Much has been made of John's neglect of his children in the duty of his country, and the John Adams miniseries in particular made a point of tracing Charles's premature death to the treatment by his father. Judging John Adams as a parent is difficult to do from a 21st-century perspective although scholars have made their feelings known on the subject. Whatever his shortcomings may have been in this area, Adams was concerned that his sons broaden their horizons, that they experience the world. He attempted to give them the opportunities that he could. The results were mixed to say the least.

Adams grew increasingly impatient with his situation in France, once again feeling frustrated by his role. He also became concerned that the United States was too reliant on the goodwill of the French. Without permission or instructions, Adams dispatched himself to Holland in the summer of 1780 in order to secure loans for the United States. At this point, he had no official standing and found it difficult to get the attention of the Dutch government. He was eventually named as official envoy. He was able to secure loans from the Dutch, but only after British General Cornwallis's surrender at Yorktown in October of 1781. At this point, the Dutch were ready to recognize the United States and loan funds to the new nation. While Adams's stay in Holland had been miserable at times—he suffered a physical collapse while he was there and was ill for quite some time—he was proud of what he was able to achieve. He was so intent on his goals in

Holland that he delayed returning to France even though peace negotiations with England had begun.

The reasons for Adams's delay have been discussed by scholars of his
diplomatic missions. Some have argued that Adams was avoiding Benjamin Franklin, a man that he had come to distrust and of whom he was
jealous.[28] Nevertheless, Adams did return to Paris and fought hard to
make sure the United States would receive its unconditional independence
and would not be under the control of the French. Once this was accomplished, in 1783, John Adams was at loose ends once again. Abigail urged
him to return home, but he hoped that there would be a further diplomatic
mission for him. Rather than going back to Braintree, Adams urged Abigail to join him in Europe, along with their daughter, Nabby. Abigail was
reluctant and was scared of ocean travel. She had never been further from
home than Salem, Massachusetts. This was a good deal to ask of her, but
when she discovered that Adams most certainly would have a diplomatic
appointment and would not return home for at least three years, she made
the decision to join him. This particular separation had put a strain on
their marriage. She was determined to be with John and hopefully repair
the damage.[29] Their time together in Europe, in France in particular, provided some of the happiest moments of their lives. Here, the Adams family
grew to love Thomas Jefferson. Adams and Jefferson went on a road trip of
sorts through the English countryside and became even closer as a result,
even though their political disagreements were beginning to emerge.

One of the most difficult diplomatic tasks Adams faced in Europe was
his service as the first minister to represent the United States at the Court
of St. James's in London. While he was greeted graciously by King George
III, the rest of the English government proved unwilling to work with
Adams. He was mocked in the press and stymied by the king's ministry.
Meanwhile, during his stay in England, a constitutional convention was
meeting in Philadelphia. Adams wanted to be there. In lieu of his presence
he wrote a series of essays entitled *Defence of the Constitutions of Government of the United States of America* in an effort to influence the proceedings of the convention. The reviews of this work are mixed, and, in these
essays, Adams expressed some ideas that would later come back to haunt
him, specifically in regard to his feelings on monarchy. Yet this effort provided Adams with a distraction from his exasperation with the English
ministry. After several years of wasted time, Adams asked the Congress to
release him from his duties in England so that he could return home. Congress granted his request and he and Abigail left Europe in March 1788.

John Adams returned to a hero's welcome in Boston. The *Massachusetts Centinel* reported on June 18, 1788: "Yesterday, after an absence of
nine years, arrived in this metropolis, from England, his Excellency JOHN

ADAMS, Esq. late Ambassadour from the United States of America, to the Court of Great Britain—with his lady."[30] The newspaper described every moment of the homecoming, noting, "The bells in the several churches rang during the remainder of the day—every countenance wore the expression of joy." Adams was greeted by the governor of Massachusetts, John Hancock, and was thanked warmly by the Massachusetts legislature.[31]

Adams was moved by this reception, but he was not sure what was next for him. His friends made it clear that he had many options and that he must serve in the new federal government in some capacity. The only office that was off limits was the presidency. That George Washington would serve as the new nation's first president was the worst-kept secret in the country. However, the vice-presidency was up for grabs. This was the office to which Adams was elected. He never turned down an opportunity to serve, but he was frustrated with the inactivity his role as vice-president required. He concluded that the vice-presidency had little to offer. Adams famously wrote to Abigail, "My Country has in its Wisdom contrived for me, the most insignificant Office that ever the Invention of Man contrived or his Imagination conceived."[32]

Adams was a man who liked to participate in debate. He enjoyed being part of the action and as vice-president, he was expected to stay quiet and break ties. Unfortunately for his reputation, he was unable to do this and in one debate in particular over how to address the president, Adams offered some suggestions that appeared monarchical. Soon, some senators had dubbed him "His Rotundity" and "The Duke of Braintree" behind his back. Despite his discomfort in the job, Adams served two full terms as vice-president. Because of this, he felt that he was heir apparent to Washington when the latter decided not to run for a third term.

In the election of 1796, Adams won the presidency, with Thomas Jefferson coming in second and therefore becoming vice-president. Adams had hoped to work closely with Jefferson, but his old friend had a different political agenda from Adams's. This would mark the beginning of the temporary but painful split between these two men who had helped to create the nation.

John Adams served one inglorious term as president. In that time, his connection to the Federalist Party solidified. However, Adams also attempted to remain above partisan strife. At this stage in his career, he abhorred the idea of political parties or factions of any kind. Historian John Howe summed up Adams's feelings on the subject. "Parties accentuated the struggle for political spoils and made personal ambition rather than social virtue the touchstone of political success. Party conflict, by exciting passions and clouding reason, corrupted elections more quickly than anything."[33] The problem for Adams was that these political parties had already formed by the time he became president and even though he was elected as a Federalist, he did not agree with many members of this party. In fact, the Federalists were clearly led by Alexander Hamilton, a man whom Adams came to despise. As a result, the party split into two factions: the Adams Federalists and the Hamiltonian or High Federalists.[34] While the two factions disagreed on several issues—including the need for an improved army versus a strong navy and the necessity for banks—much of the rancor came down to politics.

In 1796, Hamilton attempted to bring another Federalist into the presidency over Adams by reducing Adams's electoral vote. According to Howe, Adams was aware of this scheming and any trust he might have had of Hamilton disappeared in that moment.[35] This split in the Federalist Party made Adams's presidency difficult. In addition, he was also contending with the Jeffersonian Republicans. For a man who wished to remain independent and above party, these factions were impossible to navigate. Moreover, Adams did not make life easy for himself in these years.

Both John Howe and political scientist Manning Dauer believed that had Adams used political parties to his advantage rather than fight them, his presidency might have been more successful. However, he was hampered by his idea that the president should be above party, and independent. Despite this impression, Dauer contended that Adams seemed to be building a faction himself, perhaps in an attempt to take over leadership of the Federalist Party. Adams had some of the tools necessary to do this, but not all. "Honesty and forthrightness he had in abundance. He was motivated by an intense sense of trusteeship on behalf of his countrymen," contended Dauer. "In this respect he sought, like Washington, to be impartial. He stood against the extremists of his own party. But, impetuous in temperament, he lacked the ability of great political leaders like Jefferson and Lincoln to carry with him the groups necessary to political success."[36] Howe agreed, arguing, "A greater tolerance of parties and willingness to use them as agencies of the general welfare, might have saved him considerable grief." Instead, he "found himself caught between Republicans and Hamiltonians, attacked from both sides with few persons willing to speak up in his defense."[37]

In the four years he was in office, Adams made some serious mistakes as he tried to maintain his independence from party politics. He decided, for example, to retain Washington's cabinet rather than choosing his own people to serve. While Alexander Hamilton was no longer in the cabinet, he continued to pull the strings of those Federalists still serving in the government. This included some of Adams's cabinet members whose loyalties were not with Adams. They answered to Hamilton, making life difficult for the president. By the end of his presidency, Adams jettisoned those cabinet members, but the move came too late to help his reelection efforts.

In the midst of dealing with his cabinet, Adams had to contend with France, whose behavior toward the United States was less than respectful. The French were embroiled in their own revolution by the 1790s, and Adams had to navigate what had become a messy situation in Europe. After several insults from the French that Adams made public, the young nation's citizens were clamoring for war. This also led to the Federalist-controlled Congress passing a series of acts designed to crack down on French nationals in the country and curtail the civil liberties of American citizens.

Signing the Alien and Sedition Acts in 1798 was arguably the biggest error that John Adams made in his entire public career and it has stained his reputation to this day. Scholars have attempted to explain why he felt compelled to agree to them, some blaming the Federalists in Congress more than the president. Adams blamed the party, specifically Alexander Hamilton, for the acts, but maintained in later years that they were "constitutional and salutary if not necessary."[38] The HBO miniseries depicted a hesitant Adams, wrestling with the implications of the acts. There is no evidence, however, that he was reluctant to sign them into law. His support of the Alien and Sedition Acts has done damage to his legacy, even to the point where he may never receive a monument in the capital city. Various chapters later in this work include discussions of these acts and the effect they have had on Adams's reputation.

In dealing with the problems with the French, Adams understood the need to be prepared for war, but he wished to avoid it as well. "Great is the Guilt of an unnecessary War," he told Abigail.[39] Despite the fact that he was more popular than ever during this period of his presidency, Adams decided to pursue peace.

He was successful in keeping the country out of war, but not in time to win him reelection. He was defeated by Thomas Jefferson in the closely contested presidential race of 1800. Adams was out of the contest relatively early, but Thomas Jefferson's and Aaron Burr's supporters had to fight it out in the Electoral College and the House of Representatives. The election had still not been settled in January of 1801, but John and Abigail both presumed Jefferson would win, and they both preferred him to Burr. In a gesture of gracious defeat, the Adamses invited Jefferson to dinner in the winter of 1801 as a way to say good-bye to their old friend.[40]

In the midst of the contentious election, the Adamses suffered another blow, this one personal. In December of 1800, their son Charles died of complications from alcoholism. Upon receiving the news, John poured out his grief to his youngest son, Thomas. "The melancholy death of your brother is an affliction of a more serious nature to this family than any other. Oh! That I had died for him if that would have relieved him from his faults as well as his disease."[41]

Adams did not stay for Jefferson's inauguration. He left Washington in the predawn hours of March 4, 1801. As biographer Joseph Ellis noted, he has been criticized for not staying to demonstrate the peaceful transfer of power from one party to another. Yet, as Ellis argued, it was highly likely that "he did not think he was supposed to be present. There was no precedent for a defeated candidate to attend the inauguration of his successor, and he wished neither to complicate Jefferson's moment of triumph nor to lend a hand in its celebration."[42] Whatever his reason, Adams left Washington, and public life, for the last time. He was 66 years old.

One other historical milestone of Adams's presidency was the fact that he was the first president to reside in what would come to be called the White House. John Adams moved to a capital city that was still under construction in November 1800. Adams described his new residence as "habitable" upon his arrival and then added a blessing: "I pray Heaven to bestow the best of Blessings on this House and all that shall hereafter inhabit it. May none but honest and wise Men ever rule under this roof."[43] This quotation was carved into the mantel of the state dining room in 1945 at the orders of President Franklin Roosevelt.[44] How effective the Adams prayer has been in guaranteeing only "honest and wise Men" live in the house is open for debate. Still, the fact that Roosevelt honored the house's first inhabitant in this way demonstrated a certain respect for the second president.

While Adams had not anticipated it, he would live for another quarter of a century after his retirement. For the first eleven years or so at his home in Quincy, he was restless and bitter, feeling the sting of rejection and unpopularity. He worked out his feelings in several ways; none of them reflected on Adams at his best. Yet over time, he began to mellow and was even able to forgive those people who he believed had wronged him. In 1812, he famously resumed contact with Thomas Jefferson and enjoyed their correspondence for the remainder of his life. He relished his time with Abigail and was surrounded by children and grandchildren. The picture scholars paint of Adams's later years is one of peace and resignation, if not contentment.

These years were not without tragedy and loss. In August of 1813, Adams's daughter, Abigail Adams Smith, or Nabby as she was called, died of breast cancer at age 48. Five years later, in October of 1818, John lost his beloved Abigail. Two days later, Adams wrote to Jefferson, "The dear Partner of my Life for fifty four Years as a Wife and for many Years more as a Lover, now lyes in extremis, forbidden to speak or be spoken to." He signed the letter, "I am, Sir, your deeply afflicted Friend."[45] Jefferson responded that he was far too familiar with the school of Adams's affliction and that "I know well and feel what you have lost, what you have suffered, are suffering, and have yet to." He signed off by saying, "God bless you and support you under your heavy affliction."[46] Despite this deep loss, Adams lived on and enjoyed the company of friends and family when he could. He lived to see his son, John Quincy, elected to the presidency in 1824 and could not help but be proud. He was also concerned, for he knew what his son faced in the office. Like his father before him, John Quincy Adams was a one-term president.

Adams also lived to see the preparation for the celebration of the Jubilee of the Declaration of Independence. Three signers of the Declaration were still alive as the fiftieth anniversary approached in 1826: Thomas Jefferson in Virginia, Charles Carroll in Maryland, and John Adams in Massachusetts. From about 1812 on, Adams had been asked by several people to comment on the meaning of the Revolution, the drafting of the Declaration, and other aspects of the movement toward independence. As Lyman Butterfield noted in an article on the anniversary celebration, "If Americans turned their eyes towards the past at this time, it was partly because they knew they had neglected it." There was no good and complete history of the Revolution and few biographies of the Founders. Further, the 4th of July had not become a national holiday until the early 1800s.[47] Adams had become concerned with the mythology he saw growing around the founding generation, but as the big day approached, he was recognized as a mover and a shaker in the independence movement, and he received invitations to speak at various celebrations. He declined them all, being too weak to make the trips. He did offer a toast to be given on his behalf at a local commemoration. "I give you Independence Forever!" When asked if he had anything to add, Adams said, "Not a word."[48] This was a fitting toast from a man who not only fought for American independence, but also worked to maintain his own.

When the big day arrived, both Jefferson and Adams were close to death. Jefferson was the first to die, in the afternoon. Adams, whose last thoughts seemed to be of Jefferson—he whispered, "Thomas Jefferson survives," before slipping into unconsciousness—died at 6:00 that evening. It is difficult to know what a dying person is thinking as he or she approaches the last breath. Yet, given the day, it would not be at all surprising that these two men would be thinking of the time they worked together in a revolution.

John Adams, aged 90 when he died, could look back on a long and eventful life with an extraordinary life partner, Abigail. He was surrounded by family members when he passed into death, not separated from them. The one person who could not be there was his son, the president of the United States, who did not know of his father's death until a few days later. When he learned that his father was failing, he left for Quincy immediately, but would not arrive in time to say goodbye to his father. When learning of his death, he wrote, "he had served to great and useful purpose his nation, his age, and his God. He is gone, and may the blessing of Almighty Grace have attended him to his account!" Like the rest of the country, the president was awestruck by the coincidence that both Adams and Jefferson had died on the same day, the fiftieth anniversary of the Declaration. John Quincy Adams wrote, "The time, the manner, the coincidence with the decease of Jefferson has the visible and palpable marks of divine favor, for which I would humble myself in grateful and silent adoration before the Ruler of the Universe."[49]

With the passing of John Adams and Thomas Jefferson, the nation marked a milestone in its existence. One signer of the Declaration of Independence was still alive. Charles Carroll of Maryland lived until 1832. Yet the two men seen as most responsible for the birth of the United States were gone—and left the earth on the same day. John Adams, long concerned about his legacy, passed into public memory beginning with the eulogies written to honor him. Some of these were combined with memories of Jefferson as well, in order to contrast the roles of the two Founders. In these early years after his death, John Adams was not forgotten, and given the date upon which he died, his memory fit well into the usable past early Americans were embracing.

Eulogies to John Adams and Thomas Jefferson came from many places across the country. From New England to South Carolina, the two Founding Fathers were intertwined in honor. While sectionalism was prevalent in these eulogies—Northern speakers honored Adams over Jefferson and Southern eulogists Jefferson over Adams—the fact that these two giants died on the same day created a sensation across the United States. What were the odds? According to Joseph Ellis, one mathematician calculated them, concluding that "the chance that two of the signers of the Declaration of Independence in 1776 should survive half a century, and die on the 4th of July, was only one in twelve hundred millions."[50] While Americans came to terms with this astounding coincidence, speakers were preparing eulogies to both men.

John A. Shaw delivered one of the more memorable tributes, and given that he was in Massachusetts, it is to his credit that he honored both men equally. From his first sentence, he made his theme clear to his audience. The country owed gratitude to these men. Reflecting upon the services of John Adams in particular, Shaw noted his roots in Massachusetts. "This section of our country has the honor of having been the birthplace of John Adams," he stated. He then gave a review of Adams's career, beginning with his success as a lawyer. This was demonstrated by one of Adams's more difficult cases. "He was distinguished for his talents, decision, firmness, and deep sense of official duty, by the part he took … in defence of the British soldiers who perpetrated the 'Boston Massacre' in 1770." Even in 1826, members of the public were recognizing this act as one of bravery rather than betrayal to the colonial cause.[51]

Shaw continued, noting Adams's role in advocating for independence. In this part of the eulogy, Shaw made an interesting revision to events. He quoted Adams's letter to Abigail, written on the 3rd of July concerning the passage of the independence resolution by Congress on the 2nd. Yet Shaw told his audience that Adams wrote his letter on the 5th of July and was discussing the events of July 4th. The dominance of celebrating the Declaration of Independence had become so prominent by 1826 that Shaw ensured Adams's ideas concerning the celebration aligned with the public festival. The 4th of July was "a great, a good day; and with it will be forever associated the name of JOHN ADAMS."[52]

Shaw did not wish to deify either of these men, but he did tend to excuse Adams in his eulogy. While he noted that Adams "scrupulously performed all the duties of private and domestic life; and no stain can attach to his memory, as a man and Christian," he did have his weaknesses. However, asserted Shaw, "The weaker traits of his character were such as are seldom separated from an open, bold, confiding, and independent spirit."[53] He explained the difficulties of Adams's presidency by remarking upon the shadow cast by George Washington. It could not have been easy to follow Washington into the presidency. Yet Shaw would have made Adams proud by asserting, "In shewing our respect for the memory of these benefactors, it is not necessary to exhibit them as faultless: for they were subject to like passions with ourselves." In summation, Shaw said, "Poor is the tribute we can bring. Your monument is the freedom of your country, and your eulogy, the praise of ransomed millions."[54] Shaw seemed to predict that Adams would have no *physical* monument in Washington, D.C. Yet he could enjoy this more important memorial.

Daniel Webster, in honoring Adams and Jefferson, also noted the transience of stone memorials.

> But monuments and statues decay, and in the revolutions of time, history itself becomes obscure and lost. But Heaven designed them a nobler memorial; it inscribed their names on the forehead of time, and encircled them with sunbeams. As long as time shall endure—as long as the sun shall mark the year in his circuit through the heavens—whenever the Fourth of July arrives, mankind will see in his rising beams the rays of liberty, and in his meridian path the names of the two Patriots, who consecrated the day to freedom, and ascended to their rewards on its Jubilee.[55]

In these eulogies and many others like them, the speakers remembered the bravery and sacrifices of John Adams. Yet they also linked him to Thomas Jefferson, the man who would come to eclipse him in the public memory of the American people. This remained the case for some time, as younger generations of Americans were grappling with the nature of their young nation.

In 1826, the new nation was undergoing a great deal of change, but as the years went on, its people were also becoming interested in creating a past that would be usable to them as they moved into the future. According to author J.V. Matthews, this process was understandable. "In a new nation," he wrote, "an aesthetically and emotionally satisfying myth of origins is not only a necessary ingredient of an evolving national identity but a prerequisite for a sense of future direction and development." As a result, the citizens of the young nation were interested in the history of the founding of the country to the point where that story was a "national preoccupation." Matthews argued, however, that for some New Englanders, the rise of Andrew Jackson was jarring as it created a "decline in that deference on which social harmony in an economically unequal society seemed to depend."[56] To counter this trend, New Englanders looked to their own past by which they could claim their regions centrality to the founding of America. While all could agree that "George Washington was the great admonitory father figure," New Englanders argued that the Puritan founders of their region were even more important.[57] According to New England members of the Whig Party specifically, "their Puritan forefathers seemed to embody in a particularly pure form the concept of republicanism which the Whigs wished to preserve."[58] Because of their emphasis on the Puritan past, the Whigs downplayed the American Revolution. It was, in fact, "one event in a logical development." According to Matthews's reading of this interpretation of the 18th century, "this kind of historical 'placing' of the Revolution both justified and defused it as a vital force in contemporary life; the Revolution was natural, legitimate—and over."[59] The American Revolution should not be forgotten, but "it should be remembered for the heroism and self-sacrifice of its soldiers; for the wisdom of its leaders who knew that the proper outcome of revolution is the firmer establishment of government; for its place in a process of developing institutional liberty."[60]

Given such arguments, John Adams would fit nicely into this usable past. Yet for these New Englanders, placing the Revolution into a grand arc rather than marking it as a beginning of something new meant that they looked further into the past for their heroic characters. Once Adams was gone and his eulogies read, he did not serve to advance this portrait of the nation's history. Why, then, did he reemerge in national memory in later years? There are several answers to this question.

For one, the long and extraordinary life of John Adams is fascinating on many levels. As such, it became irresistible as a dramatic story. Beyond this, his diary and correspondence are a treasure trove of observations, emotions, passions, disappointments, and self-recriminations, all of which made him human and relatable. In addition, his contributions to the American Revolution and the Early Republic are numerous and noteworthy. His expectations of others and, most notably, of himself during this formative period in American history are remarkable. As a result, beginning in the mid-19th century, John Adams gained the attention of historians and other scholars who desired to understand him and explain him to their readers. Their work—sometimes but not always consulted by dramatists, actors, and other artists—provide the public with the image of this man. This "usable John Adams" surfaced in numerous places. The next several chapters discuss that portrait by analyzing how scholars and artists have remembered the life summarized above.

Two

The Historians' View
Early Biographies Through the 1960s

When examining the amount of work historians have dedicated to John Adams, it would be wrong to call him neglected. Many scholars have written on Adams and none of them have dismissed his contributions to early American history. What sets Adams apart in the historiography is his lack of Founding Father excellence. Historians of Adams are as honest as he was in recognizing his flaws as well as his strengths. John Adams is no marble man, lauded in the pantheon of the Founders. What emerges from the historiography is an earnest human being who was as likely to ruin his own reputation as others were to attack him.

Each historian who has attempted a narrative of John Adams's life comes to it with a drive to understand the man. This is the role of any scholar, but what makes Adams's biographers unique is that many of them struggle with his reputation and some feel the need to redeem it. The attributes these historians, biographers, journalists, and freelance writers choose to emphasize demonstrate a desire to place Adams squarely into the mythology of the founding generation—into a usable past—without robbing him of his humanity. The titles of these works illustrate this: *Honest John Adams; John Adams: Party of One; Passionate Sage* are some of the more interesting examples.

One biographer attempted to give his subject immortality by calling his work *This Man Adams: The Man Who Never Died*. Other biographers have taken a more standard approach: *John Adams* is the simple title of three biographies, and *John Adams: A Life* is the title of a fourth. Still other scholars have chosen to concentrate on one aspect of his life: *John Adams & the Prophets of Progress; John Adams and the American Revolution; John Adams and the Spirit of Liberty; John Adams's Republic: The One, the Few, and the Many; John Adams and the Fear of American Oligarchy*; and, most recently, *The Education of John Adams*.

All these studies indicate a fascination with the man, his character, and his mind. No one John Adams emerges from these works. Yet many of his attributes are present in all of them. For this reason, it is not necessary to discuss each work at length. How each writer has approached various aspects of Adams's life is instructive. In fact, two biographers used tactics that placed their works on the border between history and fiction. As a result, these studies will be considered in the chapter on literature.[1] Each writer has a different perspective on John Adams's personality and the many conflicts in which he was involved, a view informed by the author's own time. The question was always, "What can we learn from John Adams that will edify us today?" In other words, how might the various generations use John Adams to help them understand the United States of their own times? Tracing what was important to these writers is a fascinating journey, and the evolution of John Adams depictions is striking.

The early biographies of John Adams span several decades and pivotal events in the United States. From the upheaval of the Civil War and Reconstruction to the turmoil of the 1960s, these scholars found a way to make Adams relevant for their reading public. Whether he stood for unity, honesty, or stability, the Adams who emerges in this round of scholarship was a useful model for these writers.

To trace the many different iterations of Adams in the historiography, it is wise to start at the beginning. John Quincy Adams and Charles Francis Adams wrote the earliest biography of John Adams. Charles Francis Adams wished to preserve the writings of his grandfather and finished what his father had begun. It was a vast undertaking. He published the *Works of John Adams* (10 volumes), and the biography *The Life of John Adams* (published in 1856) completed the set.[2] It later appeared in the American Statesmen Series. While it is not necessarily an objective biography, it is thorough. The authors used incidences from their subject's life to launch into long lectures on the history of England and New England. This is typical 19th-century writing and while the perspective is valuable, it is easy to understand why later biographies are more enjoyable for the modern reader.

John Quincy Adams wrote the first two chapters before his death. Charles Francis Adams finished the work. The biography was written in tribute to the grandfather whom Charles Francis Adams called "the boldest, the most enthusiastic, the most passionate in support of liberty, of all those who figured in the history of the American Revolution."[3] Most of volume one is dedicated to Adams's work during the crisis with England that would lead to the Revolutionary War. The authors emphasized the Boston Massacre Trials and Adams's writings on the rights of the colonists as well as the British Constitution. They recounted his triumphs and tribulations at the Second Continental Congress, repeating the praise he received from his fellow delegates while arguing in favor of independence, but not ignoring his snubbing by John Dickinson after the publication of some indiscreet letters written by Adams. The volumes also contain an exhaustive narrative concerning Adams's diplomatic work during and shortly after the war as well as his role as vice-president and president of the United States. The final chapter of the two volumes covers Adams's retirement years, his renewed friendship with Thomas Jefferson, and the drama of his death on the fiftieth anniversary of the Declaration of Independence.

Throughout this biography, Charles Francis Adams made commentary on the other members of the founding generation while also taking care to advance his grandfather's reputation. Yet, in typical Adams fashion, the grandson did not gloss over the faults of John Adams. Instead, he attempted to put them in context.[4] One can forgive a grandson for wanting to defend his grandfather. What is interesting is the fact that subsequent biographies of Adams do this as well.

Following this familial biography, Theodore Parker, a minister in the Unitarian Church and a transcendentalist, wrote a series of essays on the Founding Fathers called collectively *Historic Americans*. This work, written in 1858 and published in 1871 after Parker's death, provided a brief glimpse into this New Englander's attitudes toward John Adams. Intellectually, Parker believed that, aside from Franklin, none of the founders were his equal. "He was eminent in the three departments of the Intellect," those being understanding, imagination, and reason. Despite this and his strong moral character, however, Adams had huge flaws. Parker acknowledged that he was ill-tempered and "madly impetuous." He was also a poor judge of character, according to this writer. "He often suspected the noblest of men, and put credulous faith in mean and deceitful persons, and so was unjust while he meant it not." In addition, Parker marked Adams as a "grumbler. He hated things present, and longed for the absent or the past."[5] Yet, for all this, the country owed much to John Adams. Parker, unlike other New Englanders who were more interested in their Puritan forefathers, found much that was worthy in Adams. He wrote:

> the judgment of posterity will be that he was a brave man, deep-sighted, conscientious, patriotic, and possessed of Integrity which nothing ever shook but which stood firm as the granite of his Quincy Hills. While American Institutions continue the People will honor brave, honest old John Adams who never failed his country in her hour of need and who in his life of more than ninety years, though both passionate and ambitious wronged no man nor any woman![6]

Parker's overview of John Adams was a virtual seesaw, switching from the noble to the unfortunate throughout. Yet it is a thorough summary of Adams's long life and a perceptive insight into his character. It was not, however, a full-length biography, nor would it be considered today, scholarly.

The first biography that would fit into the academic category was written in the early 20th century by a man who found much to appreciate in John Adams. For Gilbert Chinard, like many biographers, Adams's honesty was paramount. In fact, he titled his book *Honest John Adams* (1933). Writing in the years of the Great Depression, Chinard also looked to Adams as an example of what a man, from humble beginnings, could accomplish if given a chance. At a time when the American people were feeling hopelessness in the midst of the economic crisis, John Adams was a useful tool in building their confidence.

Chinard was a literary historian by trade, a fact made apparent by his assessment of Adams as a writer. He emphasized not only Adams's integrity but also the influence of his Puritan background. Chinard made no apologies for Adams, but at the same time, the neglect of Adams baffled him. In the first lines of his introduction, Chinard wrote,

> It is a strange reflection on the attitude of democracies towards their great men that America should have exalted two born aristocrats from Virginia and failed to recognize in John Adams, the descendant of humble and honest folk, a striking illustration of the principle of "equal opportunities," and the symbol of a new social order.[7]

Chinard went on to describe Adams as "Unsung, a distant and lonely figure in American history."[8] Chinard's Adams was the product of democracy, a man who rose from obscurity to shape a new nation and political philosophy. In so doing, however, Chinard argued that Adams appeared provincial to some historians, especially in comparison to Washington, Franklin, and Jefferson. For this scholar, Adams's modest origins were something to celebrate rather than ridicule. Adams was a product of the democratic movement begun in America. He was also the founder of a dynasty, belonging "to his descendants rather than to his ancestors."[9]

One of the characteristics that Chinard admired most was Adams's ability for satire. In discussing his subject's first job as a schoolmaster, Chinard gave his readers examples of Adams's wit. After one such passage, he wrote, "Had he been born in Paris, the boy who at twenty could write with such 'verve' would have been hailed as a wit of the first class...."[10] As it was, Adams was in New England and felt a need to suppress his tendency for wit. "Fortunately for us, he was never able entirely to suppress his 'righteous indignation,' and whenever the occasion presented itself gave vent to his feelings, often much to his damage, but most of the time for our great enjoyment."[11] Even as a young man, Adams had a talent for expression. While his gift in this area may not have been as exquisite as Jefferson's, his writing skills proved invaluable to him and to scholars who later studied him. His wit provides a glimpse of another side to Adams that the American people have not always recognized.

Chinard was fascinated by many passages in Adams's diary. He pointed out the young man's keen skills of observation and of what Chinard called his "talent for portraits," not painted, but written. Adams was, in fact, very good at describing the people he met. This skill grew over time, and he continued his keen observations throughout his life. In emphasizing this talent, Chinard provided an appreciative glimpse into Adams's mind and personality. Yet Chinard believed it also demonstrated Adams's work ethic. "He had for the time a remarkably rich vocabulary, the result it seems, of work and application, more than a native gift." Chinard went on to say Adams was not always good at improvising, but when he could think about what he wished to say and take pen to paper, the result was rewarding. "With his quill he seemed to pick out long strings of words from the inkstand," Chinard wrote. "His vocabulary of invectives is even richer."[12] He argued that Adams could have been one of the top writers in the colonies had he written for newspapers, but that was not what Adams wanted. His ambitions lay with the law. However, his gift for observation never failed him.

Chinard made note of Adams's writing abilities several times throughout his biography. In describing Adams's observations during the First Continental Congress, Chinard stated, "If in conversation he had learned to exercise a certain discretion, his pen was never sharper, more alert and cruel." He went on to describe John Adams's initial thoughts on Thomas Paine's *Common Sense*, calling his writings on the subject "a good page of literary criticism."[13]

Chinard was also quick to acknowledge John Adams's tendency toward self-doubt. In one instance, the biographer does this in defense of his subject. In relating the history of Adams's selection to attend the 1st Continental Congress in 1774, Chinard wrote of the delegate's nervousness to remind his readers that John Adams was a complicated man. "The 'morbid vanity' of John Adams has been so often emphasized that it is only just to call attention once more to the fundamental intellectual honesty of the man—to the hesitation, doubts, misgivings and anxiety that troubled his mind during the weeks following his appointment."[14] On this same subject, Chinard recognized Adams's sense of duty. These traits were more important to this biographer than those of vanity or ambition.

No scholar has ever disputed that Adams possessed the latter characteristics, but for Chinard, they did not provide a complete or fair portrait of the man. He saw in Adams a creature of independence and self-righteousness. He noted the moment in Adams's presidency when he decided to negotiate a peace with the French when most of the country was clamoring for war. Chinard claimed that this was the most courageous act of Adams's political career and the decision resulted from his personality, his delight "in standing alone against friend and foe...."[15] Chinard also concluded that John Adams was much more a man of the Old World of Europe than the New World of America. This biographer saw in Adams's philosophy and worldview ideas that would have resonated with the writers of Europe. Therefore, even as Adams was helping to build a new country, he was rooted in the history and culture of an older world.[16]

While the Adams family and Chinard biographies offer interesting glimpses into John Adams's life and career, they do not emphasize his friendships or his family life in the same way that later biographies will. These writers had as their agenda the need to reform the reputation of their subject and to celebrate a Founder they believed was neglected. One of the problems they faced was a lack of sources. John Quincy and Charles Francis Adams did work from John Adams's papers, and Charles Francis provided a highly edited version of John Adams's *Works*.[17] This endeavor allowed the public and scholars to see many of Adams's papers, but John's grandson was also careful in his editing.[18] A good deal was missing. This fact was explained by one scholar who approached John Adams in a different way.

In 1952, Zoltán Haraszti published *John Adams and the Prophets of Progress: A Study in the Intellectual and Political History of the Eighteenth Century*. This work was not a traditional biography but rather a study of Adams's relationship with his books. Haraszti was a Keeper of Rare Books and Editor of Publications at the Boston Public Library. This was the depository for John Adams's book collection, and Haraszti was interested in the dialogs Adams had with the various authors he was reading. He wrote an intriguing study of Adams's marginalia in order to gain a better understanding of the man. However, Haraszti also noted the one handicap that scholars faced when approaching an examination of John Adams. His papers were not openly available to the public or to scholars. As Haraszti noted, "The Adams Papers are stored in the Adams Room at the Massachusetts Historical Society," but "a member of the family is their custodian, and the Massachusetts Historical Society has no control over them."[19] This unfortunate situation, according to Haraszti, kept scholars in the dark about who Adams really was. As he lamented, "More than for any other reason, Adams is unappreciated because he is the least known of the great Americans. The immense mass of his manuscripts is still locked away."[20] Fortunately for this scholar, the Boston Public Library had Adams's books, allowing Haraszti to write his insightful investigation into the mind of John Adams.

Nevertheless, Haraszti, like other scholars of the 1950s, mourned the lack of access to the Adams papers. This would change shortly after Haraszti published his book. A new set of biographies would do more to create a complete portrait of John Adams, and the writers of these works had an advantage that Chinard and Haraszti did not. The massive collection of John Adams's papers would soon become available for scholarly use; historians rejoiced.

The man chosen to undertake the huge editorial project of the Adams papers was Lyman H. Butterfield. He was well-suited for the work. Butterfield, who had previously served as a director of the Institute of Early American History and as an associate editor for the Jefferson Papers, took on this remarkable task with enthusiasm. "Staggering as the project might have seemed to others, Mr. Butterfield called it a labor of love," wrote Dena Kleiman in Butterfield's obituary. "He would spend his days in a small, dark room of the Massachusetts Historical Society surrounded by volume after volume of family manuscripts. Enmeshed with Their Lives."[21]

Butterfield also offered a helpful glimpse into the history of the massive collection. He traced the papers from their beginnings, when John Adams realized in 1774 that he should preserve his letters. Butterfield also discussed the establishment of the Adams Manuscript Trust in 1905 and the agreement with the family to launch a microfilming program for the papers. The family members entrusted with the papers met with a group of scholars, Butterfield among them, to help make decisions about what to do with the collection. "As one of the scholars called upon," Butterfield related, "I have a confession to make. I came to the Old House in Quincy on that lovely summer day in 1952 prepared to argue a case." What he happily realized, however, is that the family members had already decided to allow the microfilming project.[22]

Butterfield's joy in this decision and in his subsequent work on the papers is clear in his narration of the history of the papers. His gratitude as an historian to the Adams family knew no bounds. "Thanks to the collective vigilance, pride, financial solvency, and wisdom of the Adams family," Butterfield wrote, "their representatives have been enabled to turn over to the public … a uniquely extensive and significant body of historical records." Because of "an act of unparalleled generosity they [the Adams papers] are now placed before those whose task and privilege it is to interpret the past to the present and future."[23]

Butterfield undertook the monumental task of editing all of Adams's writings beginning in 1954. The first works he edited were the diary and autobiography of John Adams. This project upon which Butterfield embarked was touted by the Massachusetts Historical Society, and *Life* magazine dedicated a good deal of space to the effort. There was good reason for this. *Life* provided funds for the task. "The deeds and ideas of the Adams family have led and inspired the nation since even before that great July day when independence was declared," wrote *Life*. "But the Adamses … were more than makers of history. They were brilliant reporters of it." Unfortunately, reported the magazine, those papers had long been locked away by the family, but were now turned over to the Massachusetts Historical Society and could be edited and published.[24] Scholars in the Cold War United States could now delve into the life of John Adams as never before, finding in him a model of stability and unity.

The new editor of the papers told the magazine that "reading [John Adams's] diary is like watching a display of fireworks."[25] In true *Life* magazine fashion, the article is beautifully photographed, displaying contemporary scenes of places about which Adams wrote in his early diary and his home, now part of the Adams National Historical Park. Yet the rest of the article is in John's and Abigail's words, punctuated by context notes from the magazine's editors. Remarkably, the excerpts from the Adams's letters that the magazine used were "published here for the first time."[26] Given the accessibility of the Adams papers today, it is remarkable to think that these letters were in print for the first time in 1961.

Butterfield and his staff performed a great service for researchers by putting these papers on microfilm and—with the commitment of Harvard University Press—in print; scholars took notice. Various reviews of the work highlighted its value and presented different perspectives on the picture of John Adams that emerged from them. The most remarkable yet least complete review came from President John F. Kennedy, writing in 1962. Kennedy marveled at the diverse contributions of the entire Adams family. He also noted that each member of the family, no matter what his vocation, "had a special concern to foster links between government and learning." The President did not deny certain personality traits that have always emerged in John Adams scholarship. "That Adams had considerable self-esteem and a strong propensity to self-justification is unmistakable," President Kennedy noted, diplomatically. "But the diary and autobiography do not leave an image of narrow conceit and severe austerity." Throughout these works, Kennedy discovered a man who possessed "honesty, tenacity, and pungent good sense." Finally, in assessing the value of these now published John Adams writings, the President stated, "His diaries became not a mere exercise in self-portraiture, but a faithful re-creation of an age."[27]

In addition to John F. Kennedy, two historians, students of the Revolutionary Era, wrote reviews of the edited Adams papers. Edmund S. Morgan, best known among academics for his work on the Stamp Act Crisis, wrote a review of the papers for *The New England Quarterly*. Noting the work of editors who had dedicated themselves to bringing the papers of the Founding Fathers into print, Morgan asserted these editors "recreate a man and his world in intimate detail" and because of their efforts, "we now begin to know Jefferson, Franklin, and Adams better than any man of normal memory knows himself."[28] Morgan acknowledged the work of Adams's grandson, Charles Francis, as the first editor of his papers, as did Butterfield.

The difference in this new enterprise is that little was held back from the reader. Adams's grandson tended to leave out anything that he felt "unworthy or undignified," in Morgan's words. For example, Charles Francis deleted many passages from his grandfather's diary that dealt with the farm in Braintree (now Quincy). Adams had "almost an obsession with manure," said Morgan. "Traveling in Europe he took as much pride in the superiority of his remembered piles in Braintree over those in Great Britain...." In addition to the discussions of fertilizer, Charles Francis also refused to publish passages in which his grandfather appeared jealous of others. For Morgan, this was misguided. He argued, "John Adams' vanity, however it may impair our admiration for him, was closely allied to his real strength." What the reader now saw, according to Morgan, was "the full John Adams as we have never had him before" allowing for a reassessment of him, a process that Morgan believed Adams would have welcomed.[29]

Morgan's review then shifted to a discussion of John Adams as a descendant of the Puritans. He included an interesting comparison of John Winthrop—the first governor of Massachusetts Bay and most famous for his "City Upon a Hill" analogy—and John Adams. The two men lived in different times and distinct circumstances. However, in ending his review with praise for the work of Butterfield and his team, Morgan placed Adams in the long tradition of the Protestant reformers who established Massachusetts. "Puritans looked for posthumous rewards, and it is fitting that a secularized Puritan [Adams] should receive his in the monument which Mr. Butterfield and his associates have now begun to rear."[30] For Morgan, this more complete John Adams fell in line with his Puritan ancestors and seeing this in his own words brought value to the work of Butterfield. For another historian, however, the Adams that appeared from these new, complete editions was more than a Puritan holdover.

Harvard University professor of history Bernard Bailyn wrote a review of the diary and autobiography of John Adams for *The William and Mary Quarterly*, one of the leading journals in early United States history. His review, published in April 1962, preceded Bailyn's most influential work on the American Revolution.[31] Yet Bailyn was already an expert in colonial and revolutionary Massachusetts. He brought to his review of

Butterfield's work an appreciation for the talents and background of John Adams. He, like Morgan, pointed to John Adams's Puritan background and noted the characteristics of the Calvinist faith that Adams possessed. "If he sought fame, reputation, and success," Bailyn wrote, "he despised them, too, and excoriated himself in one breath for the very efforts he urged upon himself in another."[32] This struggle was clear in Adams's diaries. Seeing these writings in all their complexities gave readers a fuller picture of who Adams was.

However, Bailyn also encountered another side of John Adams as he read these new complete editions of the diary and autobiography. Bailyn believed that a side of Adams had been missing before Butterfield's work brought to the public his fully restored writings. What Bailyn discovered was a man full of life, open to all it had to offer. "For all his mental efforts and intellectual accomplishments, his knowledge and ideas," argued Bailyn, "he responded first and fundamentally to the physical—the tangible, audible, visual—qualities of life. He felt the world, directly and sensitively, before he thought about it."[33] After experiencing the world in this way, Adams wrote about it in a way that, according to Bailyn, provided some of the most readable prose of the 18th century. Adams was capable of what Bailyn called "[s]ustained literary brilliance," an assessment with which Gilbert Chinard would have agreed.[34] Adams's diaries reveal a man adept at dramatic phrasing and dialog as well as humor.

In addition, by having the complete text of his writings, readers and scholars could now see Adams move from his uncomfortable twenties into his thirties, when Bailyn noted "a rapid growth; a sudden emergence into maturity" brought about in part because of John's marriage to Abigail Smith in 1764. Once married to this remarkable woman, the agonizing self-doubt declined. Abigail made all the difference and Bailyn wrote, "the mystery is not so much why Adams no longer poured his soul out into his notebooks after 1764 as why he did not burn the ones in which he had."[35] Yet Bailyn also stated, "For though Adams changed, around his thirtieth year, he was not transformed. The earlier characteristics were transmuted, not eliminated; and they continued to shape his, and … the nation's, history."[36]

All of this came to light with the full text of Adams's diary and autobiography. Adams's struggles, fears, insecurities, passions, and gifts came into vivid focus in a way they never had before, thanks to Butterfield and his team. Historians have benefited from this work ever since, but the first to put the collection to use was a professor of history at the University of California, Los Angeles. His work was a turning point in Adams historiography.

In 1962, Page Smith published *John Adams*. This two-volume work, while extensive, is also highly readable. In his introduction to this massive work, Smith discussed the importance of remembering individuals in history and noting their contributions. "Perhaps we, as a part of that posterity to which Adams looked for sympathy and for understanding, are at last ready to listen attentively to a voice which has preserved across the intervening generations its New England accents, its vigor of expression, its mother wit."[37] As with many other writers, Page Smith lamented the neglect of John Adams. In his bibliographical note, Smith stated, "Compared with his distinguished contemporaries, John Adams has attracted the attention of few biographers."[38] He acknowledged part of the reason for this neglect was the lack of access to Adams's writings.

As noted above, while Charles Francis Adams had published *The Works of John Adams, Second President of the United States with a Life of the Author* in 1856, this was only a part of the massive papers that John Adams generated in his lifetime. Smith believed historians were afraid of missing "important evidence which would prevent them from drawing an accurate picture of their subject."[39] This is the way in which Smith's biography differed from others that had come before it. He was the first to work from the Adams papers edited by Butterfield. These Smith called "the definitive edition of the writings of John Adams" and he put them to good use.[40] For this reason, his biography marked a watershed moment in Adams historiography.

Smith also declared that another reason for the neglect of Adams was his personality. According to this historian, Adams was "an uncongenial figure" to many writers and that "Americans preferred other heroes—Washington, Jefferson and Hamilton among them—to the prickly and outspoken New Englander."[41] Once again, the portrait of Adams is clear in the mind of a writer who, at the same time, regretted his absence from historical works. However, Smith argued that Adams was important and relevant. He applauded the availability of Adams's works "at a time when the particular truths which Adams exemplified in his life and thought are most relevant to contemporary America."[42] In this, Smith placed the life of John Adams into the context of the mid–20th-century United States and made it clear that modern citizens could learn something from the founding generation, Adams in particular.

Smith argued that he was not as interested in justifying Adams as he was in "understanding and explicating my subject's particular angle of vision." Smith stated further that "I have tried to present John Adams with all his foibles and eccentricities, his blemishes as well as his virtues, so that he may be seen in his full humanity … he would have asked no more."[43] In this way, Smith's biography was a departure from earlier works. As a result, his book is worthy of extended attention here.

Smith began his biography by introducing John Adams as an old man. The reader sees Adams as the ancient patriarch of a family and a nation who continued to think about philosophy, religion, and the meaning of his own life. "He had had a long time to consider them, a kind of second lifetime." In his first, he had been a mover and a shaker, a maker of revolutions and nations, according to Smith. Now, in his second lifetime, "he had gone back to the familiar earth of his birthplace, gone back to wait for death."[44] The opening paragraph of Smith's biography summed up the life he was about to relate, and, in literary terms, it was a great hook. The remainder of the first chapter included an extensive discussion of Adams's Puritan background, but also the discovery by an early teacher of John Adams's extraordinary mind. Adams himself related his struggle early on with learning and acknowledged the difference a good teacher made in his life.[45]

Joseph Marsh is credited with preparing Adams for Harvard, and for instilling in him a love for learning. Smith used the story of Joseph Marsh entering Adams's educational life to emphasize certain traits in Adams. "[Marsh] recognized at once that the boy had a fine mind. He was ... a curious combination of traits—sober and reserved, passionate and intense, stiff and shy yet affectionate and responsive"; in addition, according to Smith, Marsh saw that his pupil was "impulsive, headstrong, sharp-tongued, with an aggressive self-assurance balanced by an almost morbid self-doubt."[46] Whether or not Marsh observed all these things is unclear. This portion of the chapter does not include a footnote or source and much of what we know about this period of Adams's life came from Adams. Yet, in this way, Smith was able to discuss Adams's early education while also introducing those traits that were so prominent in Adams's later life. Smith wished his readers to see the entire personality of John Adams early in the biography.

As part of Smith's attempt to present the humanity of Adams, Smith wrote an extraordinary paragraph, providing a psychological analysis of the man before his marriage to Abigail. Smith argued that the unmarried Adams was paranoid and suffered from an "agonizing inferiority complex." Adams also showed signs of the "classic manic-depressive, swinging from the heights to the depths.... In addition, our psychologist would note 'a pattern of aggressive behavior,' a truculence not uncommon in small ... men of compact body structure and high energy—but tending under stress to irrational and anti-social acts." While Smith was not completely convinced of the validity of such an analysis—"Such is modern wisdom," he wrote at the end of this list—he did acknowledge Adams's issues ranging from hypochondria to mild paranoia. He also argued that Abigail provided balance and clarity for him. She "insured his sanity." In addition,

Smith stated, life with John had an interesting impact on Abigail. "If she grew through him to be more touchy, more vulnerable to the barbs of the world, the outrageous actions of men, and the accidents of fortune, she made him less so."[47]

Smith, in an exhaustive way, covered Adams's role in the American Revolution, from writings against English policy to his role in the courtroom during the Boston Massacre trial. There is no more thorough coverage of Adams's time in the Continental Congresses and the part he played in achieving American independence then in this biography. Smith also covered in depth Adams's diplomatic mission to France, Holland, and England before bringing him home to become the nation's first vice-president. What is extraordinary in Volume 2 of Smith's biography is his discussion of John Adams's presidency, specifically his coverage of the Alien and Sedition Acts and the reasons for Adams's defeat in 1800.

The Alien and Sedition Acts of 1798 have long been a stain on John Adams's legacy. These acts were in response to tensions with France which began during Washington's presidency and continued into the Adams administration. Fear and hatred of France had reached a fever pitch after the abuse of American diplomats at the hands of the French became public knowledge.[48] The strained relationship with France also created more of a partisan spirit in the young nation, with Jefferson's Democratic-Republicans[49] and Hamilton's Federalists fighting constantly over proper strategy. John Adams, while a Federalist himself, was not one to answer to party. However, when the Federalist-controlled Congress passed the Alien and Sedition Acts, Adams did not hesitate to sign them, an act that would hurt his reputation in history.

Particularly problematic to Adams's legacy was the Sedition Act, which curtailed the civil liberties of American citizens. The act read in part, that if any person

> shall write, print, utter or publish, or shall cause or procure to be written, printed, uttered or published, or shall knowingly and willingly assist or aid in writing, printing, uttering or publishing any false, scandalous and malicious writing or writings against the government of the United States, or either house of the Congress of the United States, or the President of the United States, with intent to defame the said government, or either house of the said Congress, or the said President ... shall be punished by a fine not exceeding two thousand dollars, and by imprisonment not exceeding two years.[50]

The act, written in vague terms, was open to abuse and was often used to silence political enemies. This was unfortunate for the Adams administration. In fact, Smith argued, "Perhaps he [Adams] would have had second thoughts if he could have foreseen the Pandora's box the act would open up and the cloud it would come to cast over his entire administration.

But even with such prevision, he would doubtless have supported its enactment."[51]

Smith spends a good deal of time discussing the Sedition Act by examining the context of the act (mainly aimed at the press of the time) and the reasons the Federalists felt it necessary. In an extraordinary few paragraphs, Smith not only explained the facts of the act, but also placed his biography in the context of his own Cold War era. He wrote, "The Alien and Sedition Acts have been used so persistently to indict the Federalists and the Adams administration that an effort to put them in their proper perspective is warranted."[52] Smith then recounted the threats to the new nation both from France and from factionalism within the United States. He reminded his readers, "The press, through which many ... made their voices heard, was perhaps the most violent and vituperative that was to appear in a century and a half of American history."[53] He continued by saying that the government under Adams had an expectation that "newspaper editors should tell the truth."[54] He then related the Alien and Sedition Acts to the Cold War United States:

> A hundred and fifty years later ... the greatest nation in the world ... hounded and harassed a handful of domestic Communists. Long instructed in the ways of freedom, powerful and united, the United States gave way in the twentieth century to panic fears, enacting legislation in the name of "internal security" that later historians may well judge far more harshly than the Alien and Sedition Acts.[55]

He ended this reminder to his readers by taking a jab at his fellow historians. "We can leave the Alien and Sedition Acts to the periodic indignation of righteous historians who will be happy if their own nation and their own times show no grosser offenses against human freedom."[56]

This was an amazing justification of the most misguided act of John Adams's public life. No historian writing about Adams has demonstrated comfort with the Alien and Sedition Acts. Most agree that he never should have signed them and are sorry that he did.[57] One biographer argued that while Adams saw no problem with the acts, he demonstrated a "marked reluctance" to carry the laws into action and "showed leniency in a number of instances."[58] No historian, however, spent the time and effort to vindicate Adams that Page Smith did. The Alien and Sedition Acts are a stain on the legacy of John Adams without a doubt, and to bring his positive contributions to light, Smith may have crossed the line from historian to advocate. However, this is one of many examples in which Smith delves into detail in a way many other biographers did not.

In the second volume of the biography, in writing about Adams's life after the presidency, Smith focused on Adams's feelings and continued zest for life. In writing about his subject's defeat for a second term as president, Smith wrote that Adams "lived life too passionately, cared too intensely, was involved in its hopes and anguish too inextricably to meet this final, most bitter defeat with equanimity" and that this rejection "inflicted a raw wound that would never entirely heal...."[59] Smith gave his readers an in-depth analysis of Adams's defeat as well and discussed historians' treatment of his administration in the light of Hamilton worship and Jefferson reverence.[60] Smith also devoted a great deal of time to the retirement years, noting that children were drawn to the old man, that Adams became more and more a Unitarian, and that he felt compelled to revisit his role in the Revolution as a corrective to the work of Mercy Otis Warren (whose history of the American Revolution was not kind to Adams).[61]

Smith discussed his subject's thoughts on historiography. In this summation, Smith recognized that John Adams was aware of the pitfalls of history. "One of the most serious problems of historiography was the philosophy of the historian himself. Historians were always writing histories to prove something, generally something that had little or nothing to do with attitudes and aspirations of the times and people with which they were dealing." According to Smith, Adams saw all too clearly that historians wrote to prove that an historical figure was "without blemish or imperfection." Yet, Adams believed "History, as man's collective memory must above all distinguish truth from falsehood."[62] Again, Smith took a good deal of time to discuss Adams's thoughts on history, and perhaps the biographer saw something in Adams's attitudes to which he could relate.

The John Adams that emerges in the pages of Smith's work was a man with many flaws but who possessed a drive to achieve that saved him. His work ethic, his integrity, and his honesty were as much a part of this Adams as were all his faults. Yet the humanity of Adams is a central part of Smith's portrait. In the end, Smith wanted his readers to understand the importance of John Adams. In the last paragraph of this massive work, Smith wrote, "If our history is the means by which we define ourselves, John Adams must be even more relevant to us today than he was in his own lifetime."[63] Another biographer, writing in the 1960s, agreed with Page Smith.

In 1969, freelance writer Anne Husted Burleigh published *John Adams*. In her original introduction, she expressed her belief that the philosophy of her subject was timeless. "The rare man who can sift the unchanging out of our constantly changing world is a man for the ages, a man who spans more than his own generation." Since John Adams "strove to perceive the patterns of constancy that lend a universal character to the lives of all men," he remained relevant to the tumultuous America of 1969 as well as to his own.[64]

After a period of forty years, Burleigh's biography was republished, and in the new introduction to the book, Burleigh noted the attention that Mr. Adams had received in the ensuing years. She stated, "During the four decades since this book was published, John Adams has become a much better known and appreciated member of the company of Founding Fathers." She noted not only new biographies, including the best-seller by David McCullough, but also the fame he had achieved in popular culture. "Adams himself surely would be surprised that he even has become a popular theatrical figure, playing prominently in the musical, *1776*; in the television series, *The Adams Chronicles*; and ... as the centerpiece of HBO's television series, *John Adams*."[65]

Why, then, was the Burleigh biography republished in 2009? The author offered an explanation. She believed the book still achieved its intended purpose, which was "to emphasize... John Adams' political thought and to describe his enormous contribution to the political philosophy animating the American Revolution and the early years of the young nation."[66] Burleigh's biography does indeed emphasize these things. With entire sections dedicated to his writing of the Massachusetts State Constitution as well as chapters focused on his *Defence of the Constitutions* and his *Discourses on Davila*, Burleigh's analysis of his thought is extensive.

Yet, in 1969, Burleigh also placed herself squarely in what historians have named the Republican Synthesis school of the American Revolution, best articulated by historians Bernard Bailyn and Gordon Wood. The Republican Synthesis school emphasized the ideology behind the actions of the colonial Revolutionaries and their understanding of the struggle between power and liberty.[67] For Burleigh, John Adams comprehended the conflict between these two concepts. "Adams understood," she wrote, "that the corrective to unchecked power is virtue that harnesses and directs the will to rightly ordered action." She went on to emphasize Adams's religious faith as well, arguing, "Because religious faith often provides that essential reference point and moral compass, religion, thought Adams, is the underpinning of freedom."[68]

For this biographer, in 1969 and 2009, what made Adams relevant—in addition to his faith in God—was his ability to express the ideas of the Revolution and of a republican form of government. She also saw in Adams a man keenly aware of history in the making. He could not sit by and watch.

With his capacity to be in the midst of happenings and yet perceive their relevance to the fabric of history, Adams was able ... to look back and size up, to look forward and predict—all with uncanny accuracy. Some men, it seems, ride the surface of life; others, like Adams, swim deep in the current. These are the men who feel the majesty of the events in which they partake, who see the grand workings of history in every occasion, personal or public.[69]

For Burleigh, John Adams was a model of true republicanism under the law as well as an example of a man of faith who believed that a government of laws also needed a moral compass. This required good character, and Burleigh certainly saw this in Adams. She was not the first nor would she be the last biographer to emphasize Adams's religion and morality. In fact, for many writers, these traits make Adams unique, not just in his generation, but among politicians of the 20th and 21st centuries.

The biographies of John Adams which appeared in the 19th through the mid–20th centuries were attempts to bring Adams to public attention. Grandson Charles Francis Adams did not wish for his grandfather to be forgotten, but he also hid parts of John Adams's personality apparent in his diaries. While other early biographers did not have the benefit of Adams's complete and unedited works, they were still able to see a man worthy of attention. Once the unabridged Adams papers became available to scholars, they recognized the more complete picture for what it was: a revelation into the full personality of the man. In taking advantage of this, historians such as Page Smith wished to present Adams to a country dealing with different problems from the ones Adams would know, but also argued his relevance to 1960s Americans.

These early biographies, whether apologizing for, excusing, or lauding John Adams, all argued that their subject would want to be seen, warts and all. While attempting to accomplish this, even Page Smith's massive work tended toward the laudatory. None of these monographs excused John Adams's temperament, and Smith tried to explain it. Still, one senses in these early works a need to swing Adams scholarship toward a more forgiving approach of its subject. By doing this, these writers would argue, Adams deserved a place in the past that 19th- and 20th-century Americans constructed for themselves. He could be employed in the usable past as a man who represented independence, constancy, and morality. For Burleigh in particular, this last trait was vital for the late 1960s United States.

Beginning in the late 1960s and early 1970s, many of the founding fathers were scrutinized in new ways, all thanks to the Bicentennial of the Declaration of Independence. In marked similarity to the Centennial celebration of the nation's founding, the two-hundredth anniversary of the American Revolution came at a time of war, civil unrest, and political corruption. Scholars studying the historical figures of the American Revolution continued to examine them, often with more cynical eyes than their predecessors.

For John Adams, this meant a closer analysis of his character in general and of his personality in particular. From the Bicentennial forward, Adams scholarship would move through two distinct phases, one suggesting that previous scholars had been too forgiving of him and the other asserting that he still deserved more understanding treatment. How these opposing ideas advanced in the latter part of the 20th century and into the 21st is the subject of the next chapter.

THREE

Historiography
from 1976 to the Present

The Bicentennial celebration, honoring the two-hundredth anniversary of the Declaration of Independence—with July 4, 1776, touted as America's Birthday—came at a time of division and weariness in the United States. Despite this—or more likely because of it—like their counterparts a hundred years before, Americans wanted a celebration. However, even the nature of that celebration became a matter for debate.

In 1966, the federal government created the American Revolution Bicentennial Commission (ARBC) but found it difficult to create or maintain one collective form of commemoration. In fact, the ARBC found itself under investigation by the Senate Subcommittee on Federal Charters, Holidays, and Celebrations for steering the party too much toward big business and Richard Nixon supporters.[1] Moreover, many expressed concerns about the over-commercialization of the event, understandable given the many products that the consumer could buy to demonstrate patriotism. As Tammy S. Gordon noted in her study *The Spirit of 1976: Commerce, Community, and the Politics of Commemoration*, products included "egg timers, door mats, t-shirts, engagement rings, ice cream, leisure suits, lamps, bed sheets, condoms, guns, travel tours, toilet seats, frisbees, needlepoint kits, and garage doors," leading some to dub the event "The Buycentennial Sellabration."[2]

However, there was renewed interest in the American Revolution during this period and in the Founding Fathers as well as the role played by those deemed "common people" whose lives were studied by social historians.[3] In order to review the events leading to the Declaration of Independence, Americans could tune in nightly for two years for the airing of the Bicentennial Minute. In addition, for those of the viewing audience who wished to see a dramatization of one Founding Father in particular, Public Broadcasting aired a continuing series entitled *The Adams Chronicles*, complete with study guides and a companion book.[4]

In the smaller, scholarly world, academics from different fields renewed their study of the founding generation. One of those scholars, an English Professor, Peter Shaw, chose as his subject none other than John Adams. Yet Shaw's approach to Adams differed from those of earlier biographers. In *The Character of John Adams*, Shaw sought to understand Adams's psychological make-up. In fact, one reviewer referred to the book as a psychohistory while another entitled his review "John Adams and the Psychology of Power."[5] While Shaw certainly explored patterns in John Adams's thinking and behavior, his choice of title was interesting. What emerged from Shaw's study were the patterns of thought and actions of a man deeply rooted in his Puritan background. In other words, in this case, Shaw attempted to explain Adams's personality by using literary techniques but also psychoanalysis. Since his book is cited by so many later biographers, the character of John Adams that appeared in Shaw's book deserves scrutiny.

In the preface to his book, Shaw continued the refrain about Adams's obscurity among the Founders. The first sentence reads: "John Adams's lifelong struggle with the temptations of popularity and fame was not apparent to his contemporaries, but it contributed to his lack of popularity while he lived and until recent years to his relative obscurity among the founders of the nation."[6] He went on to explain why scholars and the public had overlooked Adams in favor of Jefferson, Hamilton, and Washington. He concluded his first paragraph with an interesting commentary on an American poet who devoted one of his works to Adams. "The one exception," wrote Shaw, "was typical of Adams's bad luck with publicity. Ezra Pound, who found a version of his own cranky originality in Adams, devoted one of the longest and least known sequences in American poetry to him in his *Cantos*."[7]

Shaw proceeded through the historiography of Adams up to 1976, noting that Adams had been rediscovered by historians and biographers alike, as a "diarist, political writer, diplomat, president, and as a letter writer and sage…." Shaw remarked that Adams would have been pleased with this attention. "But I wonder if he would have noticed that, ironically, his personality is once again being lost through appreciative rehearsals of his fragmented careers."[8] This was the gap Shaw hoped to fill. By examining certain events in Adams's life, Shaw wanted to discuss his character, analyzing his thought patterns throughout his life. He discovered similarities in the ways that Adams dealt with crises, both personal and professional. Yet Shaw also wished to avoid judging Adams by 20th-century standards, stating, "As far as possible I have placed him [Adams] in the context of his time and place as well as in the light of his Puritan intellectual and emotional heritage." Shaw also expressed his wish "to introduce

Adams to readers outside the profession of American history without sacrificing the standards of historical scholarship."[9]

Throughout his biography, Shaw scrutinized Adams's inner struggle with vanity, ambition, and the need for recognition. He discovered patterns in Adams's life that suggested he fought the desire for fame and yet wished to be a great and distinguished man. He wished to be admired. Shaw stated, "Still, much as he sought the universal admiration that he felt he deserved, he never could put himself out to be popular. The truth was that from the beginning he courted not popularity but unpopularity as a mark of distinction."[10] By carefully reading Adams's diaries, letters, and political writings, Shaw attempted to define Adams's character and understand his actions. He followed Adams through his early life, his decision to become a lawyer, and his role in the independence movement, identifying models for Adams's behavior and figures of authority who he defied.

Shaw spent a large part of his study dissecting Adams's diplomatic career and his relationship with Benjamin Franklin. These two men, with similar backgrounds—both were born in Massachusetts and raised in the Puritan tradition—were nevertheless polar opposites in their approaches to life. That became apparent while the two served as diplomats in Europe. Adams's second trip to Europe, the purpose of which was to begin peace negotiations with England, was a particularly trying mission for him. He decided on his own to travel to Holland to win recognition for the United States. While there, he suffered a breakdown and was also informed that his peace commission, which was supposed to be his alone, would now be handled by him and three other men, Franklin among them.

This wounded Adams, and he blamed Franklin in part. He even reached the point of not wanting to be with the man. Because of these feelings, Adams delayed leaving Holland when he was expected in Paris for peace negotiations. As Shaw stated, "Adams's reluctance to be near Franklin had begun to have political consequences." Shaw continued his analysis of his subject's behavior by noting that "Adams still felt the wound of losing the peace commission, and he still regarded Franklin as responsible for his suffering.... A self-denier rather than a fighter, Adams responded to aggression such as Franklin's with self-doubt instead of a thirst for revenge."[11]

In the early years of his retirement, Adams was tortured by thoughts of his neglect in public memory. He wrote letters and essays attempting to explain and vindicate himself, all in the face of the rising fame of his rivals. It was difficult for him to see the growing adulation of men like Franklin and even Washington, men that at one time, Adams had admired. He was happy to acknowledge their accomplishments to a point but drew the line at making them god-like characters. Shaw wrote, "It was true that he had dropped into obscurity while they [Washington and Franklin] grew into mythical heroes celebrated in paintings and lithographs, literature and epigram. As the power of the Jeffersonians grew after 1801 Adams was mentioned less and less, his name dropping even from Fourth of July toasts."[12] The growing mythology surrounding Franklin—who died in 1790—was the most painful for Adams.

Near the end of his biography of Adams, in discussing his retirement years, Shaw wrote an interesting comparison of two autobiographies—one written by Franklin and the other by Adams. As Shaw put it, "Franklin created the image of the American of humble origin who rises through hard work to success and international prominence. The story was Adams's as much as Franklin's, but it became associated with Franklin in life, autobiography, and the historical memory of Americans."[13] Shaw continued by arguing that Franklin shared many of Adams's personality traits but made a choice early on to abandon argumentation and aggressiveness in favor of what Franklin termed humility. Shaw went one step further and compared the two autobiographies to the writings of their Puritan ancestors.[14] He wrote, "The certitude of Franklin's program has often been compared to the uplifting advice of Cotton Mather's *Essays to Do Good....* Adams's uncertainties derived from another side of Puritanism, best represented by its autobiographies."[15] What was most difficult for some of these Puritan writers—Increase Mather in particular—was what they saw as popular neglect. Adams could relate.

In his early retirement years, after what he considered a shunning by the nation he helped to create, Adams lashed out at the deification of his colleagues from the American Revolution. "With Adams the conviction grew," wrote Shaw, "that the world's lack of appreciation would be permanent."[16] Yet as the years wore on, Adams stopped fighting to vindicate himself. He was still concerned about history and posterity, but he reached a point where his overall mood toward former rivals was one of forgiveness. Shaw would not go so far as to say that Adams was at peace with himself at last. "It was not serenity that Adams achieved but an accommodation with his own craggy personality."[17] Being out of the public eye and having come to terms with his career, Adams could finally accept who he was.

The portrait that emerges from Shaw's study of John Adams is of a troubled person who struggled to come to grips with his flaws. While most biographers of Adams claim that he was self-aware and have praised this trait, Shaw saw it as a problem. Adams, in trying to avoid what he considered that great vice of vanity, appeared vain to his contemporaries and to future generations. In writing his study as he did, Shaw demonstrated that there was a fine line between vanity and self-righteousness. Adams crossed that line to his detriment. Yet the roots of that high opinion of himself ran deep into his Puritan heritage. Adams certainly was not the only Founding Father saddled with ancestral baggage. Nor was he the only leader in the Revolutionary era who did not always work and play well with others.[18] However, he was unique because of his blunt nature and his willingness to write down his thoughts about the people he encountered and worked with, either in his diary or in letters to the countless correspondents he had throughout his life. In those same writings, his own flaws were apparent and often magnified. This has allowed scholars to scrutinize his personality—his character as Shaw phrased it—in ways that they could not with the other Founders. This has also led to what might be termed "John Adams Revisionism."[19]

Shaw's portrait of Adams is different from earlier scholars in that he never dwelt on Adams's finer qualities. He did not dismiss his accomplishments, nor did he ignore his contributions to the American Revolution. Yet the nature of his study was psychological. He wrote to understand what motivated Adams and to demonstrate why he so often was his own worst enemy. If Shaw had admiration for Adams, grudging or otherwise, he rarely let it show in his work. Shaw's study was not the last word on John Adams.

How writers studied John Adams in the late 20th and early 21st centuries marked a return to a gentler approach to the man. Research on Adams and on his wife, Abigail, continued in the 1980s, but it would be the early 1990s before new biographies appeared once again, changing the nature of Adams scholarship. One of these was a study of Adams's entire life, while the other focused on his retirement years. The latter work, in particular, gave the reading public a new look at the man in his golden years and, as a result, offered a different John Adams than had appeared in earlier work. The authors of these books went to great effort to understand and explain their subject. In the case of the first author, John Adams clearly got under his skin, for he could not stop with a biography but continued his quest in various articles written for scholarly journals.

In 1992, historian John Ferling published *John Adams: A Life*. Ferling, who had written extensively on the Revolutionary and Early National periods, wrote what one blogger called "the best biography" of John Adams. The blogger noted the book "provides the perfect balance of pure insight and analysis, readability, length and hard fact versus colorful interpretation." He also enjoyed Ferling's "historical perspective interlaced with interesting character sketches and helpful political and social context."[20] Along with his biography, Ferling has written about Adams in connection with various topics, including his diplomacy, his desire to be a soldier, and—most interestingly—his health.[21] Yet Ferling admitted it took a while for him to appreciate Adams. He wrote that when he first encountered

Adams, he "did not find him endearing." Ferling used words such as "obsessive," "neurotic," and "humorless" to describe the Founder. The historian then wrote that he "rather successfully avoided Adams for the next twenty or so years" until research required him to "reacquaint myself with him."

Ferling discovered that first impressions are sometimes deceiving. "This time I found Adams very different. He seemed to be more human—and full of contradictions. Still troubled, he also seemed to be meditative, insightful, and provocative...." Adams was not the only Founder that troubled Ferling. He did not much like George Washington, either, but admitted that as his research continued on both men, his opinions of them changed. "Toward Adams, I felt esteem and affinity burgeon, although those feelings were tempered by repugnance for the way he often treated his family."[22] As a result of these changing feelings, Ferling decided to contribute his own biography to the historiography on John Adams.

What is striking about Ferling's preface to his biography of Adams is the way in which he explained his compulsion to write the book. All biographers writing about Adams felt a need to explain why they were doing it. Ferling's confession concerning his first impression of Adams and his changing feelings about him seem personal, an explanation concerning a forming friendship on some level. The fact that Ferling continued to study Adams—only one of the articles Ferling wrote on Adams appeared before this biography—suggests a lingering need to understand the man. This desire comes through in the biography in several ways.

First, Ferling reiterated what all other biographers have said concerning John Adams: as of 1992, Ferling considered Adams to be "one of the least understood of the founding fathers." Unlike earlier writers, Ferling did not contend that Adams had been neglected, but rather that he was misunderstood. In addition, the author argued, his contributions were considered less significant than those of Washington, Franklin, Jefferson, and Hamilton.

> To some he has even been a comic figure, a man full of puff and pomposity, a vain, posturing sort who took on a ridiculous cast when he sought to play a role for which he was ill suited. He has always been seen as honest and dedicated, but to the general public ... he remains little more than a "boiled shirt" or a "priggish" bore, as two popular publications recently described him.[23]

Yet Ferling also contended that the reason Adams might retain this reputation was because his thoughts, feelings, judgments, and observations were an open book. Unlike the other Founders, Adams left behind a massive record in his diary and correspondence. In noting this, Ferling made his first comparison of Adams to his contemporaries. "No other revolutionary figure left behind anything remotely akin to that preserved by Adams and his heirs." While Ferling admitted that Washington, Franklin, and Jefferson left behind "voluminous files for correspondence to historians," the men themselves were somehow veiled and protected in numerous ways. "Washington's writings were so carefully guarded that the reader can almost feel him taking pains to choose each word lest he reveal his inner self."

Ferling viewed Jefferson and Franklin as less guarded yet more private than Adams. One other key to understanding each man lay in their correspondence with their respective wives, and here again, Adams was an exception. "Whatever Washington might have written to his wife," wrote Ferling, "was lost forever when Martha burned his letters after he died." As to Jefferson, his wife died not long after Jefferson took a leading role in the Independence movement. Franklin "simply wrote home infrequently and then quite discreetly." Even the diaries of these other founders lack the introspection of Adams's. Ferling's conclusion was that this comparison was bound to put Adams at a disadvantage.

> What can be seen of Adams, therefore, is exceptional. As a consequence, the tendency of historians has been to see him as an exception. Among other things, his private writings made clear his pettiness, his ambition, his vanity, his enmities. The temptation has existed, therefore, to portray him as more petty, more ambitious, more vain, and more malicious than others.[24]

This was the first of several comparisons Ferling made of Adams to the other leaders of his day in an attempt to understand his subject. Another similarity Ferling found between Adams and the other great men of the Revolution had to do with the young Adams's obsession with recognition. As Ferling explained, this drive seemed exceptional when Adams was compared to other young men of Braintree. However, when observed alongside other "high achievers" of his time, "his behavior appears more normal." Ferling then demonstrated that Washington, Jefferson, Hamilton, and Franklin all exhibited this need to distinguish themselves in various ways. Washington wanted a commission in the British Army, while Jefferson desired a seat on the King's Council in Virginia. Hamilton dreamed of military glory, and Franklin "mapped out an extensive regimen of self-improvement, as did Adams...."[25] By comparing Adams to his counterparts in the Revolution, Ferling placed him in a larger context and demonstrated that what drove him also existed in the other Founders as well.

Another way in which Ferling attempted to understand Adams was to argue for his relevance in the United States of the 1990s. Ferling made clear in his introduction that Adams was a man of a specific time, living in two centuries that were vastly different from the 20th. Yet as Ferling argued, "John Adams's dilemmas were timeless." To demonstrate this, Ferling asked a series of questions that Adams himself had asked. "Could he succeed in his career without resorting to wickedness? Could a political leader be truly independent and genuinely serve the public? Could the demands of his work and public responsibilities be reconciled with the needs and interests of his family?" And finally, "Could he make political decisions that were personally harmful but necessary for the greater good?"[26] By using these questions as his guide, Ferling attempted to see Adams through a filter of struggles shared by many leaders in all times, including the 1980s and '90s. He wished to present the entire man—faults and all—to his readers, but he wanted to do so by connecting him to Ferling's time as well as Adams's.

Finally, in his attempt to understand Adams, Ferling reflected upon his greatness—or near greatness as the case may be. In a nine-page afterword to his biography, entitled "I am Not ... a Great Man," Ferling discussed the definition of greatness and the ways in which Adams measured up to the concept. As noted by this scholar, Adams did not claim the designation of "great man." In fact, the title of this afterword is taken from a direct quote in which Adams said, "I am not, never was, & never shall be a great man."[27] The context of this quote, however, is interesting. Adams was responding to a letter from a Dutch friend who had heard that Adams was dead. For the first half of Adams's response, he jokes about how great men are reported dead many times. Adams first admitted that he was not a great man

> ... and therefore I can conceive no Motive that any Man could have to lay me low before my time. He could not expect to gratify my Enemies, because they all know they have nothing to fear from me. They could not think of grieving or afflicting my friends for they all know they have nothing to hope from me. I conclude therefore that the report must have been owing to Some Accident and no design.[28]

Although joking about the report of his death in this way and making light of the fact that he could not be considered among the stellar actors of his time, one does sense the hurt beneath the banter. While Adams certainly wished for greatness, he did not feel that he achieved it, or rather, he did not believe the public or posterity would consider him among the great men of his generation. In his old age, he did think about his legacy a good deal.

What Ferling did with this idea of greatness was to note Adams's achievements and failures, both public and private. He praised Adams for his accomplishments in the Continental Congresses and his fight for independence. He acknowledged Adams's contribution to the forming of state governments in the new nation. Ferling also emphasized that "Adams deserves to be remembered as his country's first great nationalist, as a statesman who was more consistent in his views of America's relationship with the major powers in Europe than any other Founding Father." Finally, Ferling was effusive in his praise of Adams's bold choice to avoid war with France during his presidency, calling it a "courageous deed, an act of statesmanship that saved countless lives."[29]

In assessing Adams's private life, Ferling found much to criticize. "Adams was so consumed by a vain pursuit of recognition that, for a protracted period … his relationship with his family can only be described as indifferent, even heartless." Ferling accused Adams of being insensitive to Abigail's needs and feelings and while "Adams doubtless loved his children," his ambition left him no time to care for them.[30] Ferling acknowledged that there was a brighter side to Adams's private legacy. He did provide for his family, he opened his home to countless relatives who needed his help, and he "refused to be part of a system that reduced human beings to the status of chattel." In addition, Ferling noted Adams's capacity for friendship, stating, "behind his bilious, churlish façade, Adams could be a kind, loyal, warm individual."[31]

What was Ferling's final analysis of Adams's greatness? After writing at great length about Adams's refusal to accept democracy as the best form of government—a charge that could also be laid at the feet of a number of Founders—Ferling concluded that while Adams was not in the league of a George Washington, he certainly should be considered on equal footing with Franklin and Jefferson, just below Washington, as a great figure in his country's history. The source of his greatness, argued Ferling, "lay in his long, tireless service, undertaken at enormous personal sacrifice, and in his steadfast commitment to liberty."[32]

In his attempt to understand John Adams, Ferling presented a man with apparent flaws. In fact, he often reiterated them. Yet he also found a man he could respect and who he believed belonged with Jefferson and Franklin in particular for the work he did. While his assessment of his relationship with Abigail and the rest of his family was not as romanticized as it often was in other biographies, he did acknowledge the warmth in his subject. Moreover, Ferling stressed an important key in placing John Adams in context by highlighting the nature of his diary and his massive extant correspondence. What we know of John Adams's feelings, insecurities, struggles, judgments, loves, and hatreds is an open book. This fact, more than any other, can make John Adams a problematic figure, dismissed by many but scrutinized by others. Scholars who study Adams also sometimes find themselves so fascinated that they cannot let go. Ferling is a prime example. Once Ferling completed his biography of Adams, he went on to publish two additional articles on him, both of which demonstrated Ferling's continuing drive to understand John Adams and place him into the usable past constructed around the American Revolution.

After his biography of Adams hit the shelves, Ferling published "John Adams, Diplomat" in *The William and Mary Quarterly*. With this article, the author did a reassessment of the work Adams did in Europe during and shortly after the Revolutionary War. He began his article by restating the often-repeated Adams lament that he would not receive the proper credit for his work on behalf of his country. Ferling argued that, in his retirement, Adams remained troubled by his reputation as a diplomat and that his concerns were legitimate. Ferling cited scholars who "condemned much of his diplomatic activity between 1778 and 1781 as unwise, ruinous to himself, and of little benefit to the United States."[33] Writing in 1994, Ferling argued, "the time has arrived for a reexamination of Adams's diplomacy." Ferling's thesis statement is worth quoting in its entirety.

> This essay reconsiders Adams by exploring his motives and behavior during the War of Independence through the prism of his comprehension of how to serve America's national interest. It seeks a better understanding of Adams and his relationship with Franklin and the French and also of the difficulty with which American Independence was ultimately achieved.[34]

In this article, Ferling argued that the Model Treaty (1776), which Adams wrote in collaboration with John Dickinson, Benjamin Harrison, Robert Morris, and Benjamin Franklin, was "The most important document he authored during his congressional service." This paper was to serve as the template for treaties with the countries of Europe as the United States began its journey as an independent state. Ferling cited the opinion of one congressional delegate who believed Adams had considered the relationship between the new United States and other countries better than any man in Congress.[35] For these reasons, Adams was the perfect choice to join Franklin and his fellow envoys in France.[36]

Ferling then chipped away at the various arguments made by other scholars concerning Adams's first term of service in Europe. Ferling restated the arguments of scholars who dismissed the work Adams did in France, saying that his contributions have been portrayed as being "inconsequential." Further, Adams has been "ridiculed for wasting his time on 'work [that] other men would have relegated to their clerks.'"[37] Ferling disagreed with these conclusions, stating instead, "Adams became the administrator of an operation that had gone unmanaged" and that "he may have saved the commissioners from the acute embarrassment of bankruptcy."[38] In addition to his bookkeeping skills, Ferling cited Adams's correct assessment of French and British naval strength and that he worked in concert with Benjamin Franklin as well as Arthur Lee, the second envoy to France.[39]

The most important reexamination Ferling provided with this article concerned the relationship between Adams and Franklin. Many scholars have argued, both before 1994 and after, that Adams's disgrace as a diplomat was fueled by his hatred and jealousy of Franklin. To counter this argument, Ferling traced the working relationship between these two men and discovered that "Adams ... never once criticized Franklin in any letter penned during his first nine months in France." Even his diary was "devoid of criticism of Franklin apart from a note that Franklin's French was poor."[40] It was only when Adams's concern over the course of the war became acute that his attitude toward Franklin changed. He began to question Franklin's commitment in December 1778 and lamented that his colleague avoided confrontation, leaving Adams to fear that Franklin would not press the American cause sufficiently.

Ferling did not dismiss the fact that Adams struggled with vanity and was driven by ambition. Nor did he deny that Adams was in fact overshadowed by Franklin. Yet, Ferling claimed Adams did not detest Franklin at this stage and had even defended his colleague against charges of atheism and inability. Once Franklin reported to Congress on Adams's behavior toward the French minister Vergennes, criticizing Adams for his approach, Adams, and his allies, including Abigail, became suspicious of Franklin. Yet this did not happen until 1780–81.[41]

Ferling admitted that John Adams was not flawless as a diplomat and his biggest problem was his indiscretion. Yet Ferling also argued that none of the American envoys to Europe were perfect. "If Adams had his foibles," Ferling stated, "the same can be said of every major American envoy during the Revolution." Even Benjamin Franklin—often spared the close scrutiny given Adams—had his faults in diplomacy. According to Ferling, Franklin and his colleagues "blundered so often and so egregiously in 1777 that they aroused the ire of Vergennes [the French minister] and at times discredited the American cause."[42] By late 1780, some in Congress were ready to recall Franklin "noting Franklin's apparent lethargy and presumed servility to the French court."[43]

One interesting aspect of this article is Ferling's counter to the oft-repeated idea that Adams was not suited for diplomacy. In many ways, this was true. However, Ferling contended that Adams did have attributes that allowed him to be effective in the role. He could act in a daring manner when it was necessary, and he possessed what Ferling called "an ingrained skepticism born of his understanding of human nature."[44] He understood that French and American interests were different and that there was a connection between military and diplomatic policy. All of this led Ferling to conclude that Adams was among "the most prescient and far-sighted Americans of his day with regard to the long-term national interest of the United States."[45]

After John Ferling attempted to recast John Adams's diplomatic career, he turned to another dimension in his quest to understand Adams: he considered John Adams's health as a reason for his sometimes erratic behavior. In 1998, Ferling co-authored "John Adams's Health Reconsidered" with Dr. Lewis E. Braverman, an expert on the thyroid and a native of Quincy, Massachusetts, Adams's hometown.[46] The authors noted the many times when contemporaries of Adams questioned his sanity and called him unbalanced. The most famous of these observations came from Benjamin Franklin, who referred to Adams as "an honest man, often a wise one, but sometimes and in some things absolutely out of his senses."[47] The article also noted the assessment of scholars over time and their conclusions that Adams suffered from periodic mental breakdowns and physical illnesses that left him weak and irritable. Peter Shaw (*The Character of John Adams*, discussed earlier in this chapter) was the first scholar to argue that Adams's mental state affected his public decisions and behavior.[48] Historian James H. Hutson (*John Adams and the Diplomacy of the American Revolution*) went so far as to say that Adams suffered from an "emotional illness" and that this affected his role as a diplomat.[49]

After recapping all the possibilities put forth by scholars to explain John Adams's behavior and decisions, Ferling and Braverman advanced a new theory. "This article … suggests that Adams suffered from thyrotoxicosis, a disease of the thyroid. We do not contend that thyrotoxicosis is the only possible explanation. Indeed, we hope the article will encourage others to offer additional hypotheses."[50] This is an interesting approach to John Adams that has received little attention from scholars. James Grant (*John Adams: Party of One*) acknowledged the theory in a footnote, but few others have mentioned it. This is because, as the authors of the article concede, "The diagnosis of an illness experienced by someone who lived in the distant past is often exceedingly difficult."[51] Despite this handicap, Ferling and Braverman studied the symptoms Adams himself described and concluded that a disease of the thyroid—namely Graves' disease—could add a new dimension to the study of the Founding Father.

In order to make their case, Ferling and Braverman traced the times in Adams's life when he suffered from breakdowns, the first occurring when he was 35 years old. Adams had suffered the loss of a child (a daughter, Susanna) and had been under a great deal of stress due to the Boston Massacre trials. Noting the other times when Adams fell seriously ill, the writers (Braverman in particular) emphasized the role of stress in exacerbating thyrotoxicosis.[52] After a thorough discussion of the times in which Adams complained of various symptoms or was judged to be erratic or unbalanced, Ferling and Braverman concluded their article by stating, "We believe that John Adams's behavior was not, as many have thought, the result of problems in his head or his heart but in his thyroid."[53]

While this article asserted an interesting theory concerning John Adams's health, it is even more interesting in the way it demonstrated Ferling's continued journey toward understanding Adams. Once this historian stopped avoiding Adams, he was compelled to dive into many aspects of his life in an attempt to paint a complete picture of the man. It is true that Ferling took issue with aspects of Adams's character, his ambition at the expense of his family being the most obvious. Yet the Adams that emerges from all of Ferling's work is a man that readers can respect and with whom they can sympathize. He does not deserve to be dismissed. Rather, he should take his place alongside Franklin and Jefferson as one of the great men of the Revolution. Another historian agreed that there was room for Adams at the top.

Historian Joseph Ellis, writing in the 1990s, examined the legacy of John Adams in intricate detail. Ellis came to John Adams after establishing himself as a scholar of the New England mind and early American culture. In *Passionate Sage: The Character and Legacy of John Adams*, Ellis presented a book-length study of John Adams in retirement in an attempt to discover who Adams was and to understand him better.[54] Ellis is not the first scholar to write about Adams in retirement. All previous biographies had discussed his later years, with Page Smith devoting the most time to it. In addition, Donald H. Stewart and George P. Clark, authors of "Misanthrope or Humanitarian? John Adams in Retirement," a piece that appeared in *The New England Quarterly*, used the memoirs of Doctor John Pierce to analyze their famous subject. Doctor Pierce had visited the older gentleman on a number of occasions and found a man who retained a zest for life and learning, a kind man with a generous heart. Rather than the embittered figure that was so often painted, Stewart and Clark found in Pierce's memoirs a different soul. "We see in the *Memoirs*," they stated, "a very human individual, alert and approachable" and they found it "reassuring to perceive that his acquaintances found John Adams a figure warm, courageous and sometimes even witty, stoutly meeting life on the terms which it offered him."[55] While this is an intriguing image, these two writers did not dive as deeply into Adams's retirement years as Ellis did.

Why focus on the last twenty-five years of Adams's life? He had left public service, no longer wielding any influence on the affairs of state or diplomacy. Ellis explained it was for this very reason that he decided to explore the Founder's later years. In the preface to his book, Ellis explained, "Adams used his retirement to engage in a long and often bittersweet retrospective on his public career and personal life. That is also my purpose—to use his latter years as a perch from which to meditate on his thought and character." In doing this, Ellis hoped to find Adams's place within the revolutionary generation. Ellis also argued, as had others before him, "John Adams remains the most misconstrued and unappreciated 'great man' in American history. Not only does he deserve better; we will be better for knowing him."[56] Ellis saw a usable John Adams who could benefit 1990s Americans, if only they took the time to know him.

After a discussion of Adams's career and the moments that made it most memorable in a chapter entitled "The Education of John Adams," Ellis spent most of his book on the retirement years. Those aspects of Adams's character that emerged during the American Revolution and the Early Republic did not disappear when the man left the public eye. Adams spent the first twelve years of his retirement in an attempt to vindicate himself to the people he worked so hard to serve. He became concerned that he was being left out of the gallery of great men of the Revolution. He also felt misunderstood and was driven to set the record straight whenever he could. Ellis pointed to three distinct ways in which Adams attempted to do this: the sporadic writing of his unfinished autobiography, his correspondence with his old friend Mercy Otis Warren after the publication of her history of the American Revolution, and a long series of articles published in the *Boston Patriot*. Ellis observed that all three "showed Adams at his worst." It is true that his autobiography, in particular, offered scholars insights into his life that they would not otherwise have. However, Ellis correctly noted Adams's need to settle scores. In these attempts to vent his bitterness, Adams did his reputation more harm than good.[57]

In the midst of Adams's own resentment, Ellis noted a larger issue emerging in Adams's thought. John Adams became increasingly concerned about what we call today historical memory and the way it was used. Adams, too, understood the construction of a usable past and he was worried about the version of the American Revolution that was emerging in his later years. He was not impressed by John Trumbull's painting of the Declaration of Independence that hangs in the Capitol Rotunda today. It was inaccurate, and Adams was increasingly sensitive to what Ellis and Adams termed "bad history." What could Adams do? "By contesting these patriotic fictions Adams hoped to blow away the golden haze that was settling over the founding generation." Adams's motives, according to Ellis, were not simply born out of jealousy of men who were placed on pedestals in his stead. He was concerned about the effect this veneration would have on future generations of leaders. He wished, as Ellis termed it, to "help provide the leaders of the rising generation with more realistic expectations for themselves." The old patriarch John Adams believed there was much talent in the younger generation, but "the only problem … was that the next generation of statesmen would be transfixed by the idols being propped up by mindless devotees of patriotic mythology."[58]

This is a fascinating insight into Adams's thoughts on history and the dangers of turning the American Revolution into a mythological event. Adams was a realist and wished to see the story of the Revolution, with all its conflicts and disagreements and close votes, to be as near to the truth as possible. It was messy and Adams bristled to see it cleaned up. By changing the founding generation into demigods, the future group of leaders did not have a prayer. They could never measure up. Adams, showing a great deal of sympathy and admiration for younger men, hated to see that happen.

One of the manifestations of Adams's discomfort with the emerging mythology surrounding the American Revolution was an analysis of the meaning of the Revolution. Before, during, and shortly after the War of 1812, Adams was asked often what he believed the American Revolution was about. He became enthralled by the question and even engaged his old friends Thomas Jefferson, Benjamin Rush, and Thomas McKean in the discussion. They asked such questions as "When did the Revolution begin?" "What do we mean by the Revolution?" "Who was most responsible for beginning the colonial movement that led to the break with England?" "What was the most important moment—the watershed— when independence was a fait accompli?" Famously, Adams's answer to the second question—What do we mean by the Revolution?—written in a letter to Hezekiah Niles in 1818, was that the war itself had little to do with the real Revolution. "The Revolution was effected before the War commenced," argued Adams. "The Revolution was in the Minds and Hearts of the People. A Change in their religious Sentiments and of their Duties and Obligations."[59]

Adams was insistent on this point, perhaps because he felt that military heroes were getting too much attention or because he himself never fought in the war. Yet as Ellis observed, Adams's point of view foreshadowed scholarly work on the Revolution at the end of the 20th century, when historians "focused attention on invisible social, economic, and demographic forces operating at different speeds and in different patterns throughout the colonies.… The Whole emphasis on 'great men' was wrong."[60]

Coming out of this examination was an interesting—and unpopular—attitude concerning the American people, a mindset that explains, in part, why Adams was not as popular in public memory as other Founding Fathers. John Adams, as Ellis pointed out, did not believe in what is sometimes called "American Exceptionalism." This idea—that the United States was somehow special in the world, that God smiled on this country more than any other—was emerging in the 19th century and has remained an integral part of the American mindset ever since. However, Adams did not buy it and said so. Ellis found the evidence in Adams's own writings. He "did not think that Americans were a special people rendered immune by God's grace from the customary ravages of history." John Adams made this clear to Benjamin Rush when he wrote, "There is no Special Providence for Us [Americans]. We are not a chosen People, that I know of."[61]

This realistic assessment can explain, in part, why Adams does not fit into the model of a usable past. If Americans were attempting to create a past that would make their country and nationality exceptional in the world, Adams's blunt reality check had to be ignored. Ellis continued to examine this issue of what may be called worthy—or usable—Founders in his chapter concerning the amazing correspondence between Adams and Jefferson.

In a chapter entitled "The American Dialogue," Ellis discussed the letters exchanged by Adams and Jefferson beginning in 1812. These letters and the relationship between these two men have been the subject of many scholarly works.[62] Ellis's focus was the legacy of both men, why Jefferson's fame increased over the years and Adams was all but forgotten. While the two men worked together to create a Revolution and a new country, their approaches and visions were different. Adams was always the realist. Some would even call him a pessimist, although his overall hope for the future makes this a problematic assessment. Ellis explained their differing views in an interesting way and related them to their respective legacies.

> Whatever we choose to call them, the political values that Jefferson championed, indeed that his name came to represent, became central tenets of the American liberal tradition; the values Adams embraced became important ingredients for critics of that tradition on both the conservative and radical sides of the political spectrum. And that posture—critical realist of seductive Jeffersonian illusions—was the one Adams found most comfortable throughout his correspondence with that man at Monticello.[63]

While this focus on the letters flying between Peacefield and Monticello offered an interesting portrait of Adams as friend and critic, Ellis rounded out his picture of Adams in his later years by discussing a warmer side to the man. This part of Adams's personality came out with family and friends.

That Adams's candor and argumentative nature remained with him in his later years was undeniable, but Ellis argued that these traits endeared him to people who came to know him better. Most who encountered Adams in these later years found him, in Ellis's words, "irresistibly likable." Even old critics such as John Taylor, who in 1814 had written a withering critique of Adams's *A Defence of the Constitutions of Government of the United States of America*, by 1824 found Adams "impossible not to like."[64] Other people had found this to be true throughout Adams's life. He was never without friends. Yet in his later years, as he mellowed in his retirement, those in his inner circle found a warmth and generosity of spirit that often get lost in depictions of him. Ellis brought these elements of Adams's personality into sharp focus in discussing his renewed friendships with old college classmates and with those who had wounded him earlier in his life. Mercy Otis Warren hurt him deeply with her depiction of him in her history of the American Revolution, but Adams did not wish to die without healing their friendship. He came to her defense when someone suggested that she was not the author of a propagandistic play called *The Group*, the argument being that a woman could not have written such a play. Adams made clear that a woman *had* written that play and that it was Warren.[65]

Adams's renewed friendship with Mercy Otis Warren and his affection for his daughter-in-law, Louisa Catherine, brought another interesting aspect of Adams's character to Ellis's attention. John Adams felt comfortable with intelligent women. This, of course, was evident in his choice of a wife, but beyond Abigail, Adams treated Warren as an equal in their friendship. "And no other male member of the revolutionary generation," argued Ellis, "seemed capable of the kind of unalloyed, unromantic intimacy with strong-willed American women that Adams achieved with Warren."[66] Further, after Abigail died in 1818, Adams found comfort in his correspondence with Louisa Catherine, John Quincy's wife. Ellis noted that there were limits to Adams's views on women's equality. He opposed the franchise for women and was critical of Mary Wollstonecraft's arguments for women's rights. But Adams did believe that women should have access to the same education as men and even supported the efforts of educator Emma Willard, who wished to introduce the classics and a college curriculum to women in a new school she hoped to open.[67] This aspect of Adams's personality contrasted sharply with other men of his time and, bringing it to the forefront as Ellis did, offered a new perspective on John Adams.

Joseph Ellis presented a portrait of John Adams that was multidimensional. By comparing him to Jefferson, by emphasizing those he reached out to, by demonstrating his ability to be a warm and doting grandfather, Ellis gave his readers a likable John Adams who, in some important ways, found peace with himself. In discussing his legacy, Ellis argued that Adams was well on his way to being "securely enshrined" shortly after his death in 1826. In noting the myriad eulogies to Adams,

Ellis found respect and admiration for the man, but unfortunately, it did not last. According to Ellis, Jefferson would be the darling of even warring political camps while Adams would disappear from the picture altogether—even though he more closely represented certain ideas than did Jefferson.[68] In conclusion, Ellis wondered what would concern John Adams if he could see the nation he helped create today (in the 1990s). While he believed that Adams would be pleased to see the country had lasted so long, he would have his concerns that he would most certainly express. Among those elements that would trouble him, according to Ellis, would be "the widespread presumption of unbridled individual freedom, unencumbered by any internalized sense of social responsibility and even justified as a fulfillment of the Revolution he had fought and wrought."

While Ellis wrote in the 1990s, his words ring true for the 2020s as well. The other reality still true today is the nonexistent monument of John Adams in Washington, D.C. Ellis argued that Adams would want to know the state of his reputation, but he would not be surprised by his omission from the memorials in the capital city. In his final paragraph, Ellis implied that it was time to recognize Adams alongside Jefferson by stating what he thought Adams might recommend. He would want a monument "done in the classical style and situated sufficiently close to the Jefferson memorial that, depending on the time of day and angle of the sun, he and Jefferson might take turns casting shadows across each other's facades."[69] This is an interesting ending to a thorough biography of John Adams, one that focused on many different sides of Adams's personality and philosophy. For Ellis, like other writers in the 1990s, Adams was a man who deserved to be understood on his own terms.

If there is a common theme in the biographies of John Adams from the 1990s into the 2000s, it is that he deserves better treatment than he has received from posterity. The works of the 1990s in particular make clear that he was far from perfect, but that is the point. Unlike other Founders, Adams presented his entire soul to the world in a way that his associates did not. Further, what set the scholarly works on Adams from the 1990s apart from earlier works was the drive to understand how he might still be relevant in United States history. This is not to say that earlier biographies failed to do this. Page Smith certainly did. Yet like all history, the scholars writing about Adams in the 1960s and 1970s were products of their own times. The biographers of the 1990s, living in a different United States, developed other perspectives, and this led to a realization that John Adams should not be dismissed, nor his contributions ignored. Ferling and Ellis found Adams as relevant for the 1990s as Smith did for the 1950s and '60s.

Richard D. Brown, in writing a review essay of several works on John Adams for *The William and Mary Quarterly*, stated that "the pendulum of scholarly and popular opinion has finally swung in Adams's favor, so whatever his defects, Adams's status as an American hero of the first rank now seems assured." The question Brown addressed in his essay was: Why? Why, in the early 2000s when Brown was writing, did Adams appeal to both the scholar and the public? In answering this question, Brown—like others before him—pointed to the Adams papers. "What makes Adams a hero now is his direct, unscripted, unpretending self, endlessly visible in his diary and letters," wrote Brown. "No scandals—financial or sexual, no disreputable secrets lie buried in the archive. Long before we thought of transparency, there was John Adams, telling it like it was to the public, to his friends, to his wife, and, most important, to himself." Brown, writing in 2002, believed that "For a citizenry so nearly disillusioned by manipulation as ours, John Adams seems a precious gift."[70] The ascendancy of Adams's reputation became most apparent with the appearance of David McCullough's blockbuster biography in 2001.

McCullough's book was an important milestone in John Adams scholarship, but it was also the basis for the 2008 HBO miniseries *John Adams*. The fact that so many other biographies of Adams existed before David McCullough came to him is clear, but only McCullough's work was translated to the small screen. This biography was a bestseller and made John Adams a bit of a rock star. It did, however, have its critics. Because it is tied to the miniseries, it is best to analyze it along with the series in Chapter Seven. It is also important to note that David McCullough did not have the last word on John Adams.

In 2005, James Grant, best known as the editor of *Grant's Interest Rate Observer* and books on finance, published *John Adams: Party of One*. The title suggests Grant's approach to John Adams. He was looking to write the biography of a man known for his independent nature. Early in the book, he argued, "Throughout his political career, Adams would almost always constitute a faction of one, he had remarkably little party spirit."[71] Moreover, Grant recognized the often contradictory circumstances in which Adams sometimes found himself. "John Adams was too plainspoken for diplomacy and too honest for politics," wrote Grant in the prologue to his book. "But in no mood was he inclined to permit any compromise of American interests as he understood them."[72]

One remarkable way in which Grant's biography stands out lies in his perspective as a finance writer. He used this expertise the most when discussing John Adams's success in securing loans for the United States from Holland. He called Adams a "Junk-Bond Promoter" in the title to Chapter Eighteen of his work. Whether or not it is appropriate to use such a term in describing an 18th-century man, Grant was fascinated and impressed by this aspect of John Adams's diplomatic career. He stated, "Many have followed Adams in the capacity of junk-bond promoter. But few of his successors in speculative-grade finance have been burdened by Adams's personal scruples against debt. Down to the marrow of his Yankee bones, he hated it." Grant went on to argue that later in his career, his anti-banking, anti-debt attitude would put him at odds with the Federalist party. Other men in the new republic would criticize him for these feelings. Yet, according to Grant, his critics overlooked the fact that the loans secured by Adams "established the international credit of the United States. The anti-capitalist was the financial benefactor of his political enemies."[73]

While the loans were important to Adams, the Dutch recognition of American independence was the real achievement. Not until 1781 and the surrender of British general Cornwallis to Washington at Yorktown, did the Dutch open their doors to Adams. Once they did, however, Adams would secure the loans. Adams understood the importance of the borrowed money, but for him, the greater triumph was the recognition of the United States by the Dutch. In 1782, he wrote to Abigail, "You will see, the American Cause has had a signal Tryumph in this Country [Holland]. If this had been the only Action of my Life, it would have been a Life well spent."[74] He did not mention the loans. Interestingly, though, he began this letter with a warning to Abigail about money. "Mr. Hill is paid I hope. I will honour your Bill if you draw. But be cautious—don't trust Money to any Body. You will never have any to lose or to spare. Your Children will want more than you and I shall have for them."[75] While Grant admired Adams's achievement with the Dutch, it is doubtful that his subject would be pleased with the moniker "Junk-Bond Promoter" once the term was explained to him.

Another aspect which makes Grant's biography unique is the way in which he emphasized John Adams's religion. This theme runs throughout the book. Most Adams biographers stress his Puritan background, for it is hard to ignore. Ann Burleigh also emphasized his religion and morality. Yet Grant went a step further, examining how Adams was motivated by his faith. In one chapter, entitled "Called by Providence," Grant argued that what kept Adams moving forward on the road to independence was a belief that he had been summoned by God. Adams did, in fact, emphasize the role of a higher power in the American Revolutionary cause. In writing to his friend, Josiah Quincy, he made this belief clear. "That a great Revolution, in the Affairs of the World, is in the Womb of Providence, Seems to be intimated very Strongly, by many Circumstances: But it is no Pleasure to me to be employed in giving Birth to it," Adams wrote in 1775. Yet Adams continued by noting "by a Train of Circumstances, which I could neither foresee nor prevent, I have been called by Providence to take a larger share in active Life, during the Course of these Struggles, then is

aggregable either to my Health, my Fortune or my Inclination."[76] According to Grant, Adams believed that "Not only had God called him; He also
supported and blessed the American cause."[77]

This assessment runs contrary to the evidence presented by Ellis that
Adams rejected the idea of a providential blessing on the United States.
If Adams's attitudes about this changed between the year 1775 when he
wrote the above-quoted letter and the early 19th century, his experiences
in the 1790s could explain why. John Howe argued that his political thinking certainly did change dramatically over this period. Adams's "assump-
tions about the moral condition of the American people and the make-up
of American society altered quite significantly" between the 1770s and 1800
"essentially from an emphasis upon moral virtue and social cohesion to
notions of moral declension and social conflict."[78] With the latter mindset, Adams would not necessarily feel that God was no longer guiding the
United States, but he would wonder if the American people were in tune to
that direction.

Grant also stressed the evolving nature of Adams's belief system and
his tolerance of other religious faiths. He pointed to two examples of this.
In a story unique in Adams biography, Grant explained the founding of
the American Protestant Episcopal Church and the role Adams played in
the consecration of two American Episcopal bishops by the Archbishop of
Canterbury in 1786. "Though he [Adams] didn't love the Episcopal Church
and never would, the postrevolutionary Adams believed unwaveringly in
its right to exist."[79]

The second way in which Grant emphasized Adams's evolving
thoughts on religion focused on the revision of the Massachusetts Constitution. Adams had drafted the first state Constitution in 1780, and in it,
he had included a Bill of Rights which stated, in part, "It is the duty of all
men in society, publicly, and at stated seasons, to worship the SUPREME
BEING ... and no subject shall be hurt, molested, or restrained, in his person, liberty, or estate for worshiping GOD in the manner most agreeable
to the dictates of his own conscience...." Since Adams also made it clear
that all office holders in the state should be of the "Christian Religion,"
Grant concluded that Adams wished to protect the rights of all Christians
to practice their religions freely. "The original Massachusetts constitution," Grant wrote, "had placed the government squarely in the business
of sponsoring and supporting the protestant faith."[80] However, Grant
argued that, by 1820, Adams had become more tolerant of all religions, citing Adams's wish to amend the Massachusetts Bill of Rights. He supported
the idea of "guaranteeing equal protection under the law for 'all men of
all religions,' Jews no less than Christians."[81] Interestingly, though, historian Arthur Scherr has recently questioned this assertion, found in other

biographies as well, claiming that the evidence does not exist to support this argument.[82]

Still, for Grant, it was important to argue that Adams supported true religious freedom in his state and was disappointed when it did not come to fruition in 1820. Adams's religion was a key component of Grant's work. In fact, in ending his biography, in the last paragraph, Grant noted that Adams was thinking of God on his death bed, praying for himself and his family. Grant concluded, "he died at 6:20 p.m., a meeting-going animal to the end."[83]

Grant's John Adams was a great man. The biographer went so far as to give Adams credit for ideas and institutions that Adams did not envision. In writing about Adams's Constitution for the State of Massachusetts, Grant was intrigued by his subject's forward-thinking about the arts and education. "In the glint of Adams's eye," wrote Grant, "can be seen the National Endowment for the Humanities, the U.S. Department of Education, and the Smithsonian Institution, among myriad other public enterprises not actually provided for in the constitutions of the eighteenth century."[84] This is a stretch. However, Adams could be a visionary and did, at times, display hope for the future. His expectations for his children kept him in public service. This Grant summed up in pinpointing why Adams was a great man. "Adams's greatness lies only partly in his many contributions to the founding of the American nation; no less extraordinary is the moral achievement of his endurance in its service. His sheer tenacity of spirit is a thing of wonder."[85]

James Grant wrote the most recent full biography of John Adams, and it is a wonder that he found anything new to say. However, he did, and he gave the reading public yet another glimpse of the many sides of John Adams. Since 2005, scholars have returned to Adams, but have concentrated on various aspects of his life or development.

In 2009, Edith B. Gelles wrote the first biography of Abigail and John Adams as a couple. Gelles noted that these two people "loved each other; they enjoyed each other's company; they relied upon each other even when apart; they trusted each other and were loyal." For Gelles, all of this was worth investigating further.[86] Joseph Ellis revisited the idea of a couple's biography with his return to Adams studies in 2010. In *First Family: Abigail and John Adams*, Ellis wished to figure out how they managed as a couple in one of the most turbulent times in United States history. He believed "Abigail and John have much to teach us" about their times and about true partnership.[87] In 2019, Sara Georgini wrote *Household Gods: The Religious Lives of the Adams Family*. Only one chapter of this book is dedicated to John and Abigail, and Georgini had a specific focus for her work.[88] Finally, and most recently, Jeanne E. Abrams published *A View from Abroad: The Story of John and Abigail Adams in Europe* in which she concentrated on how these two people, who could be remarkably provincial, grew from their experiences in Europe. Like the works of Gelles and Ellis, this book is a biography of a couple, but it focuses on a certain time in their lives to offer an even deeper understanding of who these people were.[89]

In 2014 and 2018, two scholars focused on John Adams and race. Ronald Angelo Johnson, in *Diplomacy in Black and White: John Adams, Toussaint Louverture, and Their Atlantic World Alliance*, examined how two revolutionary peoples in the Atlantic World approached their situations. Four years after Johnson's book appeared, Arthur Scherr published *John Adams, Slavery and Race: Ideas, Politics, and Diplomacy in an Age of Crisis*, in which he countered the view put forward by previous scholars that Adams was anti-slavery. Both of these works offered an important addition to John Adams scholarship and filled a gap still remaining in examining Adams.[90] Two books released in 2020 provided a glimpse into John Adams as a learner and lawyer, respectively. R.B. Bernstein's *The Education of John Adams* concentrated on the growth of Adams throughout his life as what educators today would term a life-long learner. He also marked John Adams as a thinking politician.[91] In addition, in that same year, marking the two hundred and fiftieth anniversary of the Boston Massacre, Dan Abrams and David Fisher published *John Adams Under Fire: The Founding Father's Fight for Justice in the Boston Massacre Murder Trial*. In this book, the writers acknowledged John Adams as a prime mover in advocating for the rule of law in the turmoil of the imperial crisis with England. They then provided a detailed look at how he did that.[92]

Among all these later works, from the 1990s forward, John Adams appeared softer, more gentle, less repugnant. One might even call this "revised John Adams Revisionism."[93] Yet not all scholars have been willing to accept this warmer John Adams. One way in which this manifested itself is in the nature of the debate over whether Adams deserves a monument in Washington, D.C., a discussion covered in a later chapter. Moreover, one scholar in particular, has come to the forefront to reexamine ideas concerning Adams that other historians have long accepted as fact. The works of Arthur Scherr that concern Adams are important and striking, although they are not full biographies. One such work, mentioned above, concerned John Adams and slavery, and presented a reassessment of the founder's views.

The other work, an article entitled "John Adams, Political Moderation, and the 1820 Constitutional Convention: A Reappraisal," attempted to correct the mistaken idea that Adams was in favor of religious toleration for Massachusetts. In his opening paragraph, Scherr revealed his feelings regarding the gentler Adams who had emerged in the 1990s and 2000s. Because of the work of Ellis and McCullough in particular, "The literate reading public … now views him as a warm, cuddly fellow," an image perpetuated by the HBO miniseries.[94] From here, Scherr focused on the subject of John Adams and religious freedom. He remarkably admitted his own previous mistakes on the subject. What jumps off the page of this article and Scherr's book on race is a cautionary tale to scholars in particular. While trying to understand John Adams, perhaps biographers have gone too far in their attempts to make him likable. In doing so, they may not always be accurate in depicting the man.

All of these works are important to understanding certain aspects of John Adams at different times in his life. Like others before them, they offer specific ideas surrounding the many facets of John Adams. They are also most widely read amongst John Adams scholars and historians of the Revolutionary and Early National period. That is to be expected. Only David McCullough's biography of John Adams is widely read outside the scholarly community. As a result, it is not easy to comprehend John Adams as the public has seen him. In order to move beyond the scholar's view of the founder and his place in the usable past as determined by academe, it is important to analyze not only biographies and histories, but also works of popular culture. For the artists who create these works have also constructed a usable past for their time. Who is John Adams in literature, television, theater, film? How has public history depicted and used him? The following chapters will look for answers to these questions, beginning with John Adams as he has appeared in various forms of literature.

FOUR

The John Adams
of the Literary World

In 1950, on a visit to Chicago, biographer Catherine Drinker Bowen got to visit a piece of John Adams memorabilia. According to columnist Fanny Butcher, Bowen wanted to see the brown velvet suit that Adams wore when he was presented at court in Europe. Butcher described the excitement Bowen felt upon seeing the suit and the revelation the moment provided for her as a reporter. "Bowen's first sight of the outfit was not only a thrilling moment for her, but also for me as I realized that within that lifeless velvet there actually came alive for his biographer the physical presence of John Adams."[1] Bowen, unlike the biographers discussed in the previous chapters, liked to approach her subjects with literary techniques, creating scenes and dialog for her historical characters. In this way, Bowen took John Adams across the line from cold, hard scholarship into the world of artistic creation. Like the suit she was so thrilled to see, she and others in the literary world, brought Adams to life and introduced him to the public's constructed memory of the American Revolution.

As the previous two chapters demonstrate, many historians have studied the life of John Adams and have put their own spin upon his character. The historiography reveals many different perspectives on Adams. For the most part, scholars have worked diligently to discover the historical Founder. However, they do not have the freedom to create dialog or *imagine* their subject's thoughts and feelings—although they may make educated guesses about them. Writers of poetry, novels, plays, and fictionalized biography, on the other hand, can use all the techniques available to writers of fiction. They can tell the life stories of historical figures with some accuracy while also conjuring up thoughts and dialog not recorded in the records of the past. Alternatively, they can create their own worlds and insert historical figures into them without the constraints of endnotes and bibliographies.

The popularity of historical fiction, in general, allows writers to place their own stamps on events and people of the past. In the case of John Adams, writers have done this in a variety of ways. Some authors have emphasized the aspects of Adams's political philosophy that they share. Others have used him as a character in the Abigail Adams stories they have told. Still others have stressed character traits that are sometimes missing in the historiography of Adams. However these writers have approached Adams, they use their literary techniques to demonstrate his character and his inner most thoughts in intriguing ways.

In many respects, John Adams is the perfect character for fictional works. His honesty, his integrity, his arrogance, and his temper are all fodder for a writer's imagination. In addition to two biographies that are somewhat fictionalized—*This Man Adams: The Man Who Never Died* (1928) and *John Adams and the American Revolution* (1950), Adams has been the subject of poetry, novels, and plays during the 20th and 21st centuries. Each of the writers who brought him to life in this way provided creative perspectives on the man, whether he is the main subject of their work or just a supporting player in the drama of the novels. With one exception, Abigail Adams is present in these works as well. In several of the pieces it is she who is the focus. The connection between John and Abigail has always been one of the reasons the public is fascinated by him. It is no wonder that she plays such a prominent role in the fiction surrounding her husband. Yet for some writers, the poet Ezra Pound in particular, John Adams is the central figure. This is also the case with two biographies that are literary in style.

For the most part, biographies of John Adams fit squarely into the historiography of the man. However, two profiles of Adams contain fictionalized dialog and other aspects of narrative. In the first of these works, *This Man Adams: The Man Who Never Died*, Samuel McCoy did use the words of his subject. He clearly engaged in primary source research. Yet the book, published by Brentano's in 1928, does not read like other biographies. McCoy was not an historian; he was a newspaperman. He used Adams's writings throughout his book to prove to his audience that John Adams was as relevant in 1920s America as he was at the beginning of the new nation in the 1700s.

McCoy opens his work by admitting that he was not initially impressed with Mr. Adams. "This man Adams fooled me at first," he wrote. "I wasn't impressed. I saw in him only a plump, somewhat perky little man, no different from hundreds of others that one encounters and forgets."[2] He discussed his acquaintance with Adams as if they were neighbors, and in getting to know the historical character, McCoy changed his opinion. Rather than shy away from Adams's crustiness and volatility, McCoy admired it. He wrote with glee about the ability "to behold him in one of his utterly delightful tantrums" and confessed that he was grateful they were neighbors.[3]

The portrait of John Adams that McCoy painted was that of a man who possessed—and needed—a tremendous ego. In the chapter entitled "Importance of Being an Egoist," McCoy stated, "You *cannot* do the things that John Adams did unless you are possessed of enormous vitality."[4] He argued that the secret to John Adams's success was his desire for it. "And nothing on God's green earth is going to stop one of these *Me* men, these *Property* men, these *Possessions* men, these *My Rights* men, from getting what they desire.... Luckily for us, Mr. Adams yelled and howled for The Right to Keep What Belongs to You."[5]

Mr. McCoy was quick to give John Adams credit for many contributions to the Revolution and the Early Republic. In a chapter entitled "When You Need a God, Create Him," McCoy contended, "In September, 1774, it became imperative for John Adams to have a son. He wanted to bear this son; and what this man Adams *wanted*, he must have. Nine months later he bore his son...."[6] McCoy was not referring to Adams's own biological sons in this section. Instead, he was suggesting that John Adams was George Washington's figurative father. McCoy carefully noted that Adams took little notice of Washington upon their first meeting and argued, "Washington is not yet regarded as having reached a stature ... sufficient to cause the passionately anxious Adams to rank him as one of the leaders; and it was always leaders that Adams sought to win over first."[7] Yet, over time, reasoned McCoy, Adams became more aware of Washington's strengths and nominated him to be commander of the Continental Army. Through this argument, McCoy implied that John Adams created George Washington.[8]

McCoy credited John Adams with other achievements as well. He asserted,

> This man Adams placed in the hand of Thomas Jefferson the pen with which to draft the Declaration of Independence. This man Adams founded the American Navy. Either of these two achievements in itself would be sufficient to make the fame of another man, but in the case of Adams they are merely things done in passing, not to be ranked with his chief business, which is the business of eternal life.[9]

These are extraordinary statements, written by a man who wished to place John Adams in the Founding Father pantheon, not just as one of many, but as the most important of them all. However, even amid this worship, McCoy acknowledged the flaws in his subject. Rather than apologize for Adams's crustiness, he admired it, touting the founder's outspokenness as one of his great qualities. In one section of the book, McCoy chided an unnamed historian for claiming that Adams's blunt nature was his great weakness. On the contrary, claimed McCoy. "[John Adams] lives *because* he never curbed his hasty, ungovernable tongue. The softly people, who have never dared speak full truth, lie dead. Truth stings ... but never dies."[10] Later in the book, McCoy argued, "[John Adams's] title is this: The most unpopular man in all the history of America. Why? Because he never rids himself of the habit of telling people the Truth...."[11]

In the 1920s, with the rise of advertising and mass culture, some writers wished to take historical characters and place them in the early 20th century. One of the more astonishing examples of this is Bruce Barton's work on Jesus Christ. *The Man Nobody Knows,* in which Barton painted Jesus as a successful businessman, was published in 1925, three years before McCoy's book on John Adams. Both writers wished to make their subjects relevant for a 1920s audience. While Adams was certainly no Jesus Christ, the style and purpose of these writings are similar. For McCoy, John Adams was a much-needed honest man, someone who could recognize the foibles of humankind in any time. His ability and drive were important in shaping his character, but his ego and his honesty insured his immortality.

In the 1930s and '40s, not long after McCoy argued that Adams never died, an American poet dedicated a large portion of one of his major works to the Founding Father. This is fitting as the well-read Adams was also a lover of poetry. He once told his son, John Quincy, "You will never be alone, with a poet in your pocket."[12] Yet it is difficult to say what Adams would have thought of Ezra Pound, the man or his poetry. The modernist poet's work is difficult and—on the surface—nonsensical. Upon further study, however, Pound had a specific purpose in choosing Adams as a subject: the Founder fit in nicely to the emphasis on balance and governmental structure that so interested the poet.

Ezra Pound was born in Idaho in 1885 and died in Venice, Italy, in 1972. According to one biography, he was related to Henry Wadsworth Longfellow, but he suppressed this connection because Longfellow was too "establishment" for Pound's taste.[13] According to David Ten Eyck, author of *Ezra Pound's Adams Cantos*, Pound became interested in the Founding Fathers and the American Revolution while attending the University of Pennsylvania in 1901–2.[14] The future poet took extensive notes, some of which are still available to scholars. The writings of Albert Bushnell Hart on the Revolutionary period were especially influential. According to Ten Eyck, Hart "adopted an essentially Whiggish outlook, describing a steady progress towards greater individual liberty and an essential convergence between the fundamental principals of British and American constitutional law."[15] What especially struck Pound was Hart's treatment of the legal basis for the American Revolution, an idea that he would later develop in the "Adams Cantos." Ten Eyck argued then that Pound's appreciation for the history of the American Revolution came early in his life. During his time in college, he had already been thinking about the context of the American Revolution.[16]

In later years, Pound developed a fascination for fascism and for Benito Mussolini in particular. This part of Pound's life is disturbing to many readers, but according to Pound biographer Alec Marsh, there was nothing particularly unusual about the poet's choice. Marsh argued that in the 1920s, Americans did not have any reason to find fault with Mussolini and newspapers described the man as an "Italian Teddy Roosevelt."[17] Marsh then described Mussolini's form of fascism in order to understand Pound's attraction to it. As Marsh admitted, fascism is difficult to define as a political philosophy because "it is in essence a cult of the nation—just the sort of thing that does not translate well into any foreign political idiom."[18] Marsh called fascism a "pride movement, a source of strength when the state was weak and rudderless." He also made the point of connecting fascism to economic concerns in which industry serves the state. These ideas appealed to Pound who, by the early 1930s, believed "he was perfectly positioned to supply Italy with a workable economic programme" and that Italy could "solve the problem of equitable distribution of goods and services," but the government needed to remain popular.[19]

According to Marsh, Pound saw similarities between Mussolini's views on the role of government and Thomas Jefferson's. Through the decade of the 1930s, Pound thought increasingly about the 18th century and the Founders of the United States. In this context, he became more intrigued with the American Revolution and with John Adams.[20]

In the end, however, Pound took what Marsh described as a "Hard Right Turn" and, because of the writer's radio broadcasts in Italy, work on behalf of Mussolini, the United States would later charge the poet with treason. The case against Pound was confusing as were his own speeches in favor of Mussolini. Because of his lawyer's interesting tactics, Pound was committed to a mental hospital at the end of his trial.[21]

Given Pound's controversial life and his attraction to Fascism, readers sometimes find it surprising that the poet would devote part of his *Cantos* to John Adams. Yet given Pound's fascination with the American Revolution, with government, and with balance as a concept (as seen in some of his other Cantos), Adams is in many ways, the perfect subject for Pound's poetry. Despite Pound's apparent interest in the Founding Fathers in general, and Adams in particular, the "Adams Cantos" have not garnered much attention.

Just as historians have often lamented the neglect of John Adams, so

Pound scholars have bemoaned the inattention to the "Adams Cantos." Author David Ten Eyck argued, "The 'Adams Cantos' have received a proportionately small amount of critical attention."[22] In his *Ezra Pound's Adams Cantos*, Ten Eyck attributed this neglect to the scholarly attitude toward Pound's involvement with fascist politics. As a result, he maintained, many critics have failed to see the importance of the poems, perceiving them as part of a period of failure for Pound.[23] However, some critics voiced an appreciation for the poetry and believed it deserved more attention.

In 1975, the University of Maine Press published *John Adams Speaking: Pound's Sources for the Adams Cantos*. This manuscript is an exhaustive guide to the passages from Adams's own papers used by the poet in writing his work. In the introduction to the book, the author, Frederick K. Sanders, listed three reasons why the "Adams Cantos" are important works of poetry—both for Pound and for the public. First, he argued, despite Pound's controversial life and the charge of treason against him, the poet was anxious for Americans to embrace their history. He had spent a great deal of time "attempting to show those Americans who would listen that the experience of the Nation's founding belonged not simply to an archeological past but to the twentieth century as well."[24]

Pound did this in some interesting ways, to be sure. He wrote an earlier part of the *Cantos* focusing on Thomas Jefferson's correspondence. More controversial perhaps was his publication of *Jefferson And/Or Mussolini* in 1935 in which Pound cites similarities between the author of the Declaration of Independence and the fascist leader in Italy.[25] This comparison, while surprising to the post–World War II sensibilities of American readers, points to a keen interest in the early history of the United States on the part of the poet. He wished his country to appreciate their founders, especially Thomas Jefferson and, later, John Adams, because he believed his fellow Americans had "lost their hold upon the essential meanings of the American experience...."[26] Pound was formulating his ideas concerning the Founders while also appreciating what Mussolini was attempting to do for Italy.

Sanders's second argument for giving the "Adams Cantos" more attention is quite simply the *lack* of attention they had received as of 1975. Even those critics who had written extensively on *The Cantos* had spent very little scholarly effort on the "Adams Cantos." Even though Pound viewed the poems as important to the overall work, critics have not agreed with his assessment. Still, Sanders argued, their presence alone was a good reason to study them.[27]

Finally, Sanders contended that the most significant reason to call attention to the "Adams Cantos" was the neglect of John Adams himself.

According to Sanders, "the very people who should have been concerned with the career of John Adams—the historians—have been demonstrably slow about devoting their labors to his story."[28] Sanders admitted that Adams was not generally in the same heroic category as a Washington or a Jefferson, but that his influence and contributions to the American Revolution and the Early Republic deserve the attention of the American people. This writer pointed out, too, those historians who *have* studied Adams have also noted the neglect. Sanders quoted American historian and political scientist Clinton Rossiter at length, who noted that even when scholars acknowledged John Adams as one of the heroes of America, "he is left standing by himself, shy and perplexing, over to one side."[29] In this, Sanders joins a familiar refrain lamenting the absence of John Adams from historical study. For Sanders, Pound stepped in where historians had failed to tread. The poet "perceived in his own way the importance of John Adams and created out of that perception a permanent tribute to John Adams in his *Cantos*, the major work of his career."[30]

John Adams appears in the *Cantos* before the works specifically dedicated to him. In *Eleven New Cantos*, Pound focused on Thomas Jefferson as his central figure, but John Adams appears in these works as well. Ten Eyck noted that the poet had made some "offhand comments that were dismissive of Adams" but that "it was interesting to note the extent to which his attention was divided between Adams and Jefferson...."[31] Further, Pound discussed John Adams in equal measure to Jefferson in his correspondence during 1930 and 1931. According to Ten Eyck, Pound came to an interesting conclusion. "There was much to be gained ... from a more extended engagement with John Adams than was possible within the schema of *Eleven New Cantos*."[32]

The "Adams Cantos" came directly from the *Works* of John Adams, edited by his grandson, Charles Francis Adams. According to Ten Eyck, this fact is essential to understanding the material. Readers should not expect a biography when reading the poetry. Critics doing so have dismissed the work. Ten Eyck cites this biographical reading as mistaken. "The most enduring [reading strategy is] based on the notion that Pound's principal interest in the section was biographical, and that he hoped to offer as complete a portrait as possible of the American statesman he had come to admire most by the late 1930s."[33] Instead, it is an artistic piece using the chronology of John Adams's own writings in the multi-volume *Works of John Adams,* concentrating on certain themes that mattered to Pound. According to Ten Eyck, Pound meant "to demonstrate how Confucian ethics might be applied to the American scene."[34] The idea of what good government is and how John Adams worked to achieve it is paramount in the "Adams Cantos." Without this understanding of the work, the poems easily confuse readers, as they appear disjointed and random.

In addition, Sanders argued that readers would also benefit from a knowledge of the period in which John Adams lived. In fact, historical competence is key to understanding Pound's work. "A reader unfamiliar with Pound's sources [*The Works of John Adams*] would have little difficulty recognizing these key episodes and events to which Pound calls attention," argued Sanders. Knowing the history of the Revolution and Early National period would allow the reader to see the "basic clarity of the story of John Adams as Pound recounts it."[35] Historians who have dedicated themselves to the study of this period, but not to poetry, might debate this point. Yet what is most important about Sanders's argument here is the idea that Ezra Pound delivered a much more realistic portrait of John Adams than historians had.

What, exactly, did Pound choose to emphasize about John Adams? If the poems are not a biography or a chronology of Adams's life, what about the Founder did Pound want his readers to know? The poetry is not a clear narrative and in fact, it jumps around Adams's life, much as Pound's source did. Still, readers can find themes in the work.[36] Pound began his tribute to Adams by acknowledging Adams's ancestry, just as Adams himself did in his writing. The poet also noted John Adams's rejection of the ministry as his vocation and concentrated on the importance of the law to his subject. The latter is a theme throughout the "Adams Cantos" as is Adams's character and his precision in language. One of the unique aspects of this poetry about John Adams is the appearance of certain Chinese ideograms. One of these that appears several times in the poems is *cheng*, which is translated to "define the correct terms; to rectify the names or terms: a true definition."[37] By using this symbol, Pound drew the reader's attention to Adams's fascination with language and his love of precision in it.

Pound also used his "Adams Cantos" to emphasize the Founder's contributions to the American Revolution and to the Early Republic. In particular, Pound emphasized Adams's role in the two Continental Congresses, his nomination of George Washington to serve as commander of the army, his insistence that America needed a navy, and his attention to what he felt was the best form of government. On this last theme, Pound interjects the Confucian idea of balance. In Cantos LXX, the reader encounters a second Chinese ideogram that translates to "the middle, the axis, center, pivot."[38] According to Sanders and Ten Eyck, Pound saw the legalism of Confucius in the thoughts and writings of John Adams and wished to make that connection clear to his readers. Yet Ten Eyck emphasized that the Confucianism at play in the poetry is Pound's interpretation of it.[39]

In the last lines of Canto LXXI, the final of the "Adams Cantos," Pound moves from Chinese ideograms to Greek. According to Sanders, Pound quoted from Cleanthes's "Hymn to Zeus." The translated Greek reads: "Most honored of the immortals, worshipped under many names, all-powerful always, Zeus, first cause of nature, who govern all things with law."[40] Above all else, Pound was interested in John Adams's love for the law. It is not surprising that he would end his "Adams Cantos" with this quote.

Throughout the poetry, the reader hears not only John Adams's voice, but also the opinions of his grandson, Charles Francis, the man Ten Eyck called "one of the invisible heroes of the *Cantos*."[41] This is a clear indication that Pound was drawing upon the massive *Works of John Adams* compiled originally by Charles Francis Adams rather than relying on any biography of Adams. Yet looking at the poetry as a piece of art based upon this source rather than as a biographical tribute to Adams led some scholars to problematic conclusions.

In the prologue to Sanders's *John Adams Speaking*, Carroll R. Terrell argued that Pound was "dedicated to the truth about men and history." One of his main concerns in "The Adams Cantos" is to rid the record of the detritus of prejudice, cliché, and propaganda and to get to the man himself. The poet was interested in the "gestures, moods, and attitudes ... of the man himself: John Adams in action."[42] The implication here is that this is not John Adams as historians see him. This is the *real* John Adams in his own words. However, this claim is problematic. Even though Pound used Adams's own works, he still made choices. Those aspects he chose to emphasize created the John Adams that he could use to serve his purpose. To claim that an artist could present the authentic John Adams in a way that historians could not implies that a poet like Pound had no editorial preferences. In fact, he did, and Sanders admits as much. He acknowledged, "Pound does, after all, shape his sources as well as transcribe them." He continued by asking the questions, "...has the poet reported the words of his source accurately?" and "what has the source become in his art?"[43]

If Pound chose what to emphasize about Adams and used Adams's own works to create his portrait, it follows then that the John Adams he presented to his reading audience is not complete. He is as much of a creation of the poet Ezra Pound as he is of any historian or biographer who writes about him. In the end, however, what was important to Sanders as he read the "Adams Cantos" was that Pound wished to honor his subject. "The 'Adams Cantos' constitute the most elaborate tribute, as far as I know, that has ever been accorded John Adams by a major artist."[44] This is quite a statement and may have even been true according to his definition of art. Yet other literary artists have incorporated John Adams into their works since 1940 when the "Adams Cantos" were published.

Terrell included an interesting footnote in which he claimed that Ezra Pound's "Adams Cantos" had inspired a biographer of great talent. According to Terrell, Catherine Drinker Bowen emphasized the same themes as Pound in her work *John Adams and the American Revolution*. "She helped to restore him to his rightful place of importance as the main force in solving the legal and governmental problems" of the revolution. Terrell noted that Pound and Bowen had corresponded, but "Until the correspondence between Bowen and Pound is published, we cannot assess the importance of 'The Adams Cantos' on her attitude."[45] Still, Terrell saw a direct link between Pound's poetry and Bowen's biography.

Catherine Drinker Bowen (1897–1973) was the writer of several books on historical characters. The manuscripts are categorized as biographies, and Bowen did careful research for each. Yet she also allowed herself to imagine what her characters might have been thinking or feeling despite lack of evidence. She created scenes and dialog in her books that make them what are sometimes called "fictionalized biography."[46] In her biographical note in *John Adams and the American Revolution*, Bowen acknowledged the term, but made clear that she did not care for it. She preferred to think of her work as a "portrait of John Adams.... I studied the available evidence and, on the basis of it, built pictures which to me are consistent with the evidence."[47] Whatever label critics have given Bowen's works, she was a talented writer with a flair for character insight. Her work on John Adams, if somewhat fictionalized, is one of the most enjoyable biographies written about him. She also thought highly of him, calling him the "brightest, quickest, honestest man I have met in history."[48]

Bowen's is not a full biography of John Adams. Her work begins in 1745 when Adams was ten years old and continues through the approval of the Declaration of Independence by the Second Continental Congress on July 4, 1776. Bowen believed the years 1760 to 1775 were "the most important, the most significant, of John Adams's life."[49] However, rather than starting her book in the year 1760, Bowen wished to introduce her readers to the young John Adams, the small-town boy who showed few signs of the scholar he would become. As a result, Bowen spends a good deal of time writing about Adams's boyhood. The reader first meets the boy Adams in Chapter One, when the people of Braintree are anxious about a possible attack from the French during King George's War. Using this war as a backdrop to introduce John Adams and his family allowed Bowen to set the context for Adams's life as a New Englander, but also as a loyal British subject.

As Bowen wrote about Adams's early life, she used the evidence from her subject's autobiography, but also created thoughts, dialogue, and actions to present Adams as what he was in 1745: a little boy. She also used Adams's childhood to demonstrate those personality traits that remained with him his entire life. By the time Adams was ten years old, he was enrolled in the Latin School in Braintree, but Bowen emphasized how much he missed being in Dame Belcher's school, the place where his younger brother was enrolled. When walking his brother to school, John would linger for a time, according to Bowen.

> Mrs. Belcher opened school with the children singing a psalm, and John loved to sing. Mrs. Belcher let him stand in the back of the room and sing as loud as he wished; his voice came out above all the others. It was worth being late to the Latin School, worth a caning, even. John Adams did not mind a caning now and then; at least there was action in it, and resistance. What John minded was inaction, the interminable sitting from eight to five with a Latin grammar in hand.[50]

With this passage, which was Bowen's creation, the reader sees the early spark in John Adams. Noting that this ten-year-old boy hated inaction allowed Bowen to foreshadow the adult Adams, impatient for congressional action on independence, for example. What is jarring about the passage, however, is the revelation that the boy Adams hated his new school and had no love for Latin conjugation. This latter depiction does not fit the profile of the adult Adams. What Bowen did from this point was to tell a story about education that still rings true. She demonstrated the difference a good teacher made in the life of John Adams. It is an historical fact that Joseph Marsh took over the boy's education and prepared him for Harvard. However, Bowen created a vivid scene in which the young John asks Mr. Marsh if he may become his pupil. The dialogue is pure fiction, but Bowen gave her readers the chance to see the determination of Adams and the influence of Marsh. Bowen made clear that the transformation of Adams into a scholar was not immediate, but under Marsh's guidance, he was "using his brain as he would use a muscle and, in spite of himself, enjoying the exercise. What he did, he did for Joseph Marsh."[51] Because of this teacher, John Adams was prepared for Harvard, and in college he developed a love of knowledge.

Bowen spent a good deal of time on Adams's Harvard career, his stint as a schoolmaster, and his agony over choosing a career. Once Adams decided to read law with James Putnam, he dove into the study with vigor. Here again, Bowen created scenes to illustrate the character of John Adams. According to Bowen's work, Putnam was impressed with Adams's intellect, but was amazed at how clumsy and unworldly the young man was. Adams's awkwardness never left him, according to other biographers, but Putnam's concerns about Adams were pulled from Bowen's imagination. Here, as in other places, Bowen used the techniques of fiction writing to illuminate the characteristics of John Adams as they were forming.[52] For example, Bowen took a segment from John Adams's early diary to illustrate how much he agonized over his own shortcomings. In his usual introspective manner, Adams lashed out at himself, stating, "I have not conversed enough with the World, to behave rightly. I talk to Paine about Greek, that makes him laugh. I talk to Sam Quincy about Resolution, and being a great Man, and study and improving Time, which makes him laugh."[53]

The passage continued in this way for another page and a half. It is painful to read, but Bowen wove it into her narrative to make a point about this young Adams. As the omniscient narrator, Bowen wrote, "It was possible, however, that John was too sure of his failures…. John was in truth awkward, he could be stiff as a board. But there was something challenging about him … a masculine force, an aggressiveness that made itself felt even when John was silent."[54] In this way, Bowen gave her readers a portrait of a young man who was bound for great action. It is difficult to say how many of Adams's acquaintances could see this, but this author—with the advantage of 20-20 hindsight—made sure her reading audience was prepared for his role in history.

One of the writing techniques that makes Bowen's work on Adams so striking was her gift for humanizing her subject. Like a good novelist, she included facial expressions, gestures, and vivid descriptions of the people in Adams's world to bring her subject to life. Throughout the book, she also emphasized how Adams felt about the people she included in her story. It is in her biography that the reader gets the most in-depth vision of the friendship between John Adams and Jonathan Sewall. Sewall appeared regularly in the book and Bowen emphasized his importance to John almost as much as she recognized the role that Abigail played in his life. In her Chapter Sixteen, Bowen wrote, "the two [Adams and Sewall] had often ridden circuit together, shared a room at crowded inns and sat up half the night discussing their cases and talking politics. There was no man John liked so well…." Then, in parentheses and italicized, Bowen quoted a line from John Adams *Works* in which he said, "He called me John and I him Jonathan; and I often said to him, I wish my name were David."[55]

Bowen also made a point of retelling the heartbreaking story of the end of their friendship, brought about by their differing stands on the imperial crisis. To re-create this event, Bowen used another novelist technique: the flashback. John remembers the 1774 conversation he had with Sewall as he is on his way to the meeting of the First Continental Congress. "A scene came back to John as the coach rolled on…. In Falmouth lived Jonathan Sewall, still John's oldest, closest friend. Nothing had ever really come between them…. Wherever they met the two drew together naturally…. Sewall was the most congenial companion John had ever known."

Following these statements, Bowen once again inserted in parentheses the "John, Jonathan and David" line from the *Works*.[56]

She then retold the story of Sewall's attempt to dissuade Adams from going to Philadelphia. Once again, by imagining the scene, Bowen inserted details that would have been the pride of any novelist.

> After court on a July day at Falmouth, Sewall had taken John aside, invited him to walk on the hills above the sea. They had climbed high, sat at the summit on a warm rock, smoking their pipes. Even up here among the rocks and bayberry, Sewall, immaculate as always, had a look of belonging to the scene—something John admired infinitely and could never emulate.[57]

As she continued to reconstruct the conversation between the two men, she inserted small details—"From far below, the sound of the surf came faintly. A gull swooped, his wings flashed against the afternoon sky"—and the reader gets a glimpse of the thoughts swirling in Adams's mind as he attempts to respond to his friend.[58] While some biographers discuss this conversation and understand its importance, Bowen re-created it. She gave her readers the opportunity to feel John Adams's pain and understand his sacrifice in that one moment. Bowen then brought her reader back to Adams in the coach and allowed her audience into her subject's heart. "As he thought of it now in the coach, pain shot once more through John's breast, quick and bitter. He lowered his head, looking at his hands spread on his knees." In italics, the next line is from Adams's own writing. "*The sharpest thorn on which I ever set my foot.*"[59] In emphasizing this friendship, Bowen softened Adams. She brought to light a side of him that is often missing from his portrayals elsewhere.

Bowen re-created Adams's life through the approval of the Declaration of Independence. She traced his role in the Second Continental Congress, and, once again, inserted literary detail to the story of his speech in favor of independence.

> On Monday morning, July the first, 1776, John walked to the Pennsylvania State House at about half after eight. The sky was cloudless; already the bricks and cobbles gave off heat. John went up three steps and through the wide double doors that opened on Chestnut Street. The hallway was cool, the dark plank floor grateful to the eye. Through the far entrance, trees in the State House yard showed green.[60]

Setting the stage for Adams's dramatic speech in favor of the resolution on independence, Bowen provided her readers with a sense of the day in a way that other biographers have not. Then, when the resolution passed and the Declaration was approved, she ended her story with a brief dialogue between John and his cousin, Sam. Sam asks, "Is it well with you tonight?" and John replies, "It is very well with me tonight, Cousin."[61] This is the perfect ending for a novel about the years leading up to and including the Declaration of Independence. With her fictionalized biography, Bowen gave her reading audience not only a human story but also a dramatic one. Her approach to Adams—beginning in his boyhood as it does—makes her work unique. Other biographies touch on this period of his life, but she took Adams's own recollection and created vivid scenes from his childhood. Seeing his growth and development in this way explains the man he became.

For those people who are frustrated by Adams's diplomatic career or who find his years as vice-president and president painful, Bowen's is the perfect biography. Yet does her book fit well into that category? Her primary source research was well done. She included footnotes but asked her readers to peruse them all at once.[62] She created scenes and dialog based upon what she imagined had happened or been said. With all these elements, it is difficult to call Bowen's work scholarly biography. However, like any piece of good literature, it is enjoyable, dramatic, touching, and truthful to the nature of her subject. Historians and biographers acknowledged her work with respect. The fact that her book on Adams is categorized as literature does not detract from the truthful portrait she painted of her subject. She even enjoyed the respect of some academic historians. The late Julian P. Boyd, professor of history at Princeton, once wrote to Bowen: "If we differ in our interpretation, we at least agree that the historian must go to the sources…. On that issue I know that you and I stand together."[63]

The next writer to depict John Adams in his work was a true novelist, one known for his historical biographies. He was the first novelist to create a work of fiction about the marriage of John and Abigail—a practice of which John Adams would have approved. In 1795, John Adams wrote to Abigail, "To look back and recollect the Adventures of myself and my Wife and Daughter and sons, I see a kind of Romance, which, a little Embellished with Fiction or Exageration or only poetical ornament, would equal any Thing in the Days of Chivalry or Knight Errantry."[64] It would seem that Adams endorsed an historical novel about his life before the fact; 170 years later, the master of historical fiction obliged.

In 1965, Irving Stone (1903–1989) published *Those Who Love: A Biographical Novel of Abigail and John Adams*. Stone, best known for his novels based on the lives of Vincent Van Gogh (*Lust for Life*) and Michelangelo (*The Agony and the Ecstasy*), wrote *Those Who Love* from the perspective of Abigail. The reader sees John Adams and all the events of the Revolutionary and Early Republic eras through her eyes.

With Adams's first appearance, the reader sees an interesting but quirky young man. Stone painted a scene of Adams in the library of

Abigail's father, smelling books. Adams asserts to her that one can tell where a book was made by its smell. This scene is not set in historical fact, but aside from the letters John and Abigail exchanged during their court-ship, neither of them ever went into any detail about their encounters with one another. What Stone did in bringing these two characters together was to give Abigail the chance to observe John, both as a book lover and an oddity. Abigail does not swoon over his handsomeness nor fall instantly in love. Yet she is fascinated by him, and at the end of the book, she marks this peculiar moment as the time when her life began.[65]

Stone made it clear that this was not the first time John and Abigail met. What he wished to do was begin his story with their first spark. Had he commenced his novel with their first meeting in 1759, he would have had to detour several times to get to their romance. The two had known each other three years before they began courting and Joseph Ellis, in his *First Family: Abigail and John*, made an interesting point about expecta-tions. "Knowing as we do that John and Abigail Adams were destined to become the most famous and consequential couple in the revolutionary era … it is somewhat disconcerting to realize that when they first met in the summer of 1759, neither one was particularly impressed by the other."[66] Abigail was only 14 years old at their first meeting and John was 24. In addition, John was seeing Hannah Quincy at the time and by all accounts, the young Abigail just did not measure up in his mind.[67] His opinion, how-ever changed the more he got to know Abigail, and, as Stone made clear, he was drawn to her intellect and wit. She was drawn to his spirit.

While *Those Who Love* centered on Abigail, the portrait of John is intriguing. Stone gave his readers a young John Adams, struggling as an attorney and passionate about his profession. In the novel, he is anxious to marry Abigail, yet is also reluctant to do so because of his financial state. Abigail recognizes his moodiness and self-reproach. In one scene, as Abi-gail is trying to pry a wedding date from him, she tells him in no uncer-tain terms that she never imagined he was perfect. She only wishes that he would "droop a little less" as their marriage approached.[68]

Stone's novel covers John and Abigail's relationship from their court-ship, through the years of the American Revolution, and into the Early Republic. For some reason, he ended the book at the end of Adams's pres-idency rather than taking his couple through their retirement years. Per-haps this was because their letters to one another ended at this point, in 1801.[69] Still, these years and over a thousand letters gave Stone a good deal to work with. While he had to create dialog and some scenes, he was meticulous in his research.

For some reviewers, this was a detriment to the book. "Stone's 'four and a half years' of research have brought to light some intriguing bits of information, but too frequently they seem to be dragged in for the purpose of display," wrote William D. Hoyt, Jr., for the *Boston Globe*.[70] Another reviewer, Marcus Cunliffe, voiced a similar opinion, citing the completeness of the historical record. He described Stone as being "hampered" by historical facts and was also disappointed in what he saw as the incompleteness of the character, John Adams. While Cunliffe acknowledged the worthiness of Abigail, he believed John "even more worthy of study" and noted that while Stone was "fairly candid in indicating John Adams's deficiencies, he does not explore them with any great insight."[71]

Other reviewers were far less critical and found the book an excellent source for understanding this complex couple. John Barkham of *The Tucson Daily Citizen* wrote that Stone "...never lets research get into the way of his story." Stone's characters, he wrote, "live, speak and act as human beings...." Yet this reviewer also came away with a one-dimensional view of John Adams, calling him a "stern, upright, humorless Puritan."[72] Here, as in many other writings concerning Adams, the critic emphasized certain qualities over others. He was not alone in this. Lorraine Youngquist, writing for *The Marysville Advocate*, noted Stone "pictures John Adams clearly: his tempestuous outbursts for what he considers right, his scholarly writings, his unconcern for what people think and his devotion to principle" were all present in Stone's portrait of Adams. She also felt that reading the novel would be a good preface to watching *The Adams Chronicles* set to premiere on PBS.[73]

The most interesting view of Stone's novel came from gossip columnist Hedda Hopper, who reported Joe Levine was interested in adapting the novel for film and was considering Peter O'Toole and Julie Andrews for the project.[74] One would wonder if Mr. Levine had ever seen a full-length portrait of Adams in considering O'Toole for the role! The project never came to fruition, but the fact that it had caught the attention of Hollywood indicates the overall positive reaction to this novel.

Stone brought John and Abigail, one of the original power couples, to the public's attention in a new and vibrant way. However, his characterization of John Adams was a bit flat. The reader does see human moments from this Founder, most of them from the perspective of Abigail.[75] Yet Stone did give his audience glimpses into Adams's moods and reactions to the world around him. Most notably, the reader shares with John the moment he met King George III, a stunning event for Adams.[76] Most poignantly, Stone created dialog between John and Abigail after Adams's defeat for a second term as president. In the scene, Adams laments the ingratitude of the nation toward him and expresses his humiliation in a heartbreaking way that allows the reader to understand the dedication and disappointment in this man as he leaves public life.[77]

Despite all these moments, *Those Who Love* is clearly a story told from Abigail's point of view. In many respects, John Adams is a mere presence and yet readers know that these two people worked as a unit. Because of his absence for a good part of their marriage, this work of fiction keeps John Adams at a distance. Given Stone's approach to biographical fiction, this is understandable. In an obituary for Stone which appeared in the *New York Times*, the writer summed up the way Stone chose his subjects. Stone liked to write about people who he believed "had been misunderstood or unfairly misrepresented" by other authors or history. "He was also intrigued by how women in the lives of men in the public eye influenced them."[78] *Those Who Love* does capture Abigail's role in her life-long partnership with John. Another piece of literature demonstrated their partnership to theater goers.

In 1971, playwright William Gibson chose to look at the Adams marriage in a slightly different way, with both parties taking center stage. Gibson had some experience writing about historical figures. He is best known in the theater world for *The Miracle Worker*, the story of Helen Keller and her first teacher, Anne Sullivan. This work, along with a play called *Two for the Seesaw*, established Gibson as a playwright. In *American Primitive (John & Abigail)* Gibson used the words of John and Abigail Adams. These words were "put into a Sequence for the Theatre, with Addenda in Rhyme by William Gibson."[79] The Berkshire Theatre Festival first presented the play in the summer of 1969. It was subsequently revised and staged by the Circle in the Square at Ford's Theater, in Washington, D.C., in January and February 1971.[80] The year 1969 was huge for John Adams's theater career; it was also the year in which the musical *1776* opened on Broadway (see Chapter Five below). The play was revived by The Berkshire Theatre Festival's Unicorn Theatre in 2003 with updated staging and to at least one rave review.[81] In the original production, John Adams was played by James Broderick with Anne Bancroft, a veteran of Gibson's plays, taking on the role of Abigail.

In the script for *American Primitive (John and Abigail)* the dedication by Mr. Gibson reads, "to JOHN ADAMS for the pleasure of his company."[82] Along with this intriguing dedication, Gibson included a note about the nature of the work, referring to it as eyewitness history and play-like. He made it clear that he hoped directors would feel free to stage it as they liked but insisted on backdrop maps to make up for the audience's lack of geographical knowledge.[83]

The timespan covered by the play is short: 1774–1777. The audience first meets John Adams as he is heading for the First Continental Congress. Here, we see Adams expressing his insecurities and anxieties to Abigail. "A Congress. It is to be a school of political prophets, I suppose, a nursery of American statesmen.... I feel myself unequal to this business. I have four children; every lawyer grows rich who engages on the side of the crown—."[84] Not only is Adams questioning his abilities but also his means of supporting his family. It is interesting that Gibson included these two types of insecurities front and center. Meanwhile, Abigail writes of the farm and, at the same time, acknowledges the importance of his work.

While John's travels to Philadelphia in 1774 did not mark the first time John and Abigail were separated—he rode through New England often on the law circuit—what was different this time was the enormity both of John's work and Abigail's responsibilities. The audience sees their different roles throughout the work. At the same time that John expresses his impatience with Congress—"Fifty strangers, jealous of each other.... Tedious indeed is our business, slow as snails"—Abigail relates news of her mother's health and the earnestness with which John Quincy writes to his father.[85] Yet Gibson also found instances when their concerns merged. In these moments, the humanity of the two characters appears. In one scene from 1775, the frustration felt by both John and Abigail is apparent:

> **ABIGAIL:** (Turns) I want some—sentimental effusions of the heart. Are they all absorbed in the great public? Being part of the whole, I lay claim to a greater share than I have had. Johnny—Jonny says—
> **BOY:** Do you think Pappa has so many things to do that he will forget me? (A silence. John is stricken by this. Abigail takes the boy to her.)[86]

Abigail's loneliness for her husband and John's worry over his neglect of his children are palpable in this one moment. Abigail's lament here is taken from her letter of July 16, 1775, a letter in which she also described her first meeting with George Washington. While giving her impressions of the general took up a good portion of the letter, she also made clear to John that she was missing something from him. "All the Letters I receive from you seem to be wrote in so much haste," she penned, "that they scarcely leave room for a social feeling. They let me know that you exist, but some of them contain scarcely six lines. I want some sentimental Effusions of the Heart."[87]

Separation was difficult for both John and Abigail. There is also no doubt that John did worry about his absence from his children. In May of 1776, he wrote to Abigail, "It is a cruel Reflection, which very often comes across me, that I should be seperated so far, from those Babes, whose Education and Welfare lies so near my Heart." Yet he also reminded himself of what he saw as his duty to his country by adding, "But greater Misfortunes than these, must not divert Us from Superiour Duties."[88] In this same letter, Adams praised Abigail as "the best of women" who understood duty to country and bore the sacrifice well. However, he also allowed himself to retreat into his own domestic fantasy. "I want to take a Walk with you in the Garden—to go over to the Common—the Plain—the Meadow. I want to take Charles in one Hand and Tom in the other, and Walk with you, Nabby on your Right Hand and John upon my left, to view the Corn Fields, the orchards, &c."[89] In these few lines, readers can feel Adams's own loneliness and pain, feelings that Gibson captured by describing John in this scene as "stricken."

Later in the play, Gibson returned to the Adams children in a haunting glimpse of their futures. The playwright begins the scene with a quote from a letter written by John to Abigail, in February 1777. In it, he expressed anxiety for her well-being. At this point, Abigail was pregnant again and John hated to leave her. He also hated that he was separated from his children again after a brief reunion with his family. His guilt was evident in this letter: "What shall I say of or to my N.J.C. and T. [Nabby, Johnny, Charles, and Tommy]? What will they say to me for leaving them, their Education and Fortune so much to the Disposal of Chance?—May almighty and all gracious Providence protect, and bless them."[90] Using this line as a springboard, Gibson then wrote a stirring litany on the fates of the Adams children using unnamed women—perhaps Fates—like a Greek chorus as John addressed his offspring through letters. Abigail Adams the 2nd, known as Nabby in her family, was the oldest child and her future appears first in the play. The audience is told, "Romance is her lot. She will marry Washington's aide." Tommy is next and his future plainly stated as "Law will be his choice." John Quincy's future is summed up as "Haunted by a father's voice…. President at his father's death."[91] Finally, Woman 2 shares the fate of Charles:

> **JOHN:** Charles, the delight of my eyes. You are a thoughtful child, you know, your sensibility exquisite: how are your feelings affected by the times? Before you are grown—
> **WOMAN 2:** Drunkard, Sick, dirty, Homeless—
> **JOHN:** —I hope this war will be over—
> **WOMAN 2:** Dead at thirty.[92]

This is a difficult scene to read or watch. While much of the tragedy the Adams children would endure is not present here, the fate of Charles which is left for last makes the scene heartbreaking. Gibson used this foreshadowing to demonstrate the price that John and Abigail paid for their participation in the Revolution. Yet neither of them could know what the future held for their children any more than any other parent does. Who is to say, too, that the fates of their children would have been any different if the Revolution had not occurred?

What John and Abigail did know was that they expected their

children—their sons in particular—to excel. The future of the family was important to them both. Joseph Ellis argued, "It is tempting to claim that neither Abigail nor John could possibly know that they were launching a dynasty … but the evidence demonstrates beyond much doubt that they intended to do precisely that."[93] As a result, their parenting practices may seem harsh to 21st-century sensibilities, and it would be easy to blame John for Charles's fate. He was an absent father for many years. Yet John's affection for his children is evident in his letters to them. If anything, John and Abigail used a softer tone with Charles who was the "charmer of the Adams family," a child that John felt perhaps he loved too much.[94]

Adding to the sadness of this part of the play is the scene in which Abigail gives birth to a stillborn girl.[95] By depicting her pain and John's upon receiving the news, Gibson adds a level of humanity to these historical figures. He also emphasized how this couple struggled with duty versus domestic bliss and, by extension, the price the family paid for Adams's service. The message of these scenes is open to interpretation. Both the recounting of the fates of the Adams children and Abigail's strength in facing the death of her baby add drama to the piece. Yet these scenes are also thought provoking. These are the sacrifices made by people who are sometimes dehumanized by our mythology. The cost of the Revolution to John and Abigail is unmistakable.

In discussing the reasons why Gibson's play has gotten so little attention, historian Michael Kammen placed the work into its contemporary context. He described it as "a counter-culture document: a statement of disappointment with the Vietnam war and a reaffirmation of the fellowship of man."[96] Kammen is correct in his assessment and the sentiments regarding the Vietnam war were not uncommon. There is even a touch of anti-war sentiment in *1776*. Yet amongst the contemporary messages, how is John Adams used by Gibson? What portrait emerges from the play?

The John Adams that appears on the pages of Gibson's play is a man who is torn. On the one hand, he needs to be a part of the revolutionary movement. His ambition calls him to be a mover and a shaker. This is evident in all the biographies written about Adams. On the other hand, he struggles in the play with what his work is doing to his family. He needs the emotional strength his wife and children give him and coping without that causes him pain. This, too, is evident in Adams's own writing. Adams becomes a model of patriotic sacrifice in his own time and in Gibson's. What Gibson did, with more depth than any other artist depicting John Adams, was to bring this conflict within Adams into sharp focus. For this reason, the play deserves more attention than it has received.

John Adams also made appearances in shorter stage plays. In 2004, the Colonial Williamsburg Foundation in association with the Jefferson

Legacy Foundation produced a filmed version of *Jefferson and Adams: A Stage Play* written by Howard Ginsberg. The playwright expressed astonishment that nobody had written a play about the friendship of the two Founding Fathers. He also remarked that for a time, no one was interested in the work he did on them. The David McCullough biography of John Adams, published in 2001, changed that.

Ginsburg's play is not always historically accurate, but the focus of the work is on the character and friendship of these two distinct men. Thomas Jefferson, played by long-time interpreter Bill Barker, is portrayed here as a charming man, but one who hides his true self. On the other hand, John Adams, performed by Sam Goodyear, is volatile, open, and—as Goodyear observed—pure. Abigail Adams, played by Abigail Shumann, appears in the work as well. The play follows the three characters through fifty years of friendship, as it begins, flourishes, disintegrates, and resumes.[97]

The John Adams who appears here is a spiritual and emotional man. He is an optimist, but also a realist. He and Abigail are deeply hurt by the election of 1800 and Jefferson's role in it. Yet by the end of the play, their differences with Jefferson have been forgotten. In this short play, the John Adams who appears is a man who is deeply loyal to his friends and wounded when he feels they do not return that commitment. It is one of the few places in popular culture depictions where this side of Adams dominates the narrative.[98]

One genre of literature in which John Adams has appeared more than any other is the novel. In addition to *Those Who Love*, Adams has been a character in several 20th- and 21st-century works of fiction. He made brief appearances in John Jakes's Kent Family Chronicles, specifically in *The Rebels*. In addition, he appeared in murder mysteries featuring his wife and in a trilogy of books revolving around the lives of fictional women in various situations who had befriended Abigail. In many of these works, Adams is little more than a presence, but when he appeared on the page, his stereotypical characteristics dominated the depictions.

According to John Jakes, The Kent Family Chronicles was born out of a need to deal with the devastation of the Vietnam War and Watergate. The author wished to revisit the reaffirming eras of American history, including the time of the nation's founding.[99] In *The Rebels*, Jakes told the story of the Revolutionary War years and the independence movement in the Second Continental Congress. The main characters in this book are fictional, but Jakes interwove historical figures throughout. John Adams's cameos come at the Second Continental Congress, where one of the main characters, Judson Fletcher, is a delegate.

The focus of this part of the novel was on Fletcher and his behavior. Yet in the background to this drama, Benjamin Franklin, Thomas Jefferson, and John Adams are moving the Congress toward the vote on independence. Jakes used the famous exchange between Adams and Jefferson concerning who should write the Declaration with Fletcher listening in.[100] Further, the readers' impressions of Adams come from Fletcher, and the depiction of Adams is one-dimensional in the book. Still, Jakes emphasized his importance to the debate on independence and rather cleverly avoided Adams's July 1 speech in favor of independence by removing Fletcher from the room because of illness. This way, Jakes was able to evade the need to create a speech for Adams that was never written down or recalled in its entirety.[101]

Given his brief appearances and the urgency of the summer of 1776, Adams's depiction is understandable. He is not the focus of the work, nor is he present for most of the novel, but at the same time, Jakes used his July 2 letter to Abigail as part of his introduction to the book.[102] Like many authors, Jakes could not deny Adams's contribution to independence, even in a work of fiction. More recent novels depict Adams in several different ways. In one series, he provided support to his mystery-solving wife.

Placing historical figures into murder mysteries has been a popular trend for quite some time. Even Aaron Sorkin, creator and writer of *The West Wing*, recognized this in a lighthearted way. In Season 2, Episode 8 of the show, Sam Seaborn is amused by the idea of pilgrims, in their big hats, churning butter—and solving crimes.[103] This humorous moment in a television show is not off the mark. Mysteries set in historical time periods and historical figures serving as amateur detectives are abundant. One website is dedicated to the genre. "Historical Mystery Fiction" includes an exhaustive list of mysteries set in different periods of history. The historical figures who take on mysteries include Benjamin Franklin and Abigail Adams.[104]

Writing under the pseudonym Barbara Hamilton, author Barbara Hambly wrote the Abigail Adams mystery series from 2009 to 2011. There were three books in all: *The Ninth Daughter*, *A Marked Man*, and *Sup with the Devil*. The novels cover a brief period from November 1773 through May 1774, a time of tension and apprehension in Boston. With the historic events of the Boston Tea Party and its aftermath as the backdrop, Abigail solves murders. John does appear in these books, but his role is small in all of them. The focus is on Abigail and the reader sees the sharp mind she was known for work to solve the puzzles of the murders committed in the novels.

John's work as a lawyer for his clients as well as his own thoughts on crime-solving appear in these plots. For example, in the first book, *The Ninth Daughter*, Abigail discovers a body and as she is working out what to do about it, she recalls her husband's disdain for the local constables.

It is clear in this paragraph that John knew more about crime scene preservation than the law enforcement officers of Boston.[105] In addition to his thoughts on the constabulary, the reader also gets a glimpse into John's personality from Abigail's perspective.

In the instances when Abigail is thinking about John, Hamilton inserts John with his usual personality traits. While the Abigail in these mysteries loved her husband, she also acknowledged his prickly side, describing him yelling at the top of his lungs and hurling his wig about in anger.[106]

Hamilton also painted a portrait of a supportive husband who recognized his wife's sharp intellect and encouraged it. In *A Marked Man*, for example, the spouses discuss the disappearance of a young woman Abigail believes is dead. In the scene, John listens and offers his own opinions on the matter while at the same time acknowledging that her arguments are solid. As they talk, John refers to Abigail by her nickname from their courting days and beyond. John called Abigail "Portia" after the intelligent female lawyer in Shakespeare's *Merchant of Venice*.[107] In this novel, Abigail cherishes John's use of the name and the implication that she, too, would have made a great lawyer had that door been open to her.[108]

In all three of Hamilton's novels, Abigail uses her sharp intellect to solve the crimes she encounters. Her other roles as John Adams's wife and her children's mother are secondary. The focus is squarely on her, and John is in the supporting role. Because of this, Hamilton relies on those personality traits that were most prominent in all depictions of Adams. Yet in another set of novels in which he appears, the author drew a slightly different picture.

Literary depictions of John Adams appear in a series of books collectively called the Midwife Trilogy. Written between 2015 and 2017 by Jodi Daynard, the books focused on different stories within a circle of friends living during the Revolutionary War and the Early National period. In the first book, *The Midwife's Revolt*, the readers meet midwife Lizzie Boylston who befriends Abigail Adams. While the focus is on this friendship, John Adams appears from time to time and is saved from an assassination attempt near the end of the book.[109]

In the second book of the series, *Our Own Country*, Daynard shifts her narrative to tell the story of Lizzie's sister-in-law, Eliza Boylston. Eliza falls in love with a slave named John Watkins with whom she has a son. Once again, John Adams is a supporting character in the narrative, but Daynard depicts him in a way that brings out his humanity in ways that often get lost in other works. When, for example, Adams meets Eliza's son, the child turns shy and buries his face in his mother's shoulder. Eliza apologizes for this, but Adams takes it in stride, noting that he has that effect on people. In this same scene, the reader sees John's deep love for Abigail, shown through looks and gestures.[110] With this brief appearance, Daynard provides a portrait of Adams that emphasizes his awareness of his prickly reputation as well as his affection for his wife.

While historians and artists alike discuss his tenderness toward Abigail, it is not always apparent in the depictions of him. Daynard's John Adams is fully human, showing tenderness, compassion, and playfulness. Two scenes provide a picture of Adams that is refreshing. In one, he listens to Eliza's story of her son's father and agrees to help her save the man she loves. In another, he and Abigail fight playfully over a chair and later, dance.[111] John Adams is respected by the characters in this book, and he is never one-dimensional. Daynard provided a delightful portrait of the man, flaws and all. She continued to do so in the last book of the series.

A More Perfect Union tells the story of Eliza's son, Johnny. Eliza and Johnny return to the United States after Johnny's father dies in Barbados. Because of Johnny's mixed-race, Eliza has decided that he must pass for white to prove his ability in the new nation. In this endeavor, Johnny will have the help and sponsorship of none other than John Adams who is aware of his heritage. In the first scene in which Adams appears, he is vice-president, but his behavior is less than sophisticated. While assisting Adams on his farm, Johnny sees a man who is strong, stubborn—and not above urinating on trees.[112] Once again, the portrait of his humanity is striking. Yet, Johnny admires the vice-president and enjoys his company. Adams is clearly impressed with Johnny's intellect and grows to love the young man, encouraging his progress through Harvard and finding him an opportunity to clerk in a law office after graduation. Johnny assists Adams as vice-president and president while navigating his own life and career. In the novel, Adams's imperfections are clear, but so are the flaws of Hamilton and Jefferson. Of the three, the depiction of Adams is the most generous.

In an author's note, Daynard stated "John and Abigail Adams should be familiar to my readers by now; I feel that I know them intimately...." while also admitting to ambivalence about Thomas Jefferson.[113] Perhaps this explains the wonderfully three-dimensional portrait of Adams in this novel. Daynard's approach to her narrative allows her readers to see Adams in a new light and through the eyes of a fictional young man who admired him. For this reason, all three books in the series offer a delightful addition to John Adams in popular culture.

The literary depictions of John Adams—from fictionalized biography to poetry, from plays to novels—provide an engaging array of portraits. Adams was never placed on a pedestal in these works, but he was also never dismissed or condemned for his more unflattering traits. Because of the nature of literature, these writers were able to dive into Adams's point of view. Whether they created flashbacks or inner dialogs, what Adams was thinking and feeling came to the forefront. His perspective on events and what they cost him are vividly depicted. As a result, Adams's humanity shines through.

Within the literary genre, John Adams is also used in a number of ways as these authors construct the memory of his times in the context of their own. He is the mouthpiece for a strong, 1920s United States and the advocate for balance in Ezra Pound's vision for his government. He is the lively and passionate advocate for American liberties in Bowen's version of the American Revolution as well as the supporting player in Abigail's story both in the 1950s and the 2000s. He is the 18th-century patriot complete with all the angst of a man navigating the America of the early 1970s. Finally, he is the crass but delightful mentor and supporter of a young man of color in Daynard's trilogy. While this vast array of usable John Adamses is astounding, they also provide the reading audience with the nuances of Adams's character that are sometimes lost in other genres. Each author had specific reasons for choosing John Adams and what emerges from these works is a well-rounded portrait of the Founder.

It is hard to imagine that Adams would not be pleased by the variety of literary works in which he appears. As a lover of books, including poetry and fiction, John Adams understood the power of literary narrative in bringing past events to life. He could never have anticipated, however, that he would be the star of musical theater, a genre that did not yet exist in his lifetime. Yet it will be in a musical that John Adams most clearly takes center stage.

FIVE

"Obnoxious and Disliked"

The John Adams of 1776

Musical revivals are nothing new. The Tony Awards now include a category for Best Revival of a Musical. The latest reimagining of *1776* brings an entirely new perspective to the drafting of the Declaration of Independence. According to Deadline.com, the cast is composed of "performers who identify as female, non-binary and trans."[1] John Adams, played by Crystal Lucas-Perry, looks very different in this 2022 revival from the earlier portrayals of him. Yet the words given to him in the script are still there, taking on a fresh meaning for the cast and the audience alike.[2] Because John Adams is center stage in this musical, a thorough examination of the play and its history is essential to understanding how Adams is depicted and used.

It is safe to say that one of the most unlikely places to find John Adams is in a musical. Yet *1776* made the Founding Father a Broadway star. In fact, up until the HBO miniseries of 2008, this show provided the most comprehensive depiction of John Adams available in popular culture. The show and the film that followed provided a John Adams whose colleagues constantly described him as "obnoxious and disliked." The audience sees and hears a shrill and passionate advocate for independence. It also perceives a man who has extraordinary love for his wife and an amazing capacity for introspection. Many aspects of John Adams's personality are present in this depiction. Yet the nature of the show creates a caricature of John Adams, one that dominates in popular culture. This is especially interesting given the fact that this show captures Adams at a single moment in time, perhaps one of the most intense of his life. John Adams, in the summer of 1776, was driven and impatient. This is abundantly clear in his depiction on the stage. The fact that this John Adams sings and dances does not detract from the pressure the historical Founding Father was under. The added references to the heat of that summer throughout the script add to the tension. Anyone studying this important summer, can easily recognize the conditions, the intensity, and the character of John Adams at that moment in time.

The musical *1776* had a long and difficult beginning, but given the subject matter of American independence, this is appropriate. Sherman Edwards, a songwriter known for such popular ballads as "See You in September" and "Wonderful, Wonderful," conceived the show. Edwards studied history in college and was, for a time, a high school history teacher.[3] Creating *1776* allowed Edwards to bring all of his interests together, but it did not happen overnight. As Edwards told the story in 1970, the idea for the show had been on his mind for quite some time before he pursued it. He abruptly left a successful songwriting career to "do something I've had on my mind for a long time." According to John Reddy in his article, "1776: The Idea That Would Not Let Go," what Edwards wished to investigate was a "preposterous idea of doing a musical show based on the framing of the Declaration of Independence. All he had at that point was faith in the idea and a title—*1776*."[4]

Edwards was forty years old, the father of two children and an accomplished songwriter who had a deep fascination with and love for the Founding Fathers. Because of this interest—and with the support of his wife—he decided to take a chance on writing his musical. It took several years and at one point, he was obsessive about the project. It became so much a part of his daily life that one day, while driving to a recording studio in New York City, he found himself instead in front of Independence Hall in Philadelphia. "I have no idea how I got there. I was shaking so hard I got out of the car and sat on the curb."[5] After a visit to Benjamin Franklin's grave and a chance to calm his nerves, he returned home to his frantic wife and continued working on the show.

It took him five years to complete, but once he finished the work, he went looking for a producer. Finding a willing one was difficult since "Patriotism was box-office poison." Eventually, however, he met Stuart Ostrow who loved the idea and agreed to take it on.

Ostrow insisted on a revised book for the show and brought in Peter Stone to do the work.[6] Stone was an accomplished screenwriter who brought a theatrical style to the script. According to William Daniels, the actor who played John Adams, Stone was a welcome addition. Daniels was not impressed with Edwards's original script. "...when I read the script, I found the dialogue stiff and unwieldy, as if it had come straight out of a history book ... so I walked away and forgot about it." Stone was able to bring the script to life. "Peter did a powerful rewrite of this play, adding wit, speakable dialogue and a dramatic thrust that culminated in a deeply moving finale."[7]

Once the script was in place, Ostrow went in search of a director and

here again, the task proved difficult. "Stuart Ostrow couldn't find anyone to do it. Everyone turned the show down." He begged Jerome Robbins
to take it on, but the famous director turned him down flat. Yet Robbins
recalled Peter Hunt, a lighting designer he had once encountered and
encouraged Ostrow to find him and offer the show to him. Hunt had never
directed a Broadway play.[8] It was a risk, but Hunt took the job. Once the
director was in place, casting began. It was all-important to find the correct actor to play John Adams, and Ostrow knew exactly whom he wanted
in the role. William Daniels was his first and only choice.[9]

Daniels has the interesting distinction of having played many members of the Adams family over the years. He portrayed John Adams in
1776 and the television adaptation of John Jakes's *The Rebels*, John Quincy
Adams in PBS's *The Adams Chronicles*, and Samuel Adams in John Jakes's
The Bastard. As he himself phrased it, "I have now played every important
member of the Adams family, except for Abigail"[10] and *1776* was the beginning of this tradition.

By 1968, Daniels had already made a name for himself playing various
roles and originating some important characters in the theater. Yet he had
never been a leading actor and according to his memoir, he was reluctant
to take on the role of Adams. As he recalled it, his hesitation involved timing. He was not sure about the appropriateness of the show given current
events. Interestingly enough, his words to his wife about the show reflect
exactly why he was perfect to portray John Adams. "I ranted to Bonnie
[Bartlett, his wife] words to this effect: 'What is this? The founding fathers
singing and dancing up on a stage? And this in the middle of the Vietnam
War? How ridiculous!'" One can hear the John Adams quality in this reaction. Bartlett certainly did. "Bonnie looked at me and calmly said, 'Bill, it's
as if this part was written for you.'" After this gentle persuasion and some
miscommunication about where the audition would be, Daniels landed
the role. "It would be by far the largest part I'd played on Broadway," Daniels recalled. "I had nine songs, two of them solos…. My usual reaction
when I got a job was just that, it was a job; I'd try to do it to the best of my
ability. But this was something more, or at least that's what it became."[11]

The musical, like many before and after it, had a rocky out-of-town
tryout. In New Haven, Connecticut, the show opened in the midst of a
blizzard. The audiences were small, and the reviews were "forgettable."[12]
Then the show moved to Washington, D.C., and here its prospects began
to change. According to William Daniels, it was in the capital city that
the cast and creative team "realized we had a hit show on our hands. The
reviews were ecstatic and the houses sold out." Interestingly enough, in
a rather cynical tone that would have pleased John Adams, Daniels continued: "Never ones to miss a little flag waving, Congress came out in full

force to see the show." What their reactions were, Daniels did not share. He did, however, note, "My fears that it might be bad timing to mount a patriotic play in the midst of the Vietnam War were laid to rest."[13]

Despite the successful run in Washington, by the time the show moved to Broadway, the creative team and the cast were anxious. Advanced sales for the musical were dismal for opening night, March 16, 1969; "...there was just $18,000 in the box office for a show with weekly running expenses of $45,000...."[14] The only reassurance came to Peter Hunt in an unexpected moment. As the crew was working to assemble the set, "I heard our master carpenter talking to the Local men. And I heard him yell out, 'Hey guys! Don't use nails—use screws. This thing is going to be here a long time!'"[15] Why the master carpenter felt this way he did not say, but he was correct in his prediction. The sleeper hit of the season was 1776 and it ran for 1,217 performances. It closed on February 13, 1972, "one month shy of three years on Broadway."[16] Not only did the play have touring companies around the country, but also the cast was invited for a command performance in the White House—the Richard Nixon White House.

Making this happen took some persuading as many in the cast had issues with President Nixon. Stuart Ostrow, whose job it was to get the cast to the White House, sympathized. As Daniels remembered it, "Stuart, like me, was a liberal Democrat, and he listened quietly while I ranted about how much I loathed the Nixon administration."[17] Performing for this particular president was even more uncomfortable for the man playing Benjamin Franklin, Howard Da Silva. "Howard's Hollywood career had been one of those destroyed by the blacklist and the House Un-American Activities Committee (HUAC), a committee in which Nixon had actively participated."[18] Nevertheless, the cast did the performance and President Nixon greeted them afterward. The President asked Daniels if he had seen Adams's famous quotation over the fireplace in the State Dining Room. Daniels, in fact, had seen it and his fellow cast members, knowing his feelings regarding Nixon, teased him about it. The quote—"May none but Honest and Wise Men ever rule under this roof"—struck Daniels as ironic. Fortunately, Daniels told the President that he had seen the quote and quickly changed the subject.[19]

The musical received the blessing of both Congress and the White House. (Nixon's influence on the film version is a topic for later in this chapter.) What was clear in 1969 was that the show struck a chord with audiences and critics alike. For audiences, perhaps it was a reminder of a time when honest but flawed men took a bold step in the name of ideas they thought noble. Whatever the reason, the show was quite popular. Key to making the musical a hit was the performance of William Daniels as John Adams.

In discussing his approach to playing John Adams, Daniels admitted that he did not study the second president before taking on the role. He believed that he needed to concentrate on what the script gave him to work with. "If I went and read books on it, there would be information that I don't need because I have to answer the problems that are in the script to make it believable and understandable."[20] It was only during his run as Adams and afterward that he learned more about this historic figure. "After I started and went on for two years, people sent me books…. I started reading them."[21] In his memoir, Daniels remembered one book in particular. "The great historian David McCullough sent me a copy of his book *John Adams* and inscribed it with this: 'For Bill Daniels, who knows the man and the story as few do.'"[22]

Despite his lack of research, however, Daniels felt the power of the role. While he admitted to bearing no physical resemblance to the man—although both Adams and Daniels stood about five feet, eight inches—he did feel that he could relate to certain aspects of Adams's character. He shared Adams's energy and his passion. As a result, "I became committed to this role in a way I have never done with any other."[23]

Daniels's enthusiasm for the role and his care in creating it paid off. The American Theater Wing nominated him for a Tony in 1969, although he withdrew his name from contention because the committee placed him in the incorrect category of best supporting actor.[24] In addition, the critics praised his work, then and later. *New York Times* theater critic Clive Barnes wrote,

> William Daniels has given many persuasive performances in the past, but nothing, I think, can have been so effective as his John Adams here. This is a beautiful mixture of pride, ambition, and almost priggish sense of justice and yet—the saving grace of the character—an ironic self-awareness. Mr. Stone and Mr. Edwards provided Mr. Daniels with the character to play, but Mr. Daniels plays it to the hilt.[25]

Much later, in a review of the HBO miniseries *John Adams, New York Times* television critic Alessandra Stanley expressed her preference for William Daniels as John Adams over Paul Giamatti:

> Mr. Giamatti is not helped by the precedent set by William Daniels close to 40 years ago, when he played Adams in both the musical and the film version of "1776" and was pitch-perfect in the part. Mr. Daniels made a career playing brilliant, pompous and irascible men ("St. Elsewhere," "Boy Meets World"), and he was at his peak as the most confounding of the founding fathers.[26]

As a final example, theater historian Peter Filichia wrote this of Daniels's performance:

I daresay that I have seen between 80% and 90% of the Broadway musicals produced in the last half-century, but I still rank William Daniels' performance
as the best I have ever seen a male lead give in a musical. The ferocity, single-
mindedness and an ability to put aside his ego and principles to get the job
done—as well as a solid voice—made it so.[27]

Even now, many who think of John Adams or read his words connect
him with William Daniels. One comment on Facebook demonstrates this.
"Just finishing Charles Akers's biography of Abigail. Now John is in my
head twice as much—and he still sounds like William Daniels!"[28]

While the cast appears in ensemble form, the role of John Adams is
clearly the most important—thus Daniels's reaction to a Tony nomination
for best *supporting* actor in a musical. "My question was: whom was I supporting? … I had the leading role in the play and got star billing (albeit
below the title). I would have an unfair advantage against the true supporting actors in this category."[29] Even a quick glimpse at the script of *1776*
bears out Daniels's claim.

One of the striking aspects of the script is the acknowledgment of
Adams's leading role as an advocate for independence at the Second Continental Congress. While biographers of Adams are well aware of this
contribution, for many, independence will always be about Thomas Jefferson. The author of the Declaration certainly deserves the credit he is
given, but the advocate on the floor of Congress, acknowledged by his fellow delegates, was John Adams. For example, one of the New Jersey representatives, Richard Stockton, wrote this to his son: "The man to whom
the country is most indebted for the great measure of independency is Mr.
John Adams of Boston. I call him the Atlas of American independence. He
it was who sustained the debate, and by the force of his reasoning demonstrated not only the justice but the expediency of the measure."[30]

Even Thomas Jefferson acknowledged Adams's contribution to the
debate on independence, emphasizing his defense of Jefferson's Declaration. Jefferson noted that Adams "supported the declaration with zeal &
ability, fighting fearlessly for every word of it"[31] and "He was the pillar of its
support on the floor of congress, its ablest advocate and defender against
the multifarious assaults encountered."[32] Perhaps because, in later years,
George Washington and Thomas Jefferson overshadowed John Adams or
because Adams never seemed the material from which myths are made,
creative artists had overlooked his role in the days leading up to the decision on independence. The writers of *1776* corrected this error and brought
his contribution front and center for the public.

According to the historical note included with the script, the character of John Adams was a "composite of himself and his cousin Sam Adams,
also of Massachusetts."[33] There are moments in which the latter cousin is

obvious in the character. The writers noted that John Adams's reaction to the removal of the slavery clause in the Declaration was one of them. In the script, John Adams says, "Mark me, Franklin. If we give in on this issue, posterity will never forgive us." The authors noted that they had to delete part of the actual quotation from *Samuel* Adams, which read, "If we give in on this issue, there will be trouble a hundred years hence." Stone and Edwards feared that the audience would never believe Samuel Adams had so accurately predicted the Civil War and so changed the line, but they acknowledged these were Sam's words, not John's.[34] This is an interesting confession given the fact that verifying the quotation at all is difficult.[35]

There is another point in the play in which Abigail and John Adams discuss his passion for revolution. Abigail says, "Think of it, John! To be married to the man who is always first in line to be hanged!" John replies, "Yes. The Ag-i-ta-tor."[36] For scholars who have studied both John and Samuel Adams, this is a far more accurate description of Sam than John. Once John made his decision for independence, he was wholly committed to fighting for it, but Samuel was far more the agitator and had a lifelong hatred for the English that was not evident in his younger cousin. To call John Adams "the first in line to be hanged" would be inaccurate. He was a staunch supporter of colonial rights according to his reading of the British Constitution and he wrote extensively on the subject. Yet, in many respects, he was a reluctant revolutionary, concerned over the violence perpetuated by the mobs of Boston against British officials. Even as late as January 1776, he was preaching caution to his New England colleagues.

John Adams was not against independence, but he was concerned about anarchy in its wake. Adams wanted to make sure that state governments were in place to guarantee stability once independence came. According to biographer and historian Page Smith, Adams's feelings were clear. "Those hotheads who clamored for action regardless of the cost had no conception of the difficulty of political action and the dangers involved in overthrowing an established order, however imperfect it might be."[37] These are not the sentiments of an agitator.

Beyond these two examples, it is difficult to spot Samuel Adams in this character. The writers used John Adams's words many times. In addition, they captured so many of his attributes that unless an audience was aware of the historical note in the script, they would have no reason to see Samuel Adams anywhere here.

While John Adams was not the radical his cousin was, by the spring and early summer of 1776, he was growing impatient for independence. He had long insisted that the separate colonies should take over the authority on a local level to prepare for independence and, at the request of several of his colleagues, he sent *Thoughts on Government* to them. This writing proved to be a key set of instructions for the various colonies. It is clear from *Thoughts* that Adams felt the urgency of the moment and understood its importance. He wrote to a colleague, "You and I, my dear Friend, have been sent into life, at a time when the greatest law-givers of antiquity would have wished to have lived."[38] Writing on governments and constitutions occupied Adams and he enjoyed the exercise. Yet, according to Page Smith, "The strain of the delay over declaring independence began to tell on Adams. He grew increasingly edgy and impatient."[39]

He was weary but understood the importance of the work he was doing. "Objects of the most stupendous magnitude, measures in which the lives and liberties of millions, born and unborn, are most essentially interested" filled his days.[40] "We are in the very midst of a revolution, the most complete, unexpected and remarkable of any in the history of nations."[41] He was happy when, on May 15, Congress passed a resolution formally instructing the colonies to form their own governments and yet it was not enough. "The preamble [to the resolution] was more than a machine for manufacturing independence, it was the fact of independence; but, he added, 'we must have it with more formality, yet.'"[42]

It is at this very tense and frustrating period in John Adams's life that *1776* begins. The opening of the stage version is quite effective. John Adams enters the stage in front of the curtain and with his first line, the audience feels his frustration. Adams says, "I have come to the conclusion that one useless man is called a disgrace, that two are called a law firm, and that three or more become a congress. And by God, I have had *this* Congress!"[43] He continues by providing the audience with a tidy exposition for the show, reviewing the many acts and taxes that had been thrust upon the colonies without their consent. Finally, he says, "…and still this Congress won't grant any of my proposals on Independence even so much as the courtesy of open debate! Good God, what in hell are they waiting for?"

On this line, "the curtain flies up to reveal the Chamber of the Second Continental Congress…" and the members of that body immediately demonstrate to the audience their annoyance with Adams. In the opening number ("Sit Down, John!"), Congress lets Adams know that it is tired of him and his nagging on independence.[44] According to William Daniels, this opening "never failed to get the audience's attention."[45] It is in the middle of the second number ("Piddle, Twiddle and Resolve") that John Adam's frustration escalates. In the middle of this number, the singing stops for an exchange between John Hancock and James Wilson in which they discuss a petition that has come to Congress from "Mr. Melchior Meng, who claims twenty dollars, compensation for his dead mule." The issue is whether Congress should pay, and Wilson points out that "surely the beast dropped dead on its own time!" This exchange elicits yet another very adamant *"Good God!!"* from John Adams.[46]

This opening scene introduces the audience to an impatient John Adams, as well as what Adams would consider an ineffective Congress. The records of the Second Continental Congress abound with resolutions like the one quoted above, and Adams had lost all tolerance for such discussions by May of 1776. As Page Smith noted, Adams was encouraged by the May 15 resolution. Still, "Much more remained to be done and Adams was anxious to be about it."[47]

It is at this point in the play that the audience meets Abigail Adams for the first time. She was not actually in Philadelphia, but the writers could not resist the many letters that passed between John and Abigail while he served there. In order to bring her into the story and to soften John Adams, the writers decided to have them converse in what the script called "certain reaches of John Adams' mind."[48] Edwards and Stone were inspired to include these scenes and this stage setting by a brief line in one of Abigail's letters in which she wrote, "O That I could annihilate space."[49] These scenes between Abigail and John add dimension to Adams's character and allow the audience to hear, in some cases, words very similar to those the historic figures exchanged with one another.

Abigail is instantly a calming figure for John who has "such a desire to knock heads together."[50] She sympathizes, but also brings him back from the brink of his aggravation. Every time she appears, the audience sees a different John Adams from the frustrated Congressman he is in the rest of the show. No historian has ever denied that Abigail was John's salvation, that she gave him balance. This happens three times in the show with her last appearance being the most important.

It is shortly after Abigail's first appearance that Adams is described as "obnoxious and disliked" for the first time. In Scene Two, in a conversation Adams has with Benjamin Franklin, the latter says, "John, why don't you give it up? Nobody listens to you. You're obnoxious and disliked."[51] From this point on, the phrase is a running joke throughout the musical and amongst the Declaration committee who will use it cleverly, as they try to decide who will write the document. The song "But Mr. Adams" is catchy, bouncy and as a result, one of the most popular from the show. Throughout the number, Adams himself claims that he is "Obnoxious and disliked."[52] The fact that he would use this phrase to describe himself is not outside the realm of possibility. As the writers stated, "the description is his own."[53] Here, the authors were correct, but they did take some dramatic license with the actual phrase.

In August of 1822, John Adams wrote a letter to Timothy Pickering in response to some questions Pickering had about the writing of the

Declaration. It was in this correspondence that Adams labeled himself in an interesting way. In relating the conversation he had with Jefferson about who should write the document, Adams remembered:

> Jefferson proposed to me to make the draught. I said, "I will not";
> "You shall do it."
> "Oh No!"
> "Why will you not? You ought to do it."
> "I will not."
> "Why?"
> "Reasons enough."
> "What can be your reasons?"
> "Reason 1st. You are a Virginian, and a Virginian ought to appear at the head of this business. Reason 2d. I am obnoxious, suspected and unpopular; You are very much otherwise. Reason 3d: You can write ten times better than I can."
> "Well," said Jefferson, "if you are decided I will do as well as I can."[54]

It is important to note that Adams related his memory of this conversation to Pickering much later in his life and Jefferson did not recall the conversation at all. Adams's recollection also came after his stormy days as President of the United States and his failure to achieve a second term in that office. It would not be at all surprising if Adams believed himself unpopular in the Second Continental Congress because certain people who had influence (like Alexander Hamilton) did not love him in the later years of his career. Still, Adams's description of himself in the summer of 1776 as "obnoxious, suspected and unpopular" has remained part of his legacy. This was strongly reinforced by the musical and film 1776.

Yet is this a fair assessment of John Adams in the days leading up to independence? Page Smith wrote, "Adams had ample evidence of the hostility of the more conservative members toward him" but nowhere related those delegates considered Adams to be obnoxious.[55] David McCullough, in his own biography of John Adams, makes a stronger case still. McCullough discussed the days leading to the decision for independence. He related the conversation that Adams recalled in 1822, admitting that this may have been faulty memory on Adams's part. Yet what struck this biographer was Adams's self-description, "which is more that of the old man he became than the Adams of 1776, who was ... by no means as unpopular as he later said. If he was thought 'obnoxious,' it would have been only by a few, and only he himself is known to have used the word." Furthermore, McCullough argued, "there is only one member or eyewitness to events in Philadelphia in 1776 who wrote disparagingly of John Adams, and that was Adams writing long years after."[56]

Whether or not John Adams was truly "obnoxious and disliked," the description has stuck to him and in many respects has determined how the public remembers him. Adams was impatient for independence. He had no tolerance for caution by the summer of 1776. All of this comes out in the musical. The fact that John Adams's personality becomes a running joke in the script is understandable. However, it is also important to acknowledge that if Adams were unpopular with anyone, it would have been with John Dickinson. If there is an antagonist in the musical, it is Dickinson.

John Dickinson, a delegate to the Congress from Pennsylvania, was a strong advocate for the liberty of the colonies in the 1760s. He penned the lyrics to "The Liberty Song" and wrote a pamphlet entitled "Letters from a Farmer in Pennsylvania" in response to the Townshend Act of 1767, in which he argued that the colonists should not pay internal (revenue) taxes to England.[57] He was a delegate to the First Continental Congress of 1774 and resumed his duties as a delegate in the Second Continental Congress. Initially, John Adams had no animosity toward him, but as the situation in Massachusetts deteriorated in 1775, and Dickinson became more cautious about antagonizing England, Adams lost patience with him.

Although Adams heard rumors that Dickinson's seeming change of heart concerning colonial rights came because of pressure from his wife and mother, Adams could not tolerate him any longer. In a moment of aggravation, Adams wrote to James Warren, "A certain great fortune and piddling genius, whose fame has been trumpeted so loudly, has given a silly cast to our whole doings."[58] Unfortunately, the British intercepted this angry, indiscreet letter and loyalists printed it in their newspapers. This was a huge embarrassment to John Adams, and Dickinson snubbed him in public for the insult.

None of this context appears in *1776*, however. The John Dickinson in the musical is a man who would oppose any measure on independence and who was hostile to John Adams because of it. Dickinson's stand on independence is clear with his first lines. Cæsar Rodney of Delaware has been conversing with the new delegate from Georgia, Dr. Lyman Hall, when Dickinson arrives. "I trust, Cæsar, when you're through converting the poor fellow to independency that you'll give the opposition a fair crack at him." The film version of the show adds an exchange in which Dickinson makes his feelings about John Adams clear. He asks Dr. Hall where he stands on the question of treason. Hall replies that he has no stomach for it. Dickinson replies, "Ah, then be careful not to dine with John Adams. Between the fish and the soufflé, you'll find yourself hanging from an English rope."[59]

As the musical progresses, once Richard Henry Lee brings the Resolution on independence to Congress on June 7, 1776, open debate over the issue begins. The debate, with a focus on the arguments between Adams and Dickinson, dominates Scene Three of the show. At one point, Dickinson states, "My dear Congress, you must not adopt this evil measure, it is the work of the devil. Leave it where it belongs—in New England." When quietly reminded by a delegate from Connecticut, "New England has been fighting the devil for more than a hundred years," Dickinson responds, "And as of now ... the devil has been winning hands down! Why at this very moment he is sitting here in this Congress! Don't let him deceive you—this proposal is entirely his doing! It may bear Virginia's name, but it reeks of Adams, Adams, and more Adams! Look at him—ready to lead this continent down the fiery path of total destruction!"[60]

This debate continues for several pages and at one point, escalates into a physical fight in which Adams and Dickinson attack each other with their walking sticks. In many respects, the true story is no less dramatic, but it culminated on July 1. It fell to John Dickinson to speak against the resolution on independence and according to John Adams,

> He had prepared himself apparently with great Labour and ardent Zeal, and in a Speech of great Length, and all his Eloquence, he combined together all that had before been written in Pamphlets and News papers and all that had from time to time been said in Congress by himself and others. He conducted the debate, not only with great Ingenuity and Eloquence, but with equal Politeness and Candour: and was answered in the same Spirit.[61]

Once Dickinson stopped speaking, there was a pause as the delegates waited for someone to answer him. Page Smith noted, "The place was perhaps more nearly Adams' than any other delegate's.... He stood up to reply, short, stout, florid, admirable and maddening, respected even by those who most disliked him."[62] At the time, John Adams felt that the entire exercise had been a waste of time. He wrote to Samuel Chase, "That Debate took up the most of the day, but it was an idle Mispence of Time for nothing was Said, but what had been repeated and hackneyed in that Room before an hundred Times for Six Months past."[63] In the end, when Congress voted on the resolution for independence on July 2, John Dickinson stayed away, and the motion passed twelve to none with one abstention (New York).

The culmination of the tension between Dickinson and Adams in the show takes place during the vote on independence and when Dickinson is defeated, he announces that he cannot sign the Declaration. He will instead "join the Army and fight in her [America's] defense—even though I believe that fight to be hopeless." Then, in a show of respect for his opponent, John Adams rises and says, "Gentlemen of the Congress, I say ye John Dickinson!"[64] If the historical John Adams demonstrated this respect to Dickinson, nobody recorded it, but Dickinson did, in fact, join the army and in later years served as a delegate to the Constitutional Convention, representing Delaware.[65] The John Dickinson of *1776*, while not a complete villain, is a man left behind by the tide of independence. His nemesis John Adams, on the other hand, has the victory, but this only comes after great despair.

In the musical, as the delegates debate the Declaration itself, one issue comes to the forefront that threatens to sink any hope for independency. In his original draft of the Declaration, Thomas Jefferson included an indictment of the slave trade for which he blamed George III. The clause read:

> He has waged cruel war against human nature itself, violating its most sacred rights of life & liberty in the persons of a distant people who never offended him, captivating & carrying them into slavery in another hemisphere, or to incur miserable death in their transportation thither. This piratical warfare, the opprobrium of infidel powers, is the warfare of the CHRISTIAN king of Great Britain. Determined to keep open a market where MEN should be bought & sold, he has prostituted his negative for suppressing every legislative attempt to prohibit or to restrain this execrable commerce: and that this assemblage of horrors might want no fact of distinguished die, he is now exciting those very people to rise in arms among us, and to purchase that liberty of which he has deprived them, & murdering the people upon whom he also obtruded them; thus paying off former crimes committed against the liberties of one people, with crimes which he urges them to commit against the lives of another.[66]

In the play, Edward Rutledge from South Carolina asks that this clause be read aloud once again and is prepared to strike down the Declaration if it remains in the document. This is one of the most intense moments in the musical as Rutledge reminds the members of the Congress that they are all guilty in the sin of slavery. He does so with the haunting song "Molasses to Rum to Slaves," and then walks out of the Congress followed by all his fellow Southerners. John Adams, then in desperation, attempts to rally the other pro-independence congressmen, which leads to a confrontation with Benjamin Franklin. Adams is appalled that Franklin is willing to drop the clause from the Declaration to save independence. Adams believes the passage should stay, but Franklin reminds him that their top priority is a unanimous vote on independence. Later, Jefferson agrees to strike the clause, and the South supports the Declaration.[67]

The attitudes the *1776* John Adams expresses in the scene align with what many scholars believe about him—namely, that he was an abolitionist. However, at the time of independence, the historical Adams was more concerned with the break from England and a united country than he was about freeing the slaves. In later life, he did demonstrate an admiration for the anti-slavery clause. Writing to Timothy Pickering on August 6, 1822,

Adams asserted, "I was delighted with its high tone, and the flights of Oratory with which it [the Declaration] abounded, especially that concerning Negro Slavery, which though I knew his Southern Bretheren would never suffer to pass in Congress, I certainly never would oppose."[68]

As historian Arthur Scherr observed, however, in his book *John Adams, Slavery, and Race: Ideas, Politics, and Diplomacy in an Age of Crisis*, during his years in the Continental Congresses, Adams did not consider ending the slave trade a priority. "Eager to secure Southern states' participation in a struggle that at the outset primarily involved Massachusetts, Adams more than most Revolutionary leaders was willing to sacrifice emancipation measures for the common good of the war effort." Noting that Adams did express admiration for Jefferson's words against slavery, "in practice Adams considered the slaves' right to freedom an expendable goal, regarding colonial unity in winning the war as the most critical immediate issue."[69]

The statement that Adams was more willing to overlook slavery than other revolutionary leaders is heavy-handed, but the idea that Adams would have had to be reminded of his priorities in the summer of 1776—as the musical implied—does not mesh with historical evidence. More and more, scholars and the public are reassessing the Founding generation's record on slavery and African American rights. Seeing Adams in this musical act the abolitionist fits what many believe about him. Yet the historical evidence is contradictory at best.

This remarkable debate on the topic of slavery, staged dramatically in the musical, leads to one of the most moving scenes in the work and to a passionate musical rendition of one of Adams's most famous letters. The John Adams of *1776*, after seeing his hopes for independence fade because of the slavery clause in the Declaration, turns once again to Abigail for help. For the first time, Abigail comes to him in Philadelphia rather than Adams going to their home in Braintree—again, all of this in Adams's imagination. The dialog between husband and wife in Scene Seven of the musical gives the audience a remarkable glimpse into the insecurity that plagues John Adams, even though it implies that Adams never asked his wife for advice until this point.

Although the authors underestimated the role Abigail played in her husband's career, the humanity of Adams is most apparent in this scene. Stone and Edwards wrote a speech for Adams to which the historic figure could have related. "Why, Abby?" he asks her after admitting to being an agitator. "You must tell me what it is! I've always been dissatisfied, I know that; but lately I find that I *reek* of discontentment! It fills my throat and floods my brain, and sometimes—sometimes I fear that there is no longer a dream, but only the discontentment." Abigail replies that she never would have married the man he described and that John needs to remember who he really is: that he is a creature of commitment.[70]

This scene is effective because it reflects not only the vulnerability of John Adams but also the indispensability of Abigail to his life and work. In the scene's culmination, Abigail's role in lifting her husband's spirits is demonstrated further. Adams receives a delivery of some barrels of saltpeter, an item used to make gunpowder. In their first scene together, Adams directs Abigail to organize the women to make the much-needed ingredient. Just when he needs her help the most, the saltpeter arrives, and Adams, encouraged by this development, is ready to continue his fight for independence. All of this is thanks to Abigail.

Adams returns to the congressional chamber and, once he is alone, sings "Is Anybody There?"—a song that incorporated Adams's words to Abigail in his letter of July 3, 1776, which read in part:

> But the Day is past. The Second Day of July 1776, will be the most memorable Epocha, in the History of America.—I am apt to believe that it will be celebrated, by succeeding Generations, as the great anniversary Festival. It ought to be commemorated, as the Day of Deliverance by solemn Acts of Devotion to God Almighty. It ought to be solemnized with Pomp and Parade, with Shews, Games, Sports, Guns, Bells, Bonfires and Illuminations from one End of this Continent to the other from this Time forward forever more. You will think me transported with Enthusiasm but I am not.—I am well aware of the Toil and Blood and Treasure, that it will cost Us to maintain this Declaration, and support and defend these States.—Yet through all the Gloom I can see the Rays of ravishing Light and Glory. I can see that the End is more than worth all the Means. And that Posterity will triumph in that Days Transaction, even altho We should rue it, which I trust in God We shall not.[71]

In many respects, this song is the climax of the show for the character John Adams. By its end, he no longer has any doubts and is ready for the final vote on independence.

The final scene of the show is the signing of the Declaration of Independence, pulled off in dramatic fashion. As the delegates sign, "The tolling Liberty Bell begins, offstage." The actors take their places on stage to re-create the Pine-Savage engraving of the moment. A scrim curtain falls and "becomes opaque and reveals the lower half of the Declaration, featuring the signatures."[72] This ending, along with many other aspects of the musical, made it a hit. It is not surprising that a film version would follow.

Columbia Pictures released the movie of *1776* in November of 1972. Initially, audiences did not respond well, with an estimated box office total of $6,104,000 in the United States.[73] Interestingly enough, the reviews for the film have gotten better over time. Film critic Roger Ebert did not like the movie at all, giving it two stars. He did acknowledge that there were good actors in the film, singling out William Daniels (Adams) and Donald Madden (Dickinson) in particular, but "they're forced to strut and posture so much that you wonder if they ever scratched or spit or anything." Yet in a later response to this, a blogger known simply as "Jack" called this review one of Ebert's worst, saying that, although *1776* may not be a great musical, it is a great historical film.[74]

When compared to other movies depicting the revolutionary era, it has also gained reviews that are more positive. Cotton Seiler stated that *1776* is "one of the more nuanced and insightful films depicting the Revolutionary era." Vincent Canby, writing in the *New York Times* in 1986 about the release of the film *Revolution*, wrote, "The only halfway decent movie I've ever seen about the Revolution is '1776,' Peter Hunt's high-spirited, 1972 screen version of the Peter Stone-Sherman Edwards Broadway musical about the drafting of the Declaration of Independence."[75] While none of these positive statements about the film is a ringing endorsement, they are interesting in that they demonstrate a willingness to reconsider the film, especially given other movies about the period.

Since Sony released the director's cut on DVD in 2007, *1776* has made a yearly appearance on Turner Classic Movies, and a new audience has discovered it. This version of the film is complete, unlike the movie that audiences saw in 1972. According to Peter Hunt, Richard Nixon once again played a role. The president had never liked the number called "Cool, Cool Considerate Men" sung by the conservatives in Congress who wished to remain under British rule. The song refers to these men always staying to the right, never the left, and implies that they were interested only in protecting their fortunes.[76] Once the film was completed, Jack Warner, the producer, took it to the president for a viewing. Nixon asked Warner to edit out the song, and Warner did so. He also claimed that he burned the negative. Fortunately, insiders in the film industry had discovered bits and pieces of the film in the Sony vaults, and as a result, the studio restored the movie to its original form.[77]

One of the more amazing aspects of the film is that it retained, for the most part, the entire original Broadway cast. Rather than giving into the temptation to find a big-name star to play the role of John Adams, Warner decided to do the movie with William Daniels. While Daniels was not happy with the result—he walked out of the film's premiere—this is where many audiences have seen his portrayal.[78] The screenplay is faithful to the original script with a few exceptions. For instance, the opening of the film has John Adams up in the bell tower of the Pennsylvania State House, and he is not the first to speak. That honor went to Andrew McNair, Congressional Custodian. The exchange between these two men still provides audiences with a sense of who John Adams is, and when he gives his big opening speech, his point of view is clear.[79]

What the film could do that the play could not is place the story in a re-created Philadelphia and Independence Hall. Yet the characters, especially John Adams, are unaltered. There was no attempt on the part of the creative team to glamorize the story or the Founding Fathers. Over the years, as audiences have rediscovered the film, the John Adams of *1776* has become the favored portrayal of the historical figure.

While the film is the most accessible way to see *1776,* the show is staged from time to time. It is a demanding production, especially for those actors who play John Adams. The role is huge and vocally stressful. Yet for one man in particular, the opportunity to portray John Adams in this show was a dream come true. As a result, he approached the job seriously.

In July 2014, the Cape Playhouse in Dennis, Massachusetts, on Cape Cod, staged the musical for a two-week run. Actor James Beaman was cast as John Adams. Playing the role had been a lifetime goal for the actor and to prepare for it, he launched a video blog titled "Becoming John Adams."[80] In the twelve-part series, Beaman, a self-professed "history geek," traced his initial research as well as the many places he visited to prepare himself. He wished to find "the real John Adams." Beaman began his blog with a crash course on the history of the musical, noting its opening in 1969, the film version, and the 1997 Broadway revival.[81] For his second blog post, he described the process by which he approached the role. He noted that the reason great actors wanted to play John Adams was because he was a great man and a fascinating character.

Beaman also stated that, when he was playing a personality who actually lived, it was important to him to do as much research as possible. To that end, like William Daniels before him, he began with the script of the show. He had the advantage of having the historical note located at the back of the script to understand how the history was revised for dramatic purposes. Unlike Daniels, Beaman than wanted to read a narrative of Adams's life and he chose what he termed the "definitive biography"—that written by David McCullough. He then moved on to the primary sources. He read the letters of John and Abigail Adams. He even put together a Pinterest Board to help him understand the man and the period in which he lived. At the end of this post, Beaman recounted the things that he and Adams had in common, including their birth sign, their height, and their mutual love of hard cider. "Whether I am as obnoxious and disliked as Adams was," Beaman joked, "is for others to decide."[82]

In his next several posts, Beaman discussed the trips he took to Philadelphia, Quincy, and Boston as he continued his search for the "real John Adams." As he entered Independence Hall, he expressed an emotion that many historians of the Revolution feel. He simply stated, "I'm geeking out!" As he stood before the Charles Wilson Peale portrait of his character, he remarked on the many other contributions John Adams made to the Revolutionary cause, asserting, "This guy was responsible for a lot of history." From Philadelphia, Beaman's audience followed him to Quincy, where he observed that "Adams seems to be everywhere you look." He took full advantage of the Adams National Historical Park as well. He stopped in the gift shop in the visitor's center, where he noted, "John Adams is a rock star!" Afterward, he continued to the birthplaces and Peacefield.

On the final segment of his road trip, Beaman went to the Massachusetts Historical Society where he met with Peter Drummey, chief historian, and Sara Georgini, series editor for the John Adams Papers. In an interesting exchange with Drummey, Beaman expressed his desire to strike a balance between what he termed the "salty New Englander" and Adams's intellect, curiosity, and love of reading. This is a difficult task in 1776 since the play captured Adams in a moment in time. Beaman acknowledged this by stating, "The trap of the role is that you are shouting the whole time." Drummey mentioned to the actor that studying the handwritten works of Adams gives the historian—or the actor—incredible insight. When Adams was moved, apparently, his handwriting became larger. Georgini added that Adams was either writing or talking during his entire time in Congress. He never stopped. In the most interesting moment in this conversation, Beaman asked about the "obnoxious and disliked" description that followed Adams throughout the musical. Drummey made a point at this juncture to mention that that term "obnoxious" was a word Adams used to describe himself, but years later.[83]

For the remainder of his blog, Beaman captures his meetings with the wig and costume designers as well as his vocal coach as he prepared for the demanding role. The actor has the entire video blog series on his website. For anyone interested in preparing for this role or observing how an actor approaches the re-creation of an historical figure, it is a treasure.[84] Arguably, it is difficult to find who a real historical figure was years after the person has lived. Adding to this complication, in the context of 1776, is the script, which did take dramatic license. Yet the fact that James Beaman found the role so fascinating and researched the man as extensively as he did speaks volumes about the way in which this portrayal of Adams has molded the Founder's public image. As further proof of this, an interview with William Daniels and Lin-Manuel Miranda brought the 1776 John Adams full circle.

In 2016, Encores! Theater in New York City revived 1776. By this time, *Hamilton* was already a smash hit on Broadway. *Playbill* decided that it would be interesting to host a conversation between William Daniels and Lin-Manuel Miranda, two men who "have logged more hours in revolutionary-era frockcoats" than anyone else in theater history. The conversation is delightful and Miranda's admiration for Daniels was apparent. For his part, Daniels was equally impressed with Miranda and told him so. At one point in their dialog, Miranda turned to creating the characters of the Founding Fathers, specifically John Adams:

> LIN MIRANDA: That Peter Stone, went back to the texts written by these guys, who were petty, brilliant, compromised—that's more interesting than any marble saints or plaster heroes you can create. And the picture you all painted together of John Adams was so powerful; ...We don't have a John Adams in our show, but we can just refer to him and everyone just pictures *you*, Mr. Daniels.
>
> WILLIAM DANIELS: Really?
>
> LIN MIRANDA: Yeah, *1776* created such an iconic, indelible image of Adams that we just know who that is now.[85]

Miranda's final statement here is interesting. Despite all the histories and biographies of John Adams that have appeared over the years, Miranda's implication is that without *1776* and the powerful performance of William Daniels, we would not have such an immediate, multidimensional image of him. For the public that avoids history books and biographies, Miranda was certainly correct. The 2008 HBO series would also contribute to the public's knowledge of who John Adams was, yet the John Adams of *1776* has become the gold standard of depictions. This conclusion leads to certain questions about this piece of art.

First, does this particular genre of popular culture—musical theater, with its insertion of songs at just that right moment in the script—diminish the intensity of this time in John Adams's life? Roger Ebert apparently felt that it did. However, one could also argue that music, in all its forms, can only *add* to the emotions of a story. While "But Mr. Adams" is a funny rendition of a very important decision-making process, "Is Anybody There?" is one of the most moving songs in the show. The fact that Adams wrote many of the words used in that piece is a bonus.

Second, does the characterization of John Adams in *1776* mean that he will never escape being "obnoxious and disliked?" There is no doubt that this show has embedded this phrase in the minds of all who have seen it. Yet, it is important to remember that this was Adams's own assessment of himself albeit many years later. John Adams had a gift for dismissing himself and his importance while at the same time appearing quite arrogant. His diary and autobiography are full of his self-deprecating comments. A psychologist would term this defensiveness, but whatever the cause, Adams was often the first to admit his faults. Therefore, the label of "obnoxious and disliked" is not dismissive; it is insightful.

Finally, how does this piece of popular culture contribute to the idea of a "usable John Adams" to construct the memory of this moment in time? Adams's commitment, passion, impatience, and frustration are all apparent in the musical as is his reliance on and love for Abigail. The idea of commitment to a cause, emphasized in "Is Anybody There?", could resonate with people who were and are longing for a time when leaders put their nation above self-interest or loyalty to a political party. Whether or not that time ever really existed is immaterial. It is the past that was being constructed to counter the cynicism of the 1960s and '70s. Yet the play is not suggesting that the Founders were godlike. It does not dismiss the flaws in Adams or his colleagues, nor does it ignore their humanity. As Miranda pointed out, this is a better tribute than anything done in marble could be. Since Adams himself was such a realist when it came to his own character, it is hard to see how he would object to his portrayal here.

Is there more to see of John Adams in this depiction? Yes, there is and that is why this interpretation of John Adams continues to resonate with people. Beyond those traits that annoyed his fellow Congressmen, the audience sees a man willing to put everything on the line for what he believed was right. They also see a human being, struggling with his own demons in order to do a very courageous thing. There is value in seeing the Founders in this light. All of these men were highly flawed, which made their accomplishments even more remarkable. Americans enjoy the narrative of their nation's founding and often ignore or are unaware of its complexities. While not always historically accurate, 1776 does not oversimplify the Founders.

With the new production of 1776 set for Broadway in 2022 and a national tour in 2023, the cast is finding new uses for John Adams and his colleagues. According to the artistic director of the production, Diane Paulus, she wishes to use the show to grapple with certain issues surrounding the nation's founding. "How can we hold history as a predicament versus an affirming myth? How does an honest reckoning with our past help us move forward together?"[86] The cast and crew have taken 1776 to a more inclusionary level while, at the same time, maintaining the spirit of the show. Rather than accepting a past in which many groups were excluded, the production is using educational as well as theatrical techniques to make the memory of this historical moment relevant to a 21st-century audience. Hearing the words Peter Stone gave to John Adams spoken by an African American woman gives them added meaning and creates a broader use for John Adams in public memory.

The John Adams of 1776 is not larger than life; he is a person on a mission. Because he is the star of this particular show, audiences can see this much more clearly than they do in other portrayals, especially those of the small screen before the HBO miniseries. Those early television portrayals are the subject of the next chapter.

SIX

John Adams
on the Small Screen

For entire generations of Americans, television was the way they perceived the world. They learned their numbers and their letters from TV. They recognized Captain Kangaroo and Howdy Doody as good friends. Therefore, it should not be surprising that television also allowed these generations to construct a meaningful past for themselves. Shows such as *You Are There* allowed viewing audiences to live in historical moments as if seeing a news broadcast. The American Revolution also became a television moment and John Adams a TV star.

Thanks to the film version of *1776*, John Adams made an appearance on the big screen. Yet he would also appear on the small screen in the 1960s and 1970s and would reappear in the medium in the 2000s. The work that gave him the biggest audience by far was the 2008 HBO miniseries devoted to him. Because of the importance of this work, it is the focus of Chapter Seven. Before that miniseries, however, John Adams made appearances in a television version of John F. Kennedy's *Profiles in Courage* as well as a PBS series called *The Adams Chronicles* and the television version of *The Rebels*. Public Broadcasting and A&E television made documentaries about John Adams that are worth examination. In later years, Adams also appeared regularly in the PBS children's series *Liberty's Kids*. Most recently, History Channel's *Sons of Liberty* (2015) provided an interesting portrait of John Adams, comparing him to his cousin, Sam. The accuracy of these pieces varied, depending on their purposes. As with literature, John Adams is not always the star of the show. However, the portraits of him that emerge constitute a fascinating dimension of John Adams studies.

In 1964 and 1965, Robert Saudek Associations produced a television series based upon John F. Kennedy's popular book, *Profiles in Courage*.[1] The 26-episode series aired on NBC and starred a wide variety of actors from stage and screen. The historical figures covered across the episodes came from all periods of United States history, and included Anne Hutchinson, Grover Cleveland, Frederick Douglass, and Woodrow Wilson, to name a few.

Episode Seven, which aired on December 27, 1964, centered on John Adams and his role in defending the British soldiers in the aftermath of the Boston Massacre. Acclaimed actor David McCallum took on the role of John Adams in this episode. McCallum, best known for his appearances in *The Man from U.N.C.L.E.* and more recently *NCIS*, brought a calm dignity to Adams while also capturing his struggle with the changing political climate in Boston in 1770. The narrator informs the audience that John Adams is a successful lawyer and opponent to the British Crown. Yet the events of March 5, 1770, otherwise known as the Boston Massacre, will test him, for he "was to be faced with decisions that could end his political career."[2]

One of the first scenes in the show happens before the events of March 5. Adams's longtime friend Jonathan Sewall is visiting the Adams home in Boston. They discuss Adams's successful defense of John Hancock against charges of smuggling. This topic leads the two men into a debate over the larger issue of taxation without representation. Despite the fact that Adams's stance on colonial rights is clear, Sewall lets his friend know that the job of Advocate General for the colony is John's, if he wants it. Adams turns it down on the spot, but Sewall warns him about his association with the mobs of the Sons of Liberty. Adams responds hotly, "There is a difference between the Sons of Liberty and a mob!"

With this dialog, the audience sees a man who, while supporting colonial rights, does not condone violence. He has no love for the mobs that have roamed the Boston streets, harassing British soldiers. Sewall then says, "You're becoming emotional, John. It's always been your Achilles' Heel." In one brief act of this episode, the audience sees Adams, the successful lawyer, be an advocate for law and order as well as colonial rights. The scene also reveals what his friends knew about him: that he had a temper and strong emotions. While McCallum never gave full range to this side of Adams, the hint at this part of his character is interesting, coming as it did from one of his closest friends.

This conversation between Adams and Sewall laid the foundation for the decision Adams made to defend English soldiers against charges of murder stemming from the events of March 5, 1770. The Boston Massacre, as it came to be known, involved a regiment of soldiers firing into a crowd of Bostonians who had been harassing them that night. The relationship between the townspeople and these soldiers was complicated, and recent research indicates that it was not altogether hostile.[3] Still, tensions had been running high in the town, and resentment of the soldiers' presence in

Boston came to a head on March 5, when the regiment killed five people. The soldiers, including their captain, Thomas Preston, were arrested for the killings and were in desperate need of legal counsel.

Why John Adams, a known opponent to crown policy in the colonies, would agree to defend the soldiers, is still a matter of speculation. Adams related that he was approached by a friend of Preston's and responded to the man's pleas for help by saying "Council ought to be the very last thing that an accused Person should want [lack] in a free Country. That the Bar ought in my opinion to be independent and impartial at all Times and in every Circumstance. And that persons whose Lives were at Stake ought to have the Council they preferred."[4] Whether or not his motives were so pure has been questioned by historians, one stating, "How a future president of the United States, John Adams, became the leading lawyer for British soldiers has become the stuff of legend, created in large part by Adams himself through his autobiography."[5]

Biographer John Ferling believed that Adams may have been motivated by the possibility of political gain engineered by John's cousin, Samuel who "was endeavoring to further his cousin's reputation as a man who stood nobly above the fray."[6] Whatever his motives and despite what he may have gained from taking the case, he did manage to defend his clients without putting Boston on trial. How he did that was the central theme of this *Profiles in Courage* episode.

Throughout the rest of the program, Adams is confronted with the potential ramifications he faces in taking the soldiers' case. His motives are also questioned by one of his clients. Hugh Montgomery, one of the more belligerent of the soldiers wonders why Adams took on their cause. He claims that since Adams is a member of the Sons of Liberty, he intends to see the soldiers hanged. Despite this, Adams is determined to defend his clients against the charge of murder without putting the town of Boston on trial. He navigates this in court while he reminds his co-counsel, Josiah Quincy, to be careful not to condemn the actions of the Sons of Liberty. "The Sons of Liberty are not on trial," he whispers to Quincy in the courtroom.

There was, in historical fact, concern on the part of the royal government that Adams would be too soft on the town. Acting Governor Thomas Hutchinson, however, who was quite familiar with John Adams from past experience, understood Adams's strategy. According to Serena Zabin, author of *The Boston Massacre: A Family History*, "Hutchinson understood that Adams was hoping to save his clients without smearing Boston. It would be a difficult needle to thread. To do so would require a virtuoso performance."[7]

The depiction of the trial in the episode is interesting. Unlike the chaos illustrated in the 2008 HBO miniseries on John Adams, the court-room in *Profiles in Courage* is quite calm and the witnesses well-dressed. Josiah Quincy questions the witnesses, while Adams observes. The audi-ence hears his thoughts as he looks for opportunities to take a testifier to task. The only time he speaks in the courtroom is when he gives his clos-ing argument. The script writer depended upon Adams's own words in the trial of the soldiers, and here he gives that performance to which Zabin referred.[8] McCallum gave a calm but passionate interpretation of Adams's closing statement to the jury. Adams reminds the men that "The sun is not about to stand still or go out, nor the rivers to dry up because there was a mob in Boston on the 5th of March that attacked a party of soldiers." At the end of the episode, Adams wins his case and is congratulated by both Sewall and his cousin, Samuel Adams. Samuel tells John that the violence will continue. John responds, "There is still time for reason," then slumps into a chair, weary rather than triumphant.[9]

John Adams made another brief appearance in the *Profiles in Courage* series. In Episode 22, the focus was on John Quincy Adams and the stance he took against his political party and New England. In 1807, in the face of abuse from the British Navy, President Jefferson called for an embargo in an attempt to avoid war with England. This was an unpopular policy in New England as the region depended on trade from Great Britain. John Quincy Adams, serving as senator from Massachusetts at the time, had to make a choice. Either he could adhere to the Federalist party line and oppose the embargo, or he could do what he thought was best for the entire country. In the episode, as he struggles with his decision, he receives a visit from his father.

In a remarkable scene between father and son, the audience gets a brief glimpse into their relationship and the older man's regrets. When John Adams, played this time by English actor Laurence Naismith, greets his son, the two begin to hug but think better of it. This is an interest-ing commentary on the restraint with which each man showed his affec-tion. John Quincy Adams, played by Douglas Campbell, does not ask for his father's advice, but he gets it, nonetheless. John tells his son that he must tread carefully, that a man can hold principles quietly. John Quincy asks, "Is that your character?", to which John responds, "My character is out of style." He tells John Quincy that times have changed. He cautions his son to avoid modeling his behavior on John's own. He says that Jeffer-son is "a scoundrel," but that he has charm and that is what works in 1807. Even as he advises tact for his son, he also demonstrates regret, even sad-ness. In this one brief scene, Naismith was able to capture the John Adams of the early 1800s, looking back at his career and hoping to spare his son the pain he himself felt in being rejected by his country. However, John

Quincy Adams could not follow his father's counsel. He tells his wife, "I endeavor to follow my father's example, but not always his advice." John Quincy supported the embargo against the wishes of his party.[10]

The portrayals of John Adams in the *Profiles in Courage* series present a man in two different stages of his career. Both performances offered hints at Adams's personality, but they were understated. The focus of the show was on moments of courage, actions that often came with a price. The John Adams defending British soldiers did what he felt was right to protect the rule of law, but in the later episode, the older man knew what he had to sacrifice in order to follow his conscience. In looking for examples from the past of people who dared much to uphold principle, John Adams proved the perfect model for 1960s American television. However, in order to view the full trajectory of Adams's life and career, the public would have to wait for another television offering. This one was the product of Public Broadcasting and would place John Adams center stage.

In 1976, PBS produced an Emmy Award–winning docudrama called *The Adams Chronicles*.[11] This remarkable series traced four generations of the Adams family, beginning with the man who brought the name of Adams to national prominence, John. What sets the series apart from the 2008 HBO miniseries on Adams's life is that it is based solely on the Adams family papers rather than on a biography. The producers took little dramatic license yet created a popular history of the Adams family that drew critical acclaim. While George Grizzard's portrayal of John Adams is not as well known as that of Paul Giamatti or William Daniels, the nature of the series demonstrated the possibilities for delivering accurate history to the public outside the classroom without sacrificing drama and entertainment. Much of its success can be attributed to its context—namely the Bicentennial period and the evolving educational mission of Public Broadcasting in the 1970s.

The history of the Adams family is both a fascinating and a tragic story. Scholars have been drawn to the tale many times throughout the 20th and 21st centuries. Not including the companion book for the series, *The Adams Chronicles*, no less than four books cover the history of this remarkable and troubled family.

In 1930, James Truslow Adams (no relation) wrote *The Adams Family*, claiming that he had to tell the story. "In America," he wrote, "there is one family, and only one, that generation after generation has consistently and without interruption made contributions of the highest order to our history and civilization."[12] James Adams wrote as if genetics somehow flipped a switch in the Adams line with the birth of John Adams in 1735. "After four generations of simple but public-spirited yeomen," he wrote, "a something, we know not what, occurred in the blood or brain of the line and lifted it to a higher plane, from which it has never descended."[13]

Whether the change in Adams family's fortune and achievement happened because of this "something" to which the author referred or because John Adams was the first of his direct family line to attend college, the fact is that he began a long line of success. James Truslow Adams did acknowledge that this could be attributed to both of John's parents. Perhaps John Adams's rise to prominence was the consequence of "some mysterious result from the combination of Adams and Boylston blood far beyond the ken of science even to-day," the author speculated. This could be the case, given that John's mother, Susanna Boylston, came from a family known for its medical prowess in Massachusetts.[14] As discussed in Chapter One, John Adams did note that his uncle, Zabdiel Boylston, "first introduced into the British Empire the Practice of Inocculation for the Small Pox."[15] For this historian, why this shift in prominence happened is not clear. "All we shall see is that without warning, like a 'fault' in the geologic record, there is a sudden and immense rise recorded in the psychical energy of the family" and along with this, the family possessed "character and intellect far above those of the common run of their contemporaries."[16]

Forty-six years later, Francis Russell published *Adams: An American Dynasty* for American Heritage. This book, along with *The Adams Chronicles*, was one of many attempts to contribute to the Bicentennial of 1976. Russell, too, noted "with Deacon John's son and namesake some mutation altered and transformed the placid Adams stock...."[17] This book, like the previous biography of the family, lacks references of any kind and serves as a brief chronicle of the family up to the year 1976.

While these first two books on the Adams family are enlightening in certain ways, the most thorough treatment of the family from John to Brooks Adams comes from Paul C. Nagel's *Descent from Glory: Four Generations of the John Adams Family*. Nagel also refrained from using footnotes but explained why. He noted that Brooks Adams, who died in 1927, "left behind a collection of family letters and diaries extending back to the time of his famous great-grandparents" and since "every page of what I have written springs from this enormous body of manuscripts, I have not included footnotes, for their length and complexity would overpower the story."[18]

Of all the books written on the Adams family, his is by far the most thorough and heartbreaking to read. This historian told the entire story of the family, both the triumphs and the tragedies. The title of his first chapter, taken from a quote by Charles Francis Adams, is "The history of my family is not a pleasant one...."[19] With this beginning, Nagel alerted his readers to the fact that not all Adamses were successful or long-lived and the book itself is sad to read. Nagel acknowledged that whether the family members were considered successes or failures, "no Adams … made a comfortable accommodation to life."

Nagel went on to note each generation shared the trait of seeing with realistic eyes the weaknesses of humans and their societies. "The result was that while Adamses earned the attention and acclaim of the public, they rarely hesitated to scold that public and to urge it to turn in another direction."[20] This trait, argued Nagel, resulted in their neglect in the historical memory of the United States.[21] "The family provided individuals of great talent who served their country well, but whose viewpoints were usually ahead of or above those prevailing in their day." The Adamses wanted "to help, to lead, to inspire their fellow citizens," but the public did not care for their realistic attitudes concerning human nature. "Inevitably," Nagel wrote, "the Adamses were often repudiated or ignored, leaving them feeling misunderstood and unappreciated, but not surprised."[22]

The most recent history of the Adams family is 2002's *America's First Dynasty: The Adamses, 1735–1918* by Richard Brookhiser. In his brief coverage of the family, Brookhiser chose to focus on the leading member of each generation: John, John Quincy, Charles Francis, and Henry. The title of his book is an interesting reflection of the time in which he wrote. Perhaps he had in mind the Kennedys, the Bushes, or the Clintons as he studied the Adamses. This author was interested in writing about political families and argued in his introduction, "No family will ever be as famous as the Adamses, whose role in the founding gives them a leg up even on the Roosevelts, but, as long as there are elections, people will vote for candidates whose names they recognize."[23]

Brookhiser wrote brief biographies of each successful member of four generations and then ended his book with overview chapters on writing, legacy, and death, bringing each era together.[24] In attempting to sum up the Adams legacy, Brookhiser noted that most Adamses, "favored by education, experience of the world, and christening, were either simply talented, or simply normal, or simply failures."[25] Even as he focused on the successes of four generations, he also acknowledged a difficult truth about the family, noting that alcohol "laid waste two-thirds of the second and third generations."[26] This sad fact was a burden for the family, but so were the expectations of Adams parents throughout the generations. The Adams family history would make an interesting study on parenting styles.

It is safe to say, then, that the story of the Adams family has not been neglected. Yet *The Adams Chronicles* is the only example of a full-fledged dramatization of the family's history. Getting it made was no small feat. Reflecting upon the many achievements of Public Broadcasting today, it is difficult to see *The Adams Chronicles* as groundbreaking. However, in 1976, the project was ambitious and unique. The series covered four generations of the Adams family and consisted of 13 one-hour programs. The struggle for the script writers was to retain historical accuracy to the best of their abilities. According to the series' editor, Anne Howard Bailey, "the pressure from historians to make 'The Adams Chronicles' authentic in every detail sometimes placed intolerable obstacles in the dramatists' way." Bailey commented, "Trying to do a television series that is historically authentic is very difficult. When you want the support of the Adams Papers and of the Adams family themselves—without which there could not have been any television series—you have to give the historians the final word."[27] Bailey continued, "Writers yearn to tilt the scene a little. On the other hand, historians yearn to hew to the historic line. The conflict between writer and historian led to an eternal push-pull situation."[28]

The project also required substantial funding. The show was the brainchild of historian Virginia Kassel who had been working on the idea since 1969. She eventually received funding from the National Endowment for the Humanities, the Andrew Mellon Foundation, and the Atlantic Richfield Company totaling four million dollars.[29] This support allowed for filming and production to take place in the United States. As England was and is the source of many PBS offerings, the fact that *The Adams Chronicles* was the product of WNET of New York gave the series' star, George Grizzard, hope for the future of American-made shows. The success of the production would "prove Public Broadcasting can produce quality series instead of importing everything from the British."[30]

The show was indeed successful with viewers and critics alike. According to one newspaper, the program was the highest-rated continuing series in Public Broadcasting history as of 1976 "consistently quadrupling prime-time ratings for Public Television stations in the nation's 10 largest cities."[31] In addition to the ratings success, the series received notice from award committees. The show won a Peabody award and was nominated for 20 Emmy Awards, winning four.[32] However, one television critic at the time focused only on the cost of the project, which blew its budget. His article was entitled "'Adams Chronicles' A $6.7 Million Series."[33] Since the show was produced for Public Broadcasting, this emphasis on budget is not surprising. Part of the cost of the series went to securing prominent actors for the leading roles.

Of all the actors who have played John Adams, George Grizzard looked the least like him, a fact that the actor openly admitted. "It's the epitome of dress-up," said Grizzard. "With wigs and clothes like those in a John Singleton Copley portrait, they tried to make me look like John Adams, but I'm never as plump as he was as a young man. He was short and fat, a real Chubbums!"[34] Grizzard was given the unenviable task of portraying Adams over a long span of his life, from his early days as a struggling attorney to his deathbed. While Grizzard was a fine actor, he was constrained by the nature of *The Adams Chronicles*, having little opportunity to stray from the actual words of Adams himself.

The series attempted to capture the drama of the Founder's life, but it was also designed as an educational piece and despite some stellar actors in the leading roles, the show also suffered from some bad acting. The unevenness of the performances made for a stiff and awkward drama at times. Despite this problem, television audiences had a golden opportunity to learn about a family that had an impact on many periods of American history. As historian Daniel Boorstin put it in the companion book to the series, "America made the Adamses possible and … the Adamses expressed America." He went on to articulate the much repeated lament concerning the family. "We will discover why the family has not had its due in American history or patriotic lore."[35]

With *The Adams Chronicles*, the audience received the most thorough coverage of John Adams's long life to date. The series opens in 1758, and the voice-over is Grizzard as a 67-year-old Adams, quoting from the opening paragraph of Adams's autobiography. Adams said that "having been the Object of much Misrepresentation … [it is] for my children that I commit these Memoirs to writing; and to them and their Posterity I recommend … those Moral Sentiments and Sacred Principles, which at all hazards and by every Sacrifice I have endeavoured to preserve through Life."[36] While the voice of the older man explains his reason for writing his memoir, the audience sees John Adams as a young man. As historians Nancy Isenberg and Andrew Burstein remarked, his life is contrasted to the young English King, George III. This John Adams, they argue, is not a budding aristocrat, but is rather a "rustic Everyman" and that with the acts of "pitching hay and splitting rails, he is an iconic rival to Abe Lincoln as the first log-cabin president."[37]

In addition to his depiction as a young farmer, John Adams is also seen as a newly-trained lawyer, attempting to get sworn to the Boston Bar. The scenes concerning his struggles come directly from his own recollections of events in his diary. As noted in Chapter One, John had studied law with James Putnam in Worcester, Massachusetts, where he was employed as a school master. Yet when he arrived in Boston, he had no patron and had to convince three of the leading attorneys in the city to recommend him to the Bar.[38] In the series, Grizzard captured the young Adams's eagerness to prove himself and his anxiety that he could not do so to the satisfaction of those formidable lawyers.

The viewing public also saw the courtship of John Adams and Abigail

Smith, the young woman that he married in 1764. Seeing the beginning of this remarkable partnership dramatized for the first and only time is one of the unique aspects of the series. The show did not shy away from the painful experiences of the family. Here, the audience saw the only depiction of the grief John and Abigail suffered when their 18-month-old daughter, Susanna, died. She would be the first of three children John and Abigail would lose in their lifetimes, not including their stillborn daughter whom they lost in 1777. While the series showcased the family's contributions, it also demonstrated the heartbreak experienced by the first generation and the burden of greatness carried by their children, grandchildren, and great-grandchildren.

Being an Adams was never easy. The episodes dealing with John Adams's life demonstrated that his insecurity and puritanical introspection plagued the patriarch of the family. Despite the constraints placed on this dramatic series stemming from the desire for historical accuracy, the show presented an interesting portrayal of John Adams. While there were certain concessions made for the times—such as the depiction of Adams as a young, doting father—the scripts were full of Adams's insecurity and temper. "Why am I moving to Boston? Is it to fulfill my own ambitions?" "Why am I taking [the Boston Massacre] case? Is it for the prestige?" "Down Vanity!" is an almost comedic line that appears often in the script.[39]

Yet the audience also got to see John Adams as a grandfather, advising his son not to be too harsh with his children.[40] As younger generations of the family take center stage, the patriarch fades into the background, but most of the series focused on John Adams. Six of the 13 episodes were about John Adams and his long career. Even as John Quincy Adams came to the foreground, his father was there, casting a long shadow.

When George Grizzard died in 2007, his obituaries did not mention his stint as John Adams. This is because, by that time, the actor most connected to the historical figure was William Daniels of *1776* fame who interestingly played John Quincy Adams in *The Adams Chronicles*. However, in 1976, when *The Adams Chronicles* premiered, Grizzard claimed that the role changed his life. People recognized him in a way they had not before. "I can't tell you what *The Adams Chronicles* have done for me. Even on the stage in *California Suite*, I hear them: 'He's John Adams.' Twenty years on Broadway, two Tony Award nominations and that's what they remember.... But what a wonderful experience."[41] John Adams also got under the actor's skin. As he was researching the role, he admitted to becoming quite protective of him. "I started to read and I discovered that John and I have a great deal in common." Because of this affinity, Grizzard wanted the scripts to be true to the spirit of the founder. "If a line didn't seem in keeping with his character, I'd object."[42]

It is clear, then, that from the perspective of this actor, John Adams was a great role in a very long play. Yet for the series creators and for many who wrote about it, John Adams and his family were also educational material. Even before the time of its first airing, *The Adams Chronicles* was pushed as a unique way to teach the history of the United States. Journalist Betty Utterback noted, "More than 400 colleges and universities are offering a credit course in history based on the program...."[43] In addition, Educational Associates, a division of Little, Brown and Company, ran a full-page advertisement in *American Libraries*, touting all the companion books and guides accompanying the series. There was a study guide for college students as well as a guide to discussion groups for public librarians who wished to host sessions with their communities.[44]

Yet how successful was *The Adams Chronicles* as popular history? How well did it educate the public about the nation's story? It is difficult to say what college students, or the public at large, learned from the show. Yet for educators themselves, some of them historians, the results were disappointing. According to Richard W. Smith, writing on educational television, college students preferred the courses centered around *The Adams Chronicles* over history courses delivered in a traditional lecture format. However, he questioned if television was, in fact educating, citing the fact that classes focusing on the series also had study guides to go with them. He claimed that these classes were nothing more than "old fashioned home study programs with the added fillip of a TV program every week to serve as a pacer and as a motivator." He added, "Television ... is not teaching, in the traditional sense of imparting information directly to the student. Rather it is cajoling, chiding, urging the student back to his books and his serious study."[45]

A review in *The History Teacher* covered all aspects of the series, including each of the supplemental printed materials used in classrooms. The reviewer, Richard Rollins of Michigan State University, was less than impressed by this form of teaching history. He stated that The National Educational Television Network, PBS's earlier title, had spent "five years and millions of dollars" on the project. Yet, "Despite the resources expended, the television series and supplementary written materials achieve only limited success." Rollins acknowledged the project presented an opportunity at an innovative way to study the past but judged the enterprise a disappointment.[46]

What of the subject matter? Was the Adams family the best vehicle for engaging the public in the nation's Bicentennial? Given the chaos of the national Bicentennial celebration, any attempt to bring the public back to the personalities involved in the founding moment of the United States was laudable. Here, the focus of the series on John Adams made sense. The portrayal of the Founder is solid enough, although in comparison to other actors who have taken on the character, Grizzard's Adams is lackluster. Still, given the constraints he was under and the emphasis on education rather than entertainment, he can be forgiven.

In the final analysis, *The Adams Chronicles* as popular history was, on some level, a success. One critic called the show "American television at its best." Writing for the *New York Times*, John O'Connor noted, "If the first hours can be considered representative, the series gives every indication of being a Bicentennial jewel, a splendid achievement in a major anniversary year that, so far, seems to be drenched in kitsch and mediocre tribute."[47] The series presented to the public the story of a prominent family, with all its strengths and weaknesses. According to the ratings, the public watched. If academics found the series lacking, they did not always want to. As critic and historian Clifford S. Griffin noted in his review, "I wish I liked *The Adams Chronicles* more than I do. I certainly like the Adamses."[48]

The apparent struggle in the academic reviews of the series stemmed from the ever widening gap between historians in the academy and popular history as it is presented by those who are not experts in the field. The writers, producers, and actors associated with *The Adams Chronicles* were not concerned with the struggle to bridge this gap. The issue of historical accuracy versus good entertainment challenged other television offerings as well. For the most part, entertainment won out.

In 1979, Universal Television's Operation Primetime produced the miniseries *The Rebels* based upon the John Jakes novel of the same name.[49] The series was the second in the Kent Family Chronicles, following the life of Philip Kent as he joined the American Revolutionary cause. As television critics noted, *The Rebels* was not, nor did it intend to be, good history. One newspaper stated that it was "The Hardy Boys with Sword and Buckle" while another mentioned that the three main characters (all fictional) "save each other's lives a lot, get drunk and meet pretty women. Not a lot of substance here, but substance isn't the objective."[50]

In the series, Kent performs many duties for the colonial cause, but is primarily an officer in the Continental Army. Kent is made part of the dramatic mission to remove cannons from Fort Ticonderoga to Boston, an incredible success under General Henry Knox. Yet Kent is also asked to deliver messages to members of the Continental Congress. His friend, Judson Fletcher, has become a member of the Virginia delegation to the Congress.[51]

The first scene dealing with the 2nd Continental Congress is set in February 1776. In it, Thomas Jefferson, Benjamin Franklin, and the fictional Fletcher are enjoying a drink after the day's business in the Congress.

Jefferson is trying to explain to Fletcher that he lacks tact and should understand that he will not win any converts to their cause by pointing out other delegates' shortcomings. This is an interesting scene in that Fletcher seems to share the impatience of the radical members of the Congress, including John Adams. Played once again by William Daniels, Adams too, enters the tavern, greets Franklin and Jefferson, but snubs Fletcher and takes a table by himself. This encounter allows Franklin and Jefferson to explain to Fletcher that his morals and reputation are not good for the goals of the Congress. Adams, being a New Englander, will show his disapproval.[52]

In this same scene, the audience sees an interesting conversation between John Adams and Thomas Jefferson. Jefferson is concerned that the pro-independence faction is not as united as they should be. He says to Adams that the new country could have a future "beyond imagination." Adams replies, "Do we wish to create a future *beyond* imagination? Speaking for myself, I'm quite satisfied with life as it now exists—once we're rid of the King, that is." Adams is also worried about losing the support of "all men of substance and property." He defines the revolution as being "a political matter between ourselves and the king" not a social revolution. He then adds, "I tell you, Tom, this country must and will be a republic, not a democracy in the hands of the common people."[53] This interesting conversation not only foreshadowed the disagreements Jefferson and Adams would have during the years of the Early Republic, but it also painted John Adams as a true conservative. While his sentiments concerning republics versus democracies were depicted accurately, painting Jefferson as the great democrat that he will later become was a stretch. Including this conversation between the two Founders provides a great example of a series that had little regard for the authenticity of its depiction. These two men worked well together during this period and did not disagree on their main objective of independence. The show sacrificed historical accuracy to dramatic tension.[54]

Each of the remaining scenes in which John Adams appeared offer depictions of various aspects of his beliefs and personality. While Philip Kent is delivering a message to Adams from Washington concerning the situation in Boston, he also says that he wishes to see his friend Judson Fletcher. Adams acknowledges that Fletcher is a good man, but in this, he refers only to his politics. "His morals are disgusting," Adams says, and he tells Kent that he should rein in his friend before his reputation does more harm to their cause than a full regiment of King George's troops.[55]

Later, in a meeting of the committee to draft the Declaration of Independence (of which Fletcher is a member), Adams agrees with Fletcher that the document is good. "I still think we should include the original provision against slavery," argues Adams. Jefferson and Fletcher both point out that the timing is wrong for such a statement although they would love to include it if they could. Adams, conceding their point remarks, "I'm not much given to compromise on principles."[56] While the last statement is accurate concerning Adams, the history of the slavery clause in the Declaration portrayed here is inaccurate. The clause was removed by Congress, not the committee and, as David McCullough observed, "neither he [Adams] nor any other delegate in Congress would have let the issue jeopardize a declaration of independence, however strong their feelings. If Adams was disappointed or downcast over the removal of Jefferson's indictment of the slave trade, he seems to have said nothing at the time."[57]

In the final scene in which John Adams appeared, Kent has come to him to plead for help for the army. Adams acknowledges the problem. However, he's not sure he can help. "It pains me to say it, Philip, but I am, by nature, not a popular man. I sometimes feel I do our cause more harm than good." While the audience never sees why Adams views himself in this light, the depiction falls into the common "obnoxious and disliked" genre of Adams portrayals. However, in this instance, Kent reassures Adams by telling him, "Without you, we would all be lost." Kent's level of respect for Adams provided a nice balance to the oft repeated condemnation of his personality. Later in the scene, as Adams walks away from Kent and the Marquis de Lafayette, both Lafayette and Kent remark that he is both an important and impressive man.[58]

John Adams played a bit part in *The Rebels*. Yet even in the few scenes in which he appeared, an interesting portrait emerged. He was an advocate for independence, but not for democracy, an accurate description of him and many of the other Founders. He was also the go-to Massachusetts delegate in the Congress. None of the others appear here other than John Hancock whose role was as president of the Congress. This is not unlike *1776*. What we do not see in this depiction is his role in the debates of Congress. In fact, all the Congressional scenes take place after the meetings have adjourned for the day, but Judson Fletcher, the character created by John Jakes, takes on the role of the impatient advocate for independence.

It is also clear, however, that in the show, John Adams was the man trusted to argue the cause of the army and was the man to whom Washington reported the situation in Boston in 1776. Adams did meet with Washington in Cambridge, Massachusetts, in January of 1776 on his way back to Philadelphia and could see for himself the situation of the army.[59] While there is no evidence of direct correspondence between Washington and Adams during this period, Adams was, in fact keenly interested in the state of the army and its prospects for removing the British from Boston that spring. That the script writers for this series made him the recipient of direct messages from Washington does not strain the imagination.

John Adams's ideas concerning the proper form of government for the country are well-documented. The fact that he was in favor of a republic as he voiced in the series is borne out in his *Thoughts on Government*, but he also acknowledged in that famous piece "Of Republics, there is an inexhaustible variety, because the possible combinations of the powers of society, are capable of innumerable variations."[60] Therefore, his conversation with Jefferson in this script is authentic. However, Adams also voiced his concern about the obstacles to a republic, especially in the south, Thomas Jefferson country. In a letter to Horatio Gates, dated March 23, 1776, Adams wrote, "...all our Misfortunes arise from a Single Source, the Reluctance of the Southern Colonies to Republican Government." He asserted that a republic could only survive "on popular Principles and Maxims which are so abhorrent to the Inclinations of the Barons of the south." He also recognized that the South was only part of the problem, mentioning "the Proprietary Interests in the Middle Colonies," as well as "that Avarice of Land" so apparent on the continent.[61] As a result, the scripted conversation between Adams and Jefferson provided an incomplete picture of John Adams's thinking in the winter and spring of 1776. Seeing him advocate for men of property and substance in this conversation with Jefferson does not fit.

In *The Rebels* then, the audience saw glimpses of the Founders, including John Adams. All of them are depicted with respect. In the last scene in which John Adams appears—when Kent acknowledges for the audience that he is an impressive and important man—Adams is sent out of the story and off to the pantheon of the Founding Fathers.

In the early 2000s, television audiences were treated to two documentaries focusing on the relationship between John and Abigail Adams. The earliest, broadcast in 2002, was called "John and Abigail Adams: Love and Liberty." The 50-minute documentary was produced by A&E Television as part of their popular *Biography* series. This program emphasized not only the relationship between these two historical figures, but also the integral role each played in the life of the other. The back cover of the DVD noted, "Theirs was one of the greatest political partnerships in American history.... Using excerpts from their myriad letters to one another and interviews with noted colonial historians, BIOGRAPHY proudly presents the story of one of the most important couples in American history."[62] Several experts and admirers of this couple commented in the documentary, including historians David McCullough, Joseph Ellis, Edith Gellis, and Phyllis Levin. In addition, the show interviewed President George Herbert Walker Bush, former Indiana Congressman Tim Roemer, two staff members at the Adams National Historical Park, and two direct descendants of the Adamses. This was not a documentary in the style of Ken Burns in which a camera pans across a painting of the subject while an actor speaks the subject's words. Rather, using videos of the historical homes in Quincy as well as pictures of paintings of the time along with nondescript actors whose faces the audience never sees, the show re-created the lives of John and Abigail.

There is nothing outstanding about this documentary nor is the portrayal of John unique. The show begins by remarking on the fact that there is no monument to John Adams in Washington, D.C., and then moves the audience through the many contributions and sacrifices made by both John and Abigail. With such a short run-time, it was difficult for the producers to include much detail, but a strong sense of this couple's partnership emerged, making it a good starting place for anyone interested in the couple.

A far more ambitious and superior documentary was produced by the Public Broadcasting System four years later. On January 23, 2006, PBS aired "John & Abigail Adams" as part of its *American Experience* program. This two-hour show, which featured some of the same historians from the earlier documentary, also utilized reenactments by actors as well as a narration provided by David Ogden Stiers (of *M*A*S*H* fame). Weaving through the commentary of historians David McCullough, Joseph Ellis, and Joanne Freeman were scenes from the lives of the Adamses. In an open forum for Public Broadcasting Station WGBH, the writer of the program, Elizabeth Deane, explained to her audience what she hoped to achieve with the show. She called the episode "drama documentary" and stated that she wanted it to be more personal than earlier dramas about the Revolution. She watched movies and earlier documentaries about the period and found them "remote." For her, the key to changing that with John and Abigail was their letters to one another. Those letters, she said, drove her forward on the project.[63]

Also commenting on the program and on the Adamses were Kelly Cobble, curator at the Adams National Historical Park, and Jonathan Chu, University of Massachusetts, Boston. Both Cobble and Chu provided context for the documentary, Cobble stating, "We [The Adams National Historical Park] have been telling this story for a long time." Chu noted the importance of the Adamses as part of the possibility of America. He was particularly fond of a statement from McCullough, exclaiming about the moment in which John Adams, the son of a farmer, stood before King George III. Referencing this moment in the program, Chu explained, "The Adams story is not just a love story, but it's a story of the American ideals we would hope to have."[64]

The attention the producers of this documentary gave to detail, the added commentary provided by McCullough and Ellis in particular, and the acting provided for the reenactments draw an audience to the Adams story in a way that other documentaries could not. Abigail Adams was played by actress Linda Edmond, who made her Broadway debut in a revival of the musical *1776* playing Abigail. For the role of John Adams, the producers chose English actor Simon Russell Beale.

If there were an award for the actor who most looked like John Adams, it would go to Beale. His facial features and his physical build provided a television reincarnation of John Adams with little help from wigs and make-up. From the first words Beale spoke as Adams, his convincing delivery could make an audience wonder if they were hearing Adams himself. At least one critic agreed. "Beale makes Adams so visceral that it's as if you're standing beside him, feeling the heat radiating from his body and his energy displacing the air around you," wrote the blog Architecture-Chicago Plus. This blogger argued that if the show had been a feature film, Beale's work would be Oscar worthy.[65] Beale portrayed Adams from the year 1774 to his death in 1826.

While the show emphasized the partnership between John and Abigail—"Meet the original power couple," the front cover of the DVD proclaims—the depiction of Adams here is noteworthy.[66] The show does not overlook his personality, his frustration, and his flaws and Beale showcased them all. The audience sees Adams working the Continental Congress and his love of books. In fact, one of the more delightful scenes in this documentary comes at the beginning, when John is packing to leave for the First Continental Congress in 1774. As Abigail concentrates on the clothes he will need, John is packing his many books, books that he will require to make his arguments to the Congress. Adams's love for books is often glossed over in other depictions of him so this scene is especially enlightening.[67]

Beale, like George Grizzard and William Daniels before him, came to appreciate John Adams. "I've grown to admire him enormously," said Beale, "And love him."[68] This kind of attachment of an actor to an historical character led to an understanding of John Adams, warts and all. Beale could recapture the anger and bitterness of Adams in his early retirement, but also interpret his love for Abigail. The show does not shy away from Adams's ambition or the mistakes that he made although one critic chides it for apologizing for the Alien and Sedition Acts. Remarking on McCullough's explanation of the acts in the documentary, critic Verne Gay wrote, "With McCullough on Adams, there always seems to be that 'but'" and observed that while the show itself was the monument Adams never achieved in marble, it did tend to lean toward hagiography in places.

"That's O.K.," wrote Gay. "There's a lot of redressing that needs to be done with this career, but some viewers may wonder whether they're getting the full measure of the man...."[69]

This criticism is fair, for the Alien and Sedition Acts are always the stumbling block for historians and writers alike. This critic, however placed too much emphasis on this one moment in time, as have many before him. What this documentary captured as effectively as fictionalized drama was the full personality of John Adams and the true partnership he had with his wife. At the end of the program, David McCullough summed up their relationship. "A friend once said to me, she said, 'Real love isn't just gazing into each other's eyes. It's looking out together in the same direction.' And if ever there was a man and woman who were truly in love and truly looking out in the same direction, it was John and Abigail Adams."[70]

With this 2006 documentary or "drama documentary," PBS presented a nuanced and three-dimensional portrait of John Adams for its viewing audience. The goal was to bring more attention to John and Abigail Adams as fascinating and contributing members of the founding generation. This piece of television was carefully crafted for that purpose. When considering another offering from PBS, one targeting children, the agenda is quite different. Yet Abigail and John appear in this programming as well.

Liberty's Kids, a children's animated series, aired on Public Broadcasting from 2002 to 2004. It also had a successful run in syndication and on the History Channel. It is readily available for viewing on YouTube (with the addition of advertisements for children's toys) and a box set of DVDs was released in 2008.[71] This series was designed to give children an introduction to the American Revolution and focused on young people: one a journalist in training, the second an assistant and ward of Benjamin Franklin, and the third a young woman from England who came to the colonies searching for her father. She, too, lives with Benjamin Franklin in Philadelphia. One of Franklin's employees is an African American gentleman named Moses who works at the *Pennsylvania Gazette*, Franklin's newspaper.

One of the goals of *Liberty's Kids* was to give a multicultural interpretation to the American Revolution. This is admirable. However, in the process, the show is not always accurate to 18th-century cultural beliefs. Still, it went a long way in depicting the hard truths about the times. The events of the Revolution are seen through the eyes of these three young people and since one of them is English, audiences also saw the issues of the day from both the Patriot and Tory perspective. These three kids are witnesses or participants in many of the major events of the Revolution beginning with the Boston Tea Party in 1773. Throughout, historical figures, including John Adams, were also part of the show.

In this animated series, Adams was voiced by Billy Crystal. The depiction of Adams is convincing, although the accuracy of the show is often sketchy at best. The audience meets John Adams in Philadelphia where he is attending the First Continental Congress. In this episode, he will try to explain to James, the young journalist-in-training, the difference between revolutionary action and mob riot. Yet near the end of the episode, John Adams delivered a speech to the Congress using the words of Patrick Henry—who is also depicted here. The speech given to John Adams in this episode was not Henry's most famous. Yet it is often quoted. Henry said, "The Distinctions between Virginians, Pennsylvanians, New Yorkers and New Englanders, are no more. I am not a Virginian, but an American."[72]

The writers of this episode tweaked the speech so that it would be appropriate to John Adams: "I am not a New England man. I am an American. We are Americans!"[73] This was a puzzling choice. While John Adams was in the room when Henry spoke the words in question, there is no evidence that he reacted to them in any way. He did record them in his diary, but this was part of his effort to keep a record of the meeting. He made no commentary on the words spoken by Henry. Adams may have shared the sentiment, but in 1774, it was not yet clear that the colonies would be a separate nation and nationality. Very few members of the First Continental Congress would find the idea appealing. John Adams wished to win friends to Massachusetts's cause, not alienate members of Congress from other colonies. In these circumstances, John Adams would not have spoken these words. Yet throughout this episode, John Adams is a key player. Therefore, ending the episode with him speaking Henry's words made sense to the plot.

Liberty's Kids often changed historical timelines and sacrificed accuracy to teach larger lessons concerning the complexities of the Revolution. One such episode, called "Bostonians," featured John and Abigail Adams in one plot line and Thayendanegea (a Mohawk whose English name was Joseph Brant) in another. This is an interesting juxtaposition. In the episode, John Adams has returned to his family after his first mission to France and is immediately asked to attend the convention in which Massachusetts will write its state constitution. John is assigned to draft the document. All of this is historically accurate, and this is one of the few shows that depicts this part of Adams's career. As Adams struggles to write his state's constitution, young James meets Thayendanegea and comes face to face with the reality that the Revolutionary War will not end well for the Native Americans just as the historical Thayendanegea predicted.

While the audience sees Adams writing the state constitution for

Massachusetts, it also observes his relationship with Abigail. There are many touching scenes of the couple and, in the end, Abigail helps him realize what is missing from his constitution. Once he and Abigail observe their children together with Henri (the young French boy in the series), Adams writes Chapter VI, Section II of the constitution entitled "The Encouragement of Literature, etc." in which he discusses the importance of education on all levels in the commonwealth.[74] In this scene, the audience gets a glimpse of John Adams as visionary, expressing his hopes and dreams for his country and his children. This depiction of Adams lends further dimension to his character and captures a side of the historical Adams that is often missed in other television depictions.[75]

For the writers and producers of *Liberty's Kids* the goal was not always historical accuracy. According to historian Andrew M. Schocket, *Liberty's Kids* is "a reflection of its time and its agenda; that is, the recasting of the idea of America along multicultural lines."[76] In concentrating on this goal, the show did not always get the history correct. However, what the audience did see in many cases were accurate depictions of the historical characters. Focusing on John Adams and not the many historical missteps of the series, it is safe to say that the creators of the show understood who this man was and the role he played in the Revolution. Sadly, the History Channel, in its own more recent offering on the American Revolution, did not.

In 2015, the History Channel premiered a three-part miniseries entitled *Sons of Liberty*. It begins in 1765, ends in 1776, and focuses on a core group of colonists known as the Sons of Liberty. The central character is Samuel Adams. As history, the show was lacking. One might expect better from the History Channel, but the producers posted a disclaimer on the channel's website which read:

> SONS OF LIBERTY is a dramatic interpretation of events that sparked a revolution. It is historical fiction, not a documentary. The goal of our miniseries is to capture the spirit of the time, convey the personalities of the main characters, and focus on real events that have shaped our past. For historical information about the Sons of Liberty and the dawning of the American Revolution, please read the Historian's View section on history.com/sons.[77]

Stephen David, executive producer and co-writer of the series, explained his vision of the spirit of the times mentioned above. He was interested in looking at the American Revolution from a unique perspective and was inspired by the Rolling Stones song "Paint It Black." "And I was thinking, 'I wonder if there was any kind of teen angst involved with this. Like were the 1760s kind of like the 1960s?'" After asking his research team to investigate this idea, they found the historical Sons of Liberty, which formed the basis for the show.[78]

David found his so-called teen angst in men he claimed were in their 20s and 30s.[79] While this was true of some of the Sons of Liberty, it is not an apt description of Samuel Adams, who was 43 years old in 1765. Since the show claimed to "convey the personalities of the main characters," the expectation is that the characters would be portrayed accurately. When it came to Samuel Adams, this is not the case nor is it, entirely, with his cousin John.

In this series, John Adams is portrayed by Henry Thomas, best known as Elliott in *ET*. Thomas was drawn to the piece because he was "a sucker for historical pieces anyway because I'm sort of an armchair historian." Thomas saw the American Revolution as a "great piece of history and a great theater for drama."[80] Thomas found the drama of the moment and of his character given the script with which he had to work. Yet the portrait of John Adams here lacks depth. John is painted as the conservative counterpart to his roguish (and homeless) cousin, Sam.

In the special features for the DVD, John Adams is described as "basically an ambulance chaser lawyer,"[81] a metaphor that is highly inaccurate in this instance. By 1765, Adams had become in the words of biographer Peter Shaw, "one of the leading lawyers in the province."[82] As James Grant stated in his biography of Adams, *John Adams: Party of One*, riding the court circuit was not always pleasant, especially when it required travel to Maine. "A ride to the courthouse through a primeval forest was a professional ordeal of a certain time and place, but the tedium of obscure litigation is the eternal lot of the practicing lawyer."[83]

Yet by 1765, Adams's understanding of the law, as demonstrated in the courtroom and through his writing of *A Dissertation on the Canon and the Feudal Law*, composed in 1765, won him a singular honor. He was elected by the town of Boston to appear before the royal governor in support of a petition to reopen the provincial courts idled by the Stamp Act Crisis. The fact that he was chosen by the town of Boston as counsel, along with distinguished attorneys James Otis and Joseph Gridley, indicated that John Adams's reputation far exceeded the 21st-century moniker of "ambulance chaser."[84]

The *Sons of Liberty* portrayal of John Adams is closely related to the depiction of his cousin, Sam. The show's creators made the choice to re-envision Samuel Adams as a 20-something lost soul who had no direction in his life and who drank too much. His character is at the heart of the counter-culture model Stephen David had in mind. By contrast, Cousin John is sober, stiff, established, and—as a result—impatient with his ne'er-do-well relative. The first time the audience sees John Adams, he is walking from the courthouse on the day after British soldiers chased Sam all through town, attempting to arrest him. When John is approached by one of Sam's friends, Joseph Warren, John's first question is, "Where is he?" to which Warren replied, "John, it's not his fault." John then tells Warren, "You are going to have to stop protecting him. Sooner or later, he is going to have to learn his lesson."[85]

John then goes to see his cousin, who is hiding out in a cellar, and tells him that he owes £8,000 to the crown for unpaid taxes and that he needs to turn himself in because "this is the way things are." He also attempts to shame Sam by telling him that if Sam's father were here, he would tell his son to take responsibility for his actions.[86] This conservative father-rebellious teenager theme is continued when Sam rides to Braintree to seek shelter with John and Abigail. John's first reaction to Sam's appearance at his home is "He can't stay here." He believes that Sam has come to borrow money from him. John then attempts to lecture Sam, telling him, "You need to stop walking through life as if you have nothing to lose!" Sam reacts, saying that John has no right to judge him since John has "the perfect life."[87]

These scenes do not reflect the true relationship between the 43-year-old Sam and his 30-year-old cousin. While it is true that Samuel Adams was not a successful businessman, he was not a drunk nor a lost soul. Writing in 1765, the year in which these scenes take place, John Adams wrote of his cousin, "Adams I believe has the most thorough Understanding of Liberty, and her Resources" and possessed "the most correct, genteel and artful Pen." Adams continued: "He is a Man of refined Policy, stedfast Integrity, exquisite Humanity, genteel Erudition, obliging, engaging Manners, real as well as professed Piety, and a universal good Character...." Samuel Adams was also "staunch, and stiff and strict and rigid and inflexible, in the Cause."[88]

What is also missing from the *Sons of Liberty* depiction of these two men and their relationship is the complementary way Samuel and John Adams worked together in their resistance to English policy. They did this so successfully that one former Royal Governor of Massachusetts dubbed them the "brace of Adamses."[89] John was proud of his association with his cousin, saying "Is it not a Pity, that a Brace of so obscure a Breed, should be the only ones to defend the Household, when the generous mastiffs, and best blooded Hounds are all hushed to silence by the Bones and Crumbs, that are thrown to them...?"[90] John and Samuel, while using different methods, worked together well in their defense of colonial liberty. Yet in the *Sons of Liberty*, Sam's motives are unclear, and John is moved to join him only after he is threatened by British General Thomas Gage.[91]

As the series continues toward independence, the audience sees Sam and John at the Continental Congresses where Sam is blamed for all that has happened between the colonies and the crown. As the vote on independence nears, it is Sam rather than John who makes the closing argument for a new nation. Yet as he does so, he describes himself to his fellow congressman as a thug and a drunk who never did anything with his life. He says he knows this is how his fellow delegates see him and claims that these characterizations are all true. Yet he reminds the Congress that, in the eyes of the crown, they are all nothing and then asks the question, "Who do we want to be?" What they need, he says, is "a fair and equal chance." With that, the vote for independence is taken and the resolution passes. John congratulates his cousin and tells him, "Your father would be proud."[92]

In writing *Sons of Liberty* this way, Stephen David certainly discovered the teen angst he was envisioning. As a result, the depictions of these historical figures lack nuance. For some critics, this was not a problem. The *New York Times* called the show "fun and engaging" while admitting that it is not "as elegantly filmed and high minded as the HBO series 'John Adams,' but here, that's appropriate." The writer concluded, "'Sons of Liberty' isn't history exactly, but it's a well-made dramatization that brings history to life."[93] A review in the *Los Angeles Times* was not so forgiving. Mary McNamara, television critic for the newspaper, entitled her review "Never Let Facts Get in the Way" with the subtitle "'Sons' miniseries takes too many liberties on History about the American Revolution." She lamented the one-dimensional depiction of Sam Adams and other members of the Sons of Liberty, marveling that the Sons spent more time drinking than "writing innumerable political essays … or organizing and running town meetings, or forming the committee of correspondence system that led to the creation of the Continental Congress."

McNamara applauded the show for demonstrating the cleverness of the rebels, but added, "If only their intelligence and ideology had been given the same, or indeed any, attention." She continued: "Adams and the Sons of Liberty were men of action, but they were also men of amazing ideas, careful thought and continual open debate, all of which are needed to affect significant social and political change. And that's what's really cool about history."[94]

As for John Adams, McNamara summed up his characterization in the scripts by calling him "all stuffy and missing the point."[95] The John Adams that Thomas delivered certainly believed in the law and in justice as did the real Adams. However, in painting him as the scolding father figure to his cousin, the many contributions John made during the early years of colonial resistance to English policy are lost. Thomas's Adams was so busy trying to rein in Sam that his own passion for the cause of liberty is invisible. Even his contributions to the Continental Congresses and the fight for the independence vote are ignored in this representation. The historical John Adams might see certain facets of his personality in this portrayal, but he would not recognize his cousin Sam nor would he understand their relationship here. This John Adams lacked fire, determination, and depth.

The John Adams who graced the small screen in these offerings was on a spectrum beginning with his use as a model for outstanding courage. For the Bicentennial, he was spotlighted with historical authenticity based on the Adams papers. By 2015, the public saw a depiction, not of Adams himself, but of a television channel's re-creation of the American Revolution as counter-culture movement. What is interesting is that there was such a wide variety of depictions on the small screen. That John Adams made so many television appearances is surprising if one is to believe he has been neglected by the American public. From the Cold War years of the 1950s when John Adams became a model for taking unpopular stands to the 21st century when he became a mere shadow of himself to fit into a teen angst interpretation of the American Revolution, Adams morphed to fit the times and the specific usable past created by these various artists. Their agendas varied, but they were all looking for an interpretation of the American Revolution—and John Adams—that made sense for them.

Despite the many starring roles and cameos Adams had on television from the 1970s through 2015, the most thorough coverage of his life and career would appear in 2008. In that year, John Adams would have his own miniseries and would find himself in the spotlight in a way he could have never imagined. The HBO John Adams is the subject of the next chapter.

Seven

The McCullough
and HBO John Adams

In 2009, a ranger at the Adams National Historical Park gave a special tour to members of the National Council for History Education—this author among them. When asked if visitorship at the park had been affected by the release of the HBO miniseries entitled simply *John Adams*, she noted that Adams's popularity had reached new heights. In her words, the miniseries, and the biography upon which it was based, had made John Adams into their own little rock star. While this image is amusing on many levels, the success of the David McCullough biography in and of itself lends credence to the idea. While John Adams has not been neglected by historians or popular artists, McCullough's biography and the HBO miniseries that followed provided a new opportunity to bring Adams to the public. What was it about this biography that was so different from all the others? In part, the answer lies with the biographer.

David McCullough is a master storyteller. He has focused his talents on a wide variety of historical topics over the years, including the Johnstown Flood and the Brooklyn Bridge. In addition, he wrote some of the most popular biographies available in print, giving new life to historical figures such as Teddy Roosevelt and Harry Truman. When McCullough decided to turn his attention to John Adams, he practically guaranteed that Adams's memory would be vivid for the reading public once again. McCullough's biography of Adams topped the *New York Times* Best Seller list for thirteen weeks in 2001.[1] While this biography is well written, as is all of McCullough's work, many scholars believe there are better biographies of John Adams. Yet none of these other works written by lesser known historians captured the public's attention as McCullough's did. Because of this, it is not surprising that HBO wanted to adapt this book rather than any other biography written to date.

Simon and Schuster published David McCullough's biography of the second president entitled *John Adams* in 2001. According to the publisher's

145

web site, it has won more than twenty awards, including the Pulitzer Prize for biography.[2] This prize is the envy of anyone who writes biography, and many worthy books were in competition for it in 2002. McCullough's work won out in part because of the author's approach to his subject. The jury report from the Pulitzer committee stated that McCullough's biography recorded the life of Adams "close up, bringing him before the reader with intimate presence as he looks and speaks and moves." The jury went on to praise the work because it was "multilayered" and covered not only Adams's life, but also the lives of his associates as well as the history of the time, putting Adams in context. In addition, the report cited McCullough's work because of the many facets of Adams's life that the author emphasized.

In this biography, Adams was seen not only as a leading figure in the American Revolution but also as "a farmer's son, friend and lover, dotard with failing eyesight...." Finally, the jury emphasized that "For all its liveliness, *John Adams* maintains an exacting standard of scholarly research and documentation.... Technically the book is a lesson in the open-ended possibilities of the form, embodying many fresh ideas about how biographies can be constructed. The right word for this biography is 'masterful.'"[3]

The *New York Times* seemed to agree with the Pulitzer committee's assessment. In its 2001 Editor's Choice section, the times wrote, "Behold! A gentler, more quiet John Adams.... McCullough's best gift is his ability to bring such icons to life, and to make us feel the texture of life in the past."[4] Interestingly enough, though, the *Times* editor felt that something was missing from McCullough's Adams. He argued "there will always be some who will feel that the historian's subduing of Adams's noisy feistiness in this account—his rashness, stubbornness and sometimes bizarre opinions—makes him a little less himself."[5] Much of what the writer is discussing here comes down to McCullough's style. Still, it is interesting that once again, Adams cannot evade his reputation for being difficult and bad-tempered. While McCullough soft-pedaled this side of his personality—at least according to this reviewer—Adams's propensity for crustiness is inescapable.

McCullough's biography has also received good reviews from some renowned historians of the Revolutionary period. Gordon Wood, for example, called McCullough's book "the best biography of Adams ever written."[6] Historian Robert Middlekauff, author of *The Glorious Cause: The American Revolution, 1763–1789*, noted that the book

> stands as a splendid example of grand manner biography. The book is beautifully conceived and a great pleasure to read. There is a danger, however that a reader captivated by the book's literary grace will fail to see the depth of its insights. That McCullough embeds his analysis in the narrative without

breaking the flow of the story is one of his book's virtues and provides additional evidence that grand manner biography can be made to inform as well as to charm.[7]

Historian Lance Banning, while less effusive in his praise, admitted the biography has merit. He stated that much of the book is "quite perceptive, though the Adams who emerges, faults and all, is not a very different figure than the one we thought we knew." Banning continued, "McCullough has performed a major public service. We can hope that hundreds of his readers may be tempted to pursue a fuller understanding of this fascinating age." Banning wished that the biography had contained more analysis of Adams's contributions, and commented, "I would gladly have exchanged perhaps three hundred pages of such thick description for as many of analysis and richer exploration of the context of the founder's deeds."[8]

Historian John Howe echoed these sentiments. While he believed the biography deserved the praise it had received from many reviewers, he longed for more complexity in the work. By relying on Adams's own writings as much as he did, Howe argued, McCullough "loses critical perspective on a number of key issues on Adams's engagement with his times." Presenting a more balanced view on issues such as the Alien and Sedition Acts and slavery would have made the book more compelling. "To cite the less than heroic dimensions of Adams's life is not to delegitimize his many achievements. But it is to situate him more securely in his time."[9]

Because of the author's reputation, the praise for this book is not surprising. Other scholars were far more critical of the work, however. Pauline Maier, renowned historian of the American Revolution noted the quieter John Adams that the *New York Times* editor mentioned. In her discussion of the book, Maier analyzed how contemporaries and recent historians have viewed the hotheaded John Adams and argued that this trait made him admirable and even lovable. She asked her reading audience, "How can we fail to love that crotchety old man?", and argued that McCullough's portrait is of an "admirable but curiously flat John Adams."[10]

Political scientist Jean Edward Smith was more critical still. He called the book "a chatty tale, pursued in such tedious detail that is strains even McCullough's admirable prose, but sheds little insight into the early years of the republic." As a result, he claimed, "This is a biography for the coffee tables of America—a book written to be sold and not read. The numbing accumulation of trivia that substitutes for insight and analysis suggests that one should look elsewhere for an understanding of the important role Adams played in history."[11]

Historians Nancy Isenberg and Andrew Burstein were even more critical of the biography, aiming at the economic advantage McCullough's work has had. They argued, "There are far better books on Adams than McCullough's, but they haven't been hyped. There's no money in it. History is hard to sell if it's complicated."[12] Isenberg and Burstein are both academic historians who are also co-authors of a book on Jefferson and Madison. Most historians working in university settings do not get the kind of attention for their work that a David McCullough does. That stings, of course. Yet it does not change the fact that McCullough's work on Adams is accessible. Its appeal to an audience outside the walls of academia is understandable. McCullough is a talented writer who brings a passion to all of his subjects that is contagious. However, Isenberg and Burstein were not alone in their criticism.

Perhaps the most scathing review from an academic historian came from Sean Wilentz, a professor of history at Princeton University. Wilentz, a specialist in U.S. political and social history, wrote a review article in *The New Republic* in 2001. His subject was the decline of what he termed "popular history," or history written for people outside academe. By the time McCullough published his biography of John Adams, he was already a master of popular history. What Wilentz found lacking in McCullough's treatment of John Adams was a sense of who Adams was intellectually. While it is clear in his review that Wilentz favored Jefferson's vision for the country over Adams's, he does not dismiss Adams out of hand. In fact, he praised his contributions to American political theory. "No American revolutionary leader—not Madison, not Hamilton, and certainly not Jefferson—surpassed John Adams as a prolific author of systematic political theory," wrote Wilentz. He believed Adams deserved credit for "his role in crafting what he himself regarded as America's greatest gift to the world: its conceptions and institutions of constitutional government."

Wilentz stated that McCullough had written a "valentine" to Adams but had made him "less interesting than he actually was."[13] Writer and book critic Brooke Allen agreed when she wrote, "In his determination to present Adams as a lovable eccentric, rather than the three-dimensional, flawed human being he really was, McCullough cheapens the entire enterprise, turning it into a bland, Disneyfied affair." Then Allen asserted why this was unfortunate. Simply, she stated, "The real Adams needs no apologetics."[14]

What is evident in these critiques of McCullough's work is the ever widening gap between academic historians and the histories presented to the public. The latter do tend toward generalization, lacking in depth and complexity. Yet they also bring people to history who might not ordinarily wish to pursue it. When examining the work of McCullough on John Adams versus all the more scholarly works on him, those who study John Adams extensively will see gaps in the work. However, what McCullough managed to do for John Adams is bring him to the attention of a wider audience, something that academic historians have seldom been able to do. The McCullough biography is still popular and as recently as 2018, the writer was center stage at events commemorating Adams and his contributions to the United States.[15] McCullough became a fan of John Adams, and, like many scholars before him, was unable to get the Founder out of his mind.

What, then, drew David McCullough to John Adams in the first place? McCullough was not only an expert storyteller, but he had an instinct for finding the best story to tell. The biographer, when asked this question, replied that he found Adams far more intriguing than he was expecting to. In an interview with *PBS NewsHour*, McCullough stated that he began to write the story of the "intertwining" lives of Adams and Jefferson. He did worry about this approach, however. "My initial concern was that Jefferson with his fame and his aura and his glamour would outshine, outbalance, overbalance, stout short John Adams, who has been in the shadows of the two tall Virginians—Washington and Jefferson—all these years." He quickly found that "the pull … was John Adams, because to me he was a far more compelling subject, a more fascinating story…."[16]

Later in this interview, McCullough acknowledged that Adams was a difficult man, stating that he could be "abrasive, opinionated, vain" and that he was "grumpy much of the time." Yet he went on to say, "Adams was very warm hearted, affectionate, adored his friends, loved life, right up until his final days…." In a brief portion of this interview, McCullough offered a balanced view of John Adams that is often missing from discussions of him.[17] These factors enticed the producers of HBO. McCullough's name recognition, along with the attention the biography had received, guaranteed that a gentler John Adams was in the public eye. While popular culture has not neglected Adams, HBO saw an opportunity to depict Adams's drama-filled life in a way that had not been done before. The producers saw something in McCullough's version of John Adams that appealed to them, and they wanted to share that constructed past with television audiences.

Adapting an historical biography for the big or small screen is always a challenge. In her study on adaptation, Linda Hutcheon addressed this difficulty. Adapted works will be "haunted at all times by their adapted texts. If we know that prior text, we always feel its presence shadowing the one we are experiencing directly." Further, Hutcheon argued, "When we call a work an adaptation, we openly announce its overt relationship to another work or works."[18] This is the struggle scholars face when viewing a film or television series as history. Historians often feel the loss of complexity and nuance when a manuscript becomes a script.

Scholars have complained about adaptations for years, objecting to inaccuracies and omissions. The version of McCullough's biography of Adams presented by HBO is not exempt from this critique. Scholars' appraisals (discussed below) are valid. At times, the lack of complexity in the depiction of John Adams is frustrating. This is a clear demonstration of the phenomenon Hutcheon discussed. In many cases, the complexity of Adams's character is present in McCullough's work but is toned down in the series. The producer's usable John Adams was slightly more flat, less nuanced than McCullough's. For this reason, it is important to discuss what the writers overlooked, what they changed for dramatic purposes, and how the actors approached the project.

The book and the miniseries both open with John Adams on horseback, riding through the snow. David McCullough used this opening to introduce his audience to the John Adams of January 1776 as he was returning to the Second Continental Congress in Philadelphia. McCullough used this scene as a hook, and he was very good at creating a vivid picture in his readers' minds. He first mentioned his subject in the third paragraph when he wrote, "He was John Adams of Braintree and he loved to talk. He was a known talker. There were some, even among his admirers, who wished he talked less. He himself wished he talked less...."[19] McCullough then continued to describe the man and concisely introduced the subject of this work. The author gave the reader a physical description, stating "Dismounted, he stood five feet seven or eight inches tall" and says that he was "verging on portly," but that he was "surprisingly fit and solid."[20]

McCullough then turned to the inner man, discussing his studiousness, his love for his farm, his deep feelings for his friends and his wife. McCullough's readers also learn immediately of his personality traits, some of which have defined Adams for years. "He could be high-spirited and affectionate, vain, cranky, impetuous, self-absorbed and fiercely stubborn; passionate, quick to anger and all-forgiving; generous and entertaining." McCullough acknowledged his ambition, but also his honor, his Christianity, as well as his ability to be an independent thinker. He also made clear that Adams was not a wealthy man and did not possess the skills one would have with a higher social standing. "He was an awkward dancer and poor at cards."[21]

This is a masterful introduction to John Adams, delivered to the reading audience by a genius storyteller. Yet, how does such an introduction to this character translate to the small screen? When the audience sees John Adams, riding on horseback through the snow, how can it discern all that McCullough provided in his written work? The choice of scene worked dramatically, but the facets of Adams's character could not be fully displayed this way. The introduction of this man as a dramatic character would come more slowly. The key ingredient was not just the scene itself, but the actor placed there. It was important to find the right man for the role. In this, the producers at HBO struck Hollywood gold.

Paul Giamatti played Adams from the age of 35 until his death at the age of 91. Like Simon Russell Beale before him, Giamatti bears a close physical resemblance to John Adams. Yet this was not the only reason for the casting choice. While Giamatti stated in an interview that he had no idea how they came up with him for the role, the director of the piece, Tom Hooper, knew Giamatti was perfect for the part. In speaking of John Adams, Hooper explained, "He's irascible, he's got anger management problems, he's got this huge ego" and that Giamatti "fit the sense I had of Adams as an antihero, to explore the flaws of the man in addition to his greatness, [given] how brilliant Paul was at creating portraits of men struggling with demons…."[22] It is unusual to hear John Adams referred to as an antihero, but the creative team behind the miniseries wanted to stay away from making the Founder what they termed a "One-dimensional icon." For this reason, Hooper stated that Giamatti's casting would give the audience a fresh look at the American Revolution.[23]

The scope of this miniseries presented a tremendous challenge for Giamatti. Yet he never expressed any hesitation about the role. He approached it as he did any other, seeing John Adams as just another character he was playing.[24] The actor saw Adams as some sort of a misfit. In an interview with Rotten Tomatoes, Giamatti called Adams a "weird guy." He went on to say that Adams was a bit of a lunatic, "a nightmare of a guy." His description of Adams's contribution to the Revolutionary War effort demonstrated a disturbing lack of understanding of history and of Adams's character. "It's all him wandering around begging for money. I don't know how interesting that will be, but that's what he did for the whole war. He kind of traveled around Europe trying to get people to give money to finance the war. And he was sick all the time and out of his mind and depressed. He was a really weird guy."[25] None of the Adams scholars would argue that the man was a sweetheart, nor would they refute the fact that he did spend considerable time "begging for money"—especially from the Dutch. McCullough spent a good deal of space in his Adams biography discussing the mission to Holland, a quest that would eventually be successful.[26]

Yet Giamatti's apparent dismissal of a character he played is baffling. It is possible that Giamatti's comments are more a reflection of the actor's own personality rather than a contemplation of Adams's character. Giamatti could also have been implying that focusing on a character who had no role on the battlefield would be uninteresting to the public. He does say that Adams "sat the war out," meaning that he did not fight, but the mini-series does not dismiss his contributions in his role as diplomat, a position taken also by such iconic figures as Benjamin Franklin and Thomas Jefferson. Giamatti, while playing the man so thoroughly, appeared to dismiss him although there is evidence that he came to appreciate Adams a bit. According to the *Los Angeles Times*, Giamatti was intrigued to see the placement of John Adams's presidential painting in the National Portrait Gallery. "Where they have all the presidents' portraits, he really is off to the side, in a little painting. Even Buchanan has a giant great full-length portrait. It's very peculiar."[27]

This last quote could indicate a grudging admiration for John Adams on Giamatti's part although he enjoyed the role for other reasons. As late as 2018, in discussing his approach to the role, Giamatti said that Adams was for him "a fictional character" who did fascinate him. He enjoyed playing the part and ventured to say that Adams was chosen to have a mini-series based on his life because he was "an everyman kind of guy and he was everywhere." He also believed that the producers had an eye toward "subverting the mythical stature of a lot of these guys" and so they picked the man who was "notorious" for being difficult and who was a "terrible politician."[28] While Giamatti's comments indicated that he did not see all aspects of Adams's personality, he relished unpacking what the script gave him.

Not all critics appreciated Giamatti's efforts as Adams. While some saw him as brilliant in the role, others did not. Interestingly, one *New York Times* critic, Alessandra Stanley, did not like him in the role at all. In fact, this critic believed that Giamatti was the weakest link in the miniseries stating, "in this historical drama, Mr. Giamatti is a prisoner of a limited range and rubbery, cuddly looks—in 18th-century britches and wigs, he looks like Shrek." This critic also made it clear that Giamatti would always be in the shadow of William Daniels, whose performance in *1776* she much preferred.[29] Despite this and other jibes from critics, Giamatti was able to capture the complexity of John Adams over a long period of the man's life—at least to the point that the scripts allowed. The series emphasized some personality traits over others, but the John Adams that emerges is accurate if incomplete. While the series does nothing to convince an audience that Adams had likable traits, it is safe to say that Adams would recognize himself in Giamatti's portrayal.

Laura Linney, as Abigail Adams, complemented Giamatti's performance. She was brilliant in capturing the spirit and intelligence of Mrs. Adams. From the beginning of production, Linney committed herself to Abigail's journey. She explained to *The Telegraph*, "She was not a stereotypical long-suffering wife who just chastised her husband when he was grumpy and took care of the kids. She was extremely capable, and she was forward thinking. Looking back, she was clearly a feminist."[30] This last statement has been the subject of historical debates for decades. Still, Linney had a keen sense of who Abigail was and what she did for her sometimes-difficult husband.

As with all adaptations of history, this award-winning miniseries tells the most dramatic tale possible. This is not difficult to do given Adams's life and the many events in which he played a key role. The first episode opens in the year 1770. As in the book, John Adams is riding through the snow on horseback. He is returning to Boston after arguing cases out of town. The fact that the series begins much as the book does, but in a different year, says much about how the producers wished to introduce their audience to John Adams. An important year for Adams was 1770, the year in which he defended British soldiers accused of murder following the incident known as the Boston Massacre. As previous chapters have discussed, many scholars have emphasized this act, and Adams is widely admired for it. Adams's first biographers, his son, John Quincy and grandson, Charles Francis Adams referred to it as "the first and the lightest of the four moral tests which occurred in the course of Mr. Adams's public life."[31]

Given the importance of the trial to John Adams's career, beginning the miniseries here makes sense. The audience sees very quickly, a man who struggles with the decision to defend the soldiers, but who, once committed, does so with a conviction that will carry him through the future. The audience also sees through this incident the role Abigail played in Adams's life and career. Adams asks Abigail to read his closing statement and as she does, she comfortably tells him what works and what does not. There is no historical evidence that this moment took place; neither John nor Abigail ever mentioned it. Yet the writers created the scene to demonstrate the partnership between Adams and his wife. Adams repeatedly affirmed that Abigail was his chief advisor in all things. It is not outside the realm of possibility that she critiqued his work.

Within the first episode then, the audience sees a man driven to do the right thing. John Adams here is passionate, difficult, and courageous. The viewer also meets a devoted husband, but harsh father. John Adams loved his children and was committed to their education and well-being. Yet how affectionate he was with them is a matter for debate. It would also not be appropriate to expect a 21st-century image of fatherhood in this 18th-century man. The image of Adams as father in this miniseries is not always easy to watch, perhaps because the public has come to expect so much more from fathers—and perfection from the *Founding* Fathers.

It is also interesting to note here that from the first scene of Adams with his children, the series foreshadows the difficulty the couple will have with their second son, Charles. This is an intriguing dramatic choice given that Charles was born in May of 1770 and so would not have been in the picture during the events surrounding the Boston Massacre Trials. Furthermore, the writers and producers also decided to make interesting changes with all the Adams children. Abigail "Nabby" Adams would have been all of five years old in 1770 and her brother, John Quincy, only three. Yet in this opening episode, they are all older and Charles, the audience quickly sees, tries his father's patience more than the other two children do. These changes to the children's ages continue with their fourth and last child, Thomas, who was born in 1772.[32] Yet at the end of episode one, John Adams is departing a pregnant Abigail as he travels to Philadelphia in 1774.

While this maneuvering of the facts involving Adams's children seems unimportant, it is baffling. Why change the age of the Adams children? The only purpose it seems to serve is to depict Adams interacting with older children and therefore presenting him as a difficult father to love. This is one of many changes or compressions the writers and producers made in the series. The creators of this miniseries had a knack for finding the drama in Adams's life but had to choose what to emphasize here and their choices were sometimes unfortunate.

The writers of the miniseries faced a challenge that Adams himself acknowledged as he journeyed to Philadelphia in 1774. Adams wrote, "There is such a quick and constant Succession of new Scenes, Characters, persons, and Events turning up before me that I cant keep any regular Account."[33] Adams attempted to record all of his impressions and, as a result, readers have one of the more fascinating portions of John Adams's diary. McCullough included Adams's observations in his biography, but it would have been difficult for the miniseries to depict them all.

Once in Philadelphia, Adams made keen observations of the city and his fellow delegates. His description of John Dickinson, who would soon become a major advocate for delay in Congress, was brilliant. "Mr. Dickenson ... is a Shadow—tall, but slender as a Reed—pale as ashes. One would think at first Sight that he could not live a Month. Yet upon a more attentive Inspection, he looks as if the Springs of Life were strong enough to last many Years."[34] What the show could do is provide its audience with the Dickinson Adams described. Actor Željko Ivanek captured that Dickinson brilliantly and, in this way, the series used Adams's diary to good effect.[35]

Another aspect of Adams's diary that the series included was his growing impatience with the Congress. By October, he was clearly irritated with the proceedings. The most remarkable expression of his growing frustration came in a letter to Abigail on October 9, 1774.

I am wearied to Death with the Life I lead. The Business of the Congress is tedious, beyond Expression. This Assembly is like no other that ever existed. Every Man in it is a great Man—an orator, a Critick, a statesman, and therefore every Man upon every Question must shew his oratory, his Criticism and his Political Abilities. The Consequence of this is, that Business is drawn and spun out to an immeasurable Length. I believe if it was moved and seconded that We should come to a Resolution that Three and two make five We should be entertained with Logick and Rhetorick, Law, History, Politicks and Mathematicks, concerning the Subject for two whole Days, and then We should pass the Resolution unanimously in the Affirmative.[36]

This quotation revealed John Adams at his cynical and humorous best. Fortunately, the writers of the miniseries used it in its entirety at the beginning of one of the best episodes, entitled simply "Independence."

In this episode, the audience sees the frustration and impatience of Adams with some of his fellow colonials. Once John Adams was committed to the cause of the American colonies, whether it was fighting for their rights as Englishmen or full independence, he never looked back. He was sure of the rightness of the movement and, being from Massachusetts, knew the first experiences of the war. All of this comes through in this episode.

While the writers do take liberties (there is no record that he saw anything of Lexington and Concord, for example), the episode builds the tensions and Adams's impatience vividly. When the Congress finally reaches the debate on independence, the writing team had to be creative in putting words in Adams's mouth. Much to the distress of many historians, the secretary of the Congress did not record what Adams said in this debate on July 1, 1776. What the record shows is brief. "Resolved, That this Congress will resolve itself into a committee of the whole, to take into consideration the resolution respecting independency." A few lines later, the record reads, "The Congress resolved itself into a committee of the whole. [After Some Time,] the president resumed the chair."[37]

Adams did speak for two hours, but what he said has been lost. Yet the moment was too dramatic and important for the writers of the miniseries to ignore. Therefore, they did what they could to capture Adams's sentiments. "The hour has come. My judgment approves this measure and my whole heart is in it. All that I have, all that I am and all that I hope for in this *life* I am now ready to stake upon it! While I live, let me have a country. A *free* country!"[38] In that moment, Giamatti captured Adams's urgency and passion for the cause of independence. There are several moments like this over the seven episodes. However, the series also missed opportunities to bring both drama and humanity to their story.

One of the more frustrating aspects of the miniseries is the omissions from Adams's life, clearly covered by McCullough. While HBO would never agree to a 30-part series, there are certain moments that would have enhanced the production. Their absence is puzzling, especially given how much these moments mattered to Adams. One involved the sacrifice of a friendship for the sake of his commitment to the cause of the colonists.

As noted in Chapters One and Four of this book, Jonathan Sewall played a huge role in John Adams's early life and career, and yet he is strangely missing from most popular culture depictions of Adams. The HBO miniseries is one of the exceptions, but even here, it downplays his friendship with Adams. Sewall appears in the first episode; the list of characters includes his name. However only those scholars who have studied Adams or Sewall would know who he was. Further, the writers changed the history in which he appears with Adams. There are two examples of this that are most striking.

Sewall's conversation in which he offers Adams the post of Advocate General is here, but it happens after the Boston Massacre trials rather than in 1768. Adams is speaking to his friend and even addresses him as "Jonathan" but that is the only time he calls him by name. In addition, there is little sense that Sewall is looking to save his friend from committing treason. Likewise, the dramatic departure the two men took from one another is missing. Interestingly enough, the writers did include a scene in which the two men part company in 1774. In comparison to what really happened, it is muted and disappointing. Anyone who knows the dramatic story could find themself waiting for the moment in this scene. Yet it never comes.

As noted above in the introduction and in Chapter Four, the moment Adams and Sewall said goodbye to one another is an emotional exchange. In 1774, Jonathan Sewall warned Adams not to attend the First Continental Congress, that the power of Great Britain was too great. To see the end of this valued friendship dramatized would give John Adams an added dimension and demonstrate Adams's commitment to the cause. The writers at HBO certainly had reason to include it since McCullough himself wrote about it. "As long as they lived, neither man would forget the moment. Adams told Sewall he knew Great Britain was 'determined on her system,' but 'that very determination, determined me on mine.' The die was cast, Adams said. 'Swim or sink, live or die, survive or perish, [I am] with my country.... You may depend upon it.'"[39] This conversation was all the more dramatic because the two men had climbed a hill outside of Falmouth (now Portland), Maine, overlooking Casco Bay. What a filming opportunity! Yet the scene is missing from the adaptation.

The conversation between Sewall and Adams was alluded to in an indoor scene in which Sewall warns Adams that obedience to the crown is the only course of action. He adds, "The crown has ruled, John. The only reasonable course left is obedience, and YOU would do well to remember that and act accordingly, old friend." Adams's only reply delivered with hesitation and sadness is, "Good Day, old friend."[40] This is the moment in which Adams sacrificed a long friendship for what he believed was right. Yet the miniseries version lacks warmth.

Losing this friendship was heartbreaking for Adams. Making more of it would have humanized him further. It would have also offered dramatic opportunity—as would their reunion years later. The two men were reunited in London after the war while Adams served as the first U.S. minister to the Court of St. James's in the 1780s. The reunion, too, was heartbreaking.

Adams made a point to find Sewall and greeted him warmly, taking Sewall's hand in both of his and asking, "How do you do, my dear old friend?" The two men talked for a couple of hours. It was as if they had never parted company. In a letter, recounting the reunion, Sewall observed, "Adams has a heart formed for friendship and susceptible of its finest feelings. He is humane, generous and open—warm in the friendly attachments though perhaps rather implacable to those whom he thinks his enemies."[41] Once again, the drama of this moment would have played well in the miniseries, but after episode one, Sewall disappears from the Adams story.

The omission of these heartbreaking scenes from the miniseries robs John Adams of that part of his humanity. McCullough covers the stories of these two encounters with Jonathan Sewall in his biography. They give a reading and viewing audience another dimension of Adams that is often lacking. Perhaps they do not fit into the agenda to depict Adams as an antihero or perhaps the writers and producers wanted to avoid the complication of demonstrating Adams's softer side. Whatever the reason, the creators of *John Adams* decided to tone down their subject's deep love for his friends. The choice is unfortunate given how important friendship was to Adams. McCullough emphasized this early on. "'Friendship,' Adams had written to his classmate and cousin, Nathan Webb, 'is one of the distinguishing glorys of man…. From this I expect to receive the chief happiness of my future life.' When … Webb became mortally ill, Adams was at his bedside keeping watch through several nights before his death."[42] Ignoring this side of Adams's personality is one of the failings of the miniseries.

One other glaring omission from the show is the remarkable "Remember the Ladies" exchange between Abigail and John. Had the creators chosen to include it, such a scene would have shed more light on the relationship between John and Abigail. This exchange between these

two extraordinary people is so famous, even U.S. History survey readers include this dialog in their American history units.[43] McCullough did
discuss the exchange in his biography, although briefly. He also came to
an interesting conclusion about it. Noting that Abigail was writing in the
spring of 1776, shortly after the British had evacuated Boston, McCullough
emphasized her admission that she was feeling happier and more optimis-
tic about life. After quoting the famous letter at length, he concluded, "She
was not being entirely serious. In part, in her moment of springtime *gai-
ety*, she was teasing him. But only in part."[44] This is an interesting analysis of the letter and McCullough does not give it much attention. Still,
he did include it in his work on John Adams. However, this most famous
conversation is missing from the miniseries. There are many points in the
show in which the audience sees John and Abigail writing to one another
or reading letters. Why the writers chose to exclude this correspondence
is unclear.

The series did create a conversation between John and Abigail in
which she reminds him that women are important in the movement toward
independence. Abigail argues that sending a woman to the Congress
would knock sense into John Dickinson and his kind. Adams tells her that
it is a matter of politics. She replies, "Politics? Do women not *live* politics,
John Adams? When I go to the cupboard and I find no coffee, no sugar, no
pins, no meat, am I not living politics?"[45] The writers did a superb job creating this dialog. Giamatti and Linney perform it superbly, but this is as
close as the series gets to the "Remember the Ladies" exchange from 1776.
Throughout the series, the writers provide many instances of Abigail bal-
ancing John, giving him perspective and counsel. One has to wonder why
her most famous nudge to her husband is absent from the drama.

The show is guilty of other compressions, omissions, and changes
from the biography that are puzzling. For example, it compresses John
Adams's two trips to Europe into one. This particular creative license is
unfortunate, as the viewer is not aware that on the second trip to Europe,
Adams took both John Quincy and Charles with him. As is made clear in
one critic's commentary, this omission is an important one for the depiction of Charles Adams.

> Throughout the series, John and Abigail's dissipated son Charles makes much
> of his childhood separation from his parents, as first John and then Abigail left
> for Europe, "abandoning" him, he says, to the care of tutors. This purported
> desertion is made the central fact of Charles's life, the root of his eventual per-
> sonal dissolution, and a seemingly justified reproach that John struggles to
> evade.[46]

This particular compression also serves, once again, to emphasize Adams
as a neglectful father. The long separations from his family weighed heavily

on Adams. While he was away, he sent letters to his children, offering advice to them—even when they were too young to understand it.[47] He knew all too well what his absence meant in their lives, and he carried that guilt. Why the writers missed an opportunity to show him as a father who wanted his *two* oldest sons with him is baffling.

The writers and producers also omitted John Adams's return home in time to write the Massachusetts State Constitution. Granted, this may not have been the most dramatic event of his live, but the moment adds to the list of his many contributions to the new nation, and he was very proud of this accomplishment. McCullough spent five pages on it, calling it "one of the most admirable, long-lasting achievements of John Adams's life." Moreover, McCullough argued, "As time would prove, he had written one of the great, enduring documents of the American Revolution. The constitution of the Commonwealth of Massachusetts is the oldest functioning written constitution in the world."[48] Perhaps this particular achievement did not fit nicely into the dramatic narrative. Yet it was a job for which Adams was ideally suited, and it would have provided more "home and hearth" scenes as well. To see John Adams writing about and discussing those principles of government that were so important to him would have contributed to a deeper understanding of his character.

There is another change made by the production team that is more glaring if not more understandable. On New Year's Day, 1812, John Adams wrote a letter to Thomas Jefferson. This action in and of itself seems unimportant. Yet this letter would mark the beginning of the 14-year correspondence between the two Founders and would begin a remarkable reconciliation between the two men whose friendship had suffered great damage because of the politics of the early republic. Here again, the value Adams put on friendship and the mending of former bonds would have been clear to the audience.

The reunion was the work of Benjamin Rush, who wrote to both men, begging them to forgive and forget. Rush used every strategy at his disposal, even resorting to writing about his dreams in which he saw their reconciliation. John Adams found these dreams amusing and wrote to Rush, "A Dream again! I wish you would dream all day and all Night, for one of your Dreams puts me in spirits for a Month. I have no other objection to your Dream, but that it is not History."[49] At the time that Adams wrote this letter to Rush (1809), the reconciliation was still three years off, but Rush never gave up. Once the correspondence between Adams and Jefferson had resumed, Adams could not help but tease Rush. "Mr Mediator! You have wrought Wonders! You have made Peace between Powers that never were at War! You have reconciled Friends that never were at Enmity!"[50] Despite this ribbing, Rush was thrilled. "I rejoice in the correspondence which has taken place between you and your Old friend Mr Jefferson. I consider you and him, as the North and South poles of the American Revolution.—Some talked, some wrote—and some fought to promote & establish it, but you, and Mr Jefferson thought for us all."[51]

The producers of the John Adams miniseries would have been remiss had they not included this dramatic reconciliation. It is there and in a very moving way. However, the writers made a change that is perplexing. Rather than using the correct date for the resumption of communication between these two old friends, the writers decided that Adams would first reach out to Jefferson upon the death of Abigail in 1818. Dramatically, placing the impetus for the reconciliation on Abigail's death is enough to bring an audience to tears. Unfortunately, it did not happen that way. In fact, Abigail was involved in the exchange of letters. Historian Jeremy Stern was unforgiving in his critique of this change:

> Arbitrarily changing history, bringing Rush into the story years after his death, pushing Abigail out of the renewed friendship with a man who had, as the program itself had emphasized, been her friend as well—what possible reason can be given for such unnecessary distortions? The real story is even more dramatic, and could have been presented in just as compact and televisually practical a fashion.[52]

What the writers of the miniseries failed to see in making this change was that Jefferson had been important to both John and Abigail. While Abigail did not push for a reconciliation between the two men, she was there to see it. When Abigail died at the age of 74, Adams did pour out his grief to Jefferson and Jefferson responded in a comforting way. The miniseries depicts all of this and does not alter Adams's image here in any fashion.

Episode Seven covers Adams's retirement years and is, in fact the most moving episode of the series. In it, Adams loses Abigail; reconciles with Jefferson; and then dies on July 4, 1826, 50 years to the day after the Second Continental Congress adopted the Declaration of Independence. Since, famously, Thomas Jefferson died on that same day, the writers of the series take the audience back and forth between Monticello and Peacefield, Adams's home. Once Adams had died, the audience sees him walking with Abigail once more with a voiceover of some of their letters to one another. The final lines are Adams's, taken from a letter he wrote to Abigail in April of 1777. "Posterity! You will never know, how much it cost the present Generation, to preserve your Freedom! I hope you will make a good Use of it. If you do not, I shall repent in Heaven, that I ever took half the Pains to preserve it."[53] It is an artistic and dramatic end to the series.

Whatever quibbles historians may have with this miniseries, it is a powerful depiction of a complex man. Scholars who study the past will always have problems with popular culture adaptations such as this. Yet, despite the changes and the omissions, the essence of who John Adams was does come through on the small screen. If historians wish the public to be interested in a character like John Adams, they must accept a certain amount of dramatic license. Still, what bothered one historian is worth noting. Jeremy Stern wrote,

> [John] Adams does not need such revision: he was a great man despite his flaws, a fascinating and important man without being the sole driver of events. He would emerge quite well from an accurate account of his life—one that respected McCullough's factually solid narrative, rather than recasting reality to suit the scriptwriters' own sense of drama.[54]

Stern's is a fair criticism of the series although the HBO production was not the huge offender to history that the History Channel's "Sons of Liberty" was. In fact, as biopics go, *John Adams* was quite good in many respects. Historian James T. Kloppenberg noted the enormity of depicting Adams's life on screen and stated, "Capturing in seven episodes the complex sensibility of John Adams and the still greater complexity of late eighteenth-century American politics is impossible. [Kirk] Ellis's screenplay and Hooper's direction give us the best rendition yet on film."[55] Yet Kloppenberg did take issue with the factual errors. He argued that "avoiding or at least acknowledging such examples of poetic license might help guard against the cynical (and, in this case, largely unwarranted) assumption that films never get history right."[56]

Historian Andrew Schocket, in his book *Fighting Over the Founders: How We Remember the American Revolution*, offered another interesting critique of the HBO miniseries. In studying the Revolution in collective memory, Schocket observed two different approaches to the history. One, which he called "essentialism," advocates that there was one Revolution "led by demigods, resulting in an inspired governmental structure and leaving a legacy from which straying would be treason and result in the nation's ruin."[57] The other approach to remembering the Revolution Schocket called "organicist," the idea that "there are many pasts that may share elements but no one fixed truth."[58]

In his analysis of HBO's *John Adams*, Schocket saw what he called "a fascinating amalgam of essentialism and organicism." While, on the one hand the emphasis of the series was on one Founding Father and presented an "Adams's-eye view of Revolutionary America and the early republic,"[59] the writers and producers of the series wanted to include an acknowledgment of slavery. Schocket stated, "Subtle details indicate an organicist sensibility: crowd scenes always include African American faces, and city scenes pan by exterior walls plastered with fliers offering bounties for capture of run-away slaves."[60] In the end, according to Schocket, the series leans more toward the essentialist approach to the Revolution, with John and Abigail, becoming "composite characters ... standing in for every Revolutionary couple and their experiences" and also as "witnesses to the grand scope of the American Revolution."[61] This explains the times in which the miniseries inserted John and Abigail into incidences the historical couple did not see.

For two other historians, the changes made to history in this miniseries were unforgivable. Nancy Isenberg and Andrew Burstein, who were not fans of McCullough's biography, also did not care for the television adaptation of his work. In a section of their chapter "The Adamses on Screen" in *A Companion to John Adams and John Quincy Adams*, entitled "The Frog and the Princess: HBO's *John Adams*," these scholars take the series to task for its mangled chronology and its emphasis on "gore and trauma." They stated, "If *The Adams Chronicles* had the sterile feel of colonial Williamsburg, the overall atmosphere of the HBO is no closer to reality." They also found the physical appearances of Laura Linney and Paul Giamatti disconcerting. "The glaring contrast between husband and wife reminds one of fairytale characters—*Shrek*, for instance. Giamatti can't help but look like a warty frog next to her." In summing up their critique of the show, Isenberg and Burstein, wrote, "In sum, the highly acclaimed HBO series *John Adams* is not history. It is not even close. It distorts both characters and basic facts. Beyond engaging in dramatic license, it bowdlerizes history, because scriptwriters and producers knew they could get away with it."[62] These historians and others quoted above give the series harsh condemnations and their frustration with it are understandable. Yet, what about the portrayal of John Adams here?

Beyond the changes to history made by the miniseries, the characterization of John Adams is also troubling. Schocket argued that the series gave the HBO audience a complex John Adams. "He's principled and irascible, brilliant and insecure, and occasionally a little ridiculous."[63] In this case the usable John Adams is intended to counter the depiction of Washington and Jefferson, founders whom, Giamatti argued, we all know and love. The problem with this is that it is an incomplete picture of Adams. What is sometimes missing, in glaring ways, is John Adams's warmth, his humor, and his love of life. The staff at the Adams National Historical Park took note of this.[64]

Is HBO's *John Adams* a precise biography of the man? Furthermore, should it be? Robert A. Rosenstone in his book *History on Film/Film on History,* observed, "historical adaptations are as complex as historiography itself." He argued, "It is time ... to stop expecting films to do what (we imagine) books do." He continued to discuss the nature of film itself. He contended that "films are not mirrors that show some vanished reality, but constructions, works whose rules of engagement with the traces of the past are necessarily different from those of written history."[65]

One further question: Given the limitations of the medium, is it possible to construct accurate dramatic portrayals for characters as complex as John Adams? For that matter, how does one accomplish this on the page? Countless biographers and historians have tried, as this book has so far demonstrated. Each has had his or her own purpose for writing about Adams.

If the purpose of biography is to illuminate certain characters or the times in which they live, screen biopics are just as useful as written ones. In the case of the HBO John Adams miniseries, the character of Adams, with all of his flaws, is present if incomplete. For a post–9/11 American public, he is a flawed man, doing the best he can in extreme circumstances. He is both hero and anti-hero, a fully human man who continues to speak truth to power. As for the people who think about John Adams or read his works, perhaps at some point Giamatti's voice will be the one they hear in their heads.

David McCullough, discussing the art of writing biography, said that it was important to "write for the ear as well as the eye" and to tell stories.[66] Print biographies do this, but so do biopics. If every word of a biography does not appear as an on-screen moment, the essence of the biography, the heart and soul of it can still exist. In some cases, a biopic can be better in terms of bringing a certain character to the attention of an audience. As hard as some historians have tried, only David McCullough with his art of storytelling along with the cast and crew of the miniseries *John Adams* could transform the man into the rock star to which the park ranger at the Adams National Historical Park referred. Yet the attachment to the story of John Adams and his family evident at this park demonstrates a commitment to the man that no scholar or artist can rival. The depictions—and uses—of John Adams seen in his hometown of Quincy, Massachusetts, and at the Adams National Historical Park are the subjects of the next two chapters.

EIGHT

John Adams of Quincy

In 2018, Congressman Stephen H. Lynch (D–Massachusetts) spoke to the House of Representatives concerning the need to build a monument to John Adams in Washington, D.C. Lynch remarked, "President Adams was a remarkable leader and a steadfast public servant. It's a glaring oversight that there is no memorial in our nation's capital honoring John Adams and his family for their role in shaping our nation."[1] Congressman Lynch is not the first person who has attempted to get an Adams memorial built. Given that this latest authorization expired on December 2, 2020, it is likely he will not be the last. As the article in *Roll Call* pointed out, the Adams National Memorial Foundation has been authorized three times to move ahead with plans for a monument.[2] Yet as of this writing, the memorial has neither been planned nor built. It is almost as if John Adams's own prediction about his memorialization has cursed the project.

Outside of Washington, D.C., it would be difficult to argue that Adams has been neglected in U.S. public history. There are statues to Adams in Rapid City, South Dakota, and even in Bilbao, Spain.[3] By far, the most evident commemoration of John Adams is found in his hometown of Quincy, Massachusetts. The citizens of the city and the staff of the Adams National Historical Park (discussed in Chapter Nine) have lovingly preserved his memory.

John Adams is remembered in Rapid City, South Dakota, because he was one of the presidents of the United States. Rapid City is noted for Mount Rushmore and the town calls itself "The City of Presidents." Not only do they honor the four men carved into their famous mountain, but they pay tribute to the other presidents as well. There are statues to various presidents scattered throughout the city center. The bronzes of the presidents were sculpted by John Lopez and dot the streets of Rapid City. The John Adams statue is located at the corner of 6th Street and Main Street. In it, Adams is demonstrating his oratorical skills, perhaps arguing for independence from England. This statue has a corresponding listing on the Visit Rapid City Website. Here, the city has included information about

Adams as well as the location of his statue and the name of the sculptor.[4] With this recognition, John Adams is honored because of his role as President of the United States. That is the only reason the statue exists here, and he is lumped in with all the other people who have held that office. So where might one find an extensive commemoration of John Adams as an individual? Not surprisingly, the answer is in Massachusetts.

The largest and most important public history celebration of John Adams is in the town of Quincy, Massachusetts. The area that became Quincy—the place in which Adams was born, raised, and died—is a continuous memorial to the man who gave a great deal back to it. The fact that Adams came from this place is important in understanding him. His connection to what is now Quincy is essential. According to Dr. Edward Fitzgerald, executive director of the Quincy Historical Society, the fact that Adams came from this particular place was relevant to what he did and how he did it. His motives and strategies in helping to move the colonies to states and establish a new nation were tied to the virtues he saw in his hometown. "He has a relationship to a place that I don't know who else does in that group [the Founding Fathers]," said Dr. Fitzgerald.[5] Washington is tied to Mt. Vernon and Jefferson to Monticello, yet Adams's connection was to more than just his own property.

Adams recognized his ties to his region of New England and the town where he grew up. Writing from The Hague in 1782, Adams reflected on the area for which he was homesick. "I know not the Reason but there is some Strange Attraction between the North Parish in Braintree and my Heart. It is a remarkable Spot. It has vomited Forth more Fire than Mount Etna. It has produced three mortals, Hancock and two Adams's, who have, with the best Intentions in the World, set the World in a blaze."[6] Interestingly enough, John Adams referred to himself and his cousin Samuel, who is more often associated with Boston. In fact, Adams acknowledged that it was Samuel's father who was born in the north parish of Braintree, not Samuel himself.[7] These ties to place continued for at least four generations of the Adams family. That relationship between the town and Adams as well as his descendants creates an interesting dynamic that is unique. Further, the history of the area that is now Quincy speaks to John Adams's observation that his roots are in an area remarkable for spewing fire. Contention was nothing new to the area by Adams's time.

Tracing the history of rebellion in Quincy begins with the first Englishman in the region, who arrived in 1625. Thomas Morton, a lawyer who had initially settled in the Plymouth colony, found himself at odds with the strict ideas of the elders there. As a result, he decided to look elsewhere for a place to settle. He sailed with Captain Wollaston who, upon landing in the Quincy region, left Morton in charge of a group of indentured servants. Morton liked the place so much that he decided to stay and established a trading post there. According to the introduction to Morton's own work, *The New England Canaan,* edited by Charles Francis Adams, Jr., Morton fit in well in the area. Adams wrote,

> Passionately fond of field sports, Morton found ample opportunity for the indulgence of his tastes in New England. He loved to ramble through the woods with his dog and gun, or sail in his boat on the bay. The Indians, too, were his allies, and naturally enough; for not only did he offer them an open and easy-going market for their furs, but he was companionable with them. They shared in his revels.[8]

Morton enjoyed his fun and even erected a May pole, a tradition common for the English.

Yet in the eyes of the Separatists in Plymouth, William Bradford among them, May-Day festivities had distinctly pagan origins. "It represented all there was left of the Saturnalia and the worship of the Roman courtesan."[9] Morton was viewed with suspicion by the leaders of Plymouth and when the larger migration of Puritans arrived in the area in 1630 to establish the colony of Massachusetts Bay, Morton would become a target. John Winthrop, Puritan governor of Massachusetts Bay, saw him as a "blasphemer and troublemaker." Winthrop arrested Morton, confiscated his land, and burned the homes in the trading post to the ground. Hoping to establish a Godly settlement there, Winthrop redistributed the land to those whom he saw as God-fearing, Edmund Quincy among them. This was the first Quincy associated with the region.[10]

Having rid himself of Thomas Morton, who was sent back to England, Winthrop had hoped to restore peace to the area, but this was not to be. As writer Nina Sankovitch, author of *American Rebels: How the Hancock, Adams, and Quincy Families Fanned the Flames of Revolution*, stated it, "It was as if the hills themselves breathed rebellion into their inhabitants."[11] This region of the Massachusetts Bay colony also became associated with an extraordinary woman named Anne Hutchinson, who famously caused no end of trouble for Winthrop and his model colony. Hutchinson was directly connected to the so-called Antinomian Crisis in Massachusetts Bay and was banished from the colony in 1637.[12] Edmund Quincy would avoid entanglement with the Hutchinson controversy since he died in 1637, but he was connected to the area, and his family would become important members of the community. In 1640, the selectmen decided to change the name of their settlement from Mount Wollaston, named for the captain who initially left Morton in charge, to Braintree.[13]

The north parish of Braintree was long associated with the Quincy family. This part of the settlement was incorporated as Quincy, in honor of Colonel John Quincy, in 1792. The town in which John Adams grew up, the town he knew as Braintree, was not free of controversy or litigation. Adams witnessed many of these tensions firsthand as his father was dedicated to public service for the town.

It is not surprising that John Adams would develop his independent spirit in such a place. While the villagers valued community, they had also developed a sense of independence, setting themselves off from the larger settlement of Boston.[14] As Sankovitch noted, "The people of Braintree believed not only in their individual abilities but also in their collective duty to determine their own fates and the shared future of their village."[15] While, on the one hand the settlers wished to advance their community by working together, they also demonstrated an independent streak that Adams himself would emulate throughout his life. Whether he was fighting for American independence or his own freedom from political parties, Adams could look to his hometown for inspiration.

Adams acknowledged his deep roots in Quincy. In a rough draft of his autobiography, he wrote, "My Father, Grandfather, Great Grandfather, and Great Great Grandfather all lived and died in this Town of Quincy, for so many Years the First Parish in the Ancient Town of Braintree, and are buried in the Congregational Church Yard."[16] That Adams always returned to his hometown, even after living in Boston, Philadelphia, New York, Paris, Amsterdam, and London, demonstrated his love for and commitment to the area. On the one hand, this connection marked Adams as provincial. On the other, his dedication to Quincy and his family's continued connection to it has allowed his legacy to thrive in the town. Adams's love for the village was further demonstrated by deeds in which he donated lands and funds to various projects in the town. These deeds would guarantee that he made a permanent mark on Quincy.

In the first of three deeds, Adams donated land to the city of Quincy because of the "veneration I feel for the residence of my ancestors and the place of my nativity, and of the habitual affection I bear to the Inhabitants with whom I have so happily lived for more than eighty six years." He wished the proceeds of this land—meaning any rents or profits from the sale of products from the property—to "promote their happiness, and the instruction of their posterity, in religion, morality, and all useful arts and sciences." To that end, he asked that the funds raised be used to build a stone temple for the Congregational Church.[17] Any funds left over, he said, should go to the building of a school "for the teaching of the Greek and Latin languages, and any other languages, arts and sciences, which a majority of the ministers, magistrates, lawyers, and physicians, inhabiting in the said Town may advise." These profits from the deeded land became the Adams Temple and School Fund with his son, Thomas Boylston Adams, and four others as trustees.[18]

Along with the gift, Adams issued a warning to the town: "If there should be any gross corruption or mismanagement in the care of this interest" or any negligence and waste "knowingly permitted, or connived by the said Town, or by the Selectmen thereof," the property would revert to the "oldest male person, at the time living among my posterity."[19] While John Adams wished to show his gratitude to the place that formed him, he would not tolerate any dishonesty or bungling. Adams had carefully and frugally acquired the property he was now donating to the town; he would not let it be misused.

Shortly after this first deed was signed, town officials expressed thanks to Adams. They accepted the gift "with gratitude, affection, and respect" and also stated that "they regard it with sentiments of peculiar veneration, as the gift of one, whose patriotism and virtues have cast a lustre upon the place of his nativity." They continued by acknowledging Adams's contributions to the independence of the nation as well as his instrumental influence in creating "free and well balanced constitutions of government, which alone can secure and perpetuate our inestimable privileges."[20]

At a time when Adams was still concerned about his legacy, these expressions of gratitude must have done wonders to reassure him. His pleasure was expressed in a letter to the town read into the minutes of the August 6, 1822, town meeting. "The harmony and unanimity with which the town have accepted the instrument of conveyance, and their approbation of the restrictions, limitations and conditions, expressed in it, are very gratifying to me, and receive my best thanks."[21] John Adams had to know that, locally, he was a revered member of the Founding generation. Yet he never stopped worrying about his legacy. Through his gift to the town and the town's grateful acceptance of it, he could rest assured the town of Quincy would not forget him, even if the nation did. While it is impossible to know Adams's motives behind this gift, it is safe to say that he was, in part, attempting to be remembered in some way. He did not stop with this first deed.

In the second deed, also dating to 1822, Adams, "in consideration of the kindness with which my former conveyance … has been accepted," donated more land to the town. One parcel of land included an "ancient cellar and well." Here Adams was referring to the birthplace of John Hancock that had burned to the ground. Adams instructed the town to build the classical academy referred to in the first deed on the site of Hancock's birthplace to honor "that great, generous, disinterested, bountiful benefactor of his Country once President of Congress and afterwards Governor of this state." In this way, Adams wished to memorialize his old friend, a man he had known since childhood.

In the deed, he went on to discuss the history of the house, even managing to mention James Otis, Jr., in the document. Otis was a hero of Adams's, a man who, according to Adams, never received proper recognition for his role in the Revolutionary movement. While Otis had no ties to Quincy, Adams was always ready to teach the history of the Revolution any way he could. He further instructed that as soon as the funds were sufficient to cover the cost, the town should hire a schoolmaster who could teach the classics. In true John Adams fashion, he suggested the way in which the subjects should be taught.

> I hope the future M[...] will not think me too presumptuous if I advise them to begin their lessons—in Greek and Hebrew, by compelling their pupils to take their pens and write over and over again copies of the Greek and Hebrew Alphabets in all their Variety of Characters, over and over again until they are perfect masters of those Alphabets and Characters, this will be as good an exercise in chirography as they can use, and will stamp those Alphabets and characters upon their tender minds and vigorous memories so deeply that the impression will never wear out, and will enable them at any period of their future lives to study those languages to any extent with great ease.[22]

The building that was built on the site of Hancock's birthplace became the Adams Academy. There is a plaque noting the Hancock connection to the building and a bust of Hancock on the front lawn of the property.

Even though Adams later specified in a third deed that the school be built before the church—the town already had a church building—this was not the way the town proceeded. The church, known at the time as the Stone Temple, was built first and completed in 1828. The school was not built until the early 1870s. By that time, any idea of a classical academy was an anachronism. The school did open and did well for approximately thirty years, but there was not room to expand the school because of its location. It was fine for translating Homer, but by the late 19th century, science education was also important, and the school could not add labs to its existing space. Enrollments declined and in 1907, the school closed its doors. The building now houses the Quincy Historical Society.[23]

Also in a third deed, John Adams left his library to the town of Quincy. Adams loved his books and specified that he was not ready, in 1822, to part with them all. He wished to retain "a few that I shall reserve for my consolation in the few days that remain to me," but all the rest would go to Quincy, providing that they be cataloged and stored in the Adams academy.[24] He also asserted "That none of the books shall ever be sold, exchanged or lent, or suffered to be removed from the apartment [in the academy], without a solemn vote of a majority of the superintendents."[25] He did, however, stipulate that "The books may be removed to any place the Committee of the town shall direct, or remain where they are, at the pleasure of the Committee of the town; locked up and the keys held by the Committee during my life, and the pleasure of my Executors afterwards."[26] This last item concerning his library may explain how the books came into the possession of another institution later in the century.

Interestingly enough, the collection did not remain in Quincy but was donated to the Boston Public Library in 1894. The John Adams Library contains over 3000 volumes that belonged to Adams while he lived as well as volumes donated by members of the family. The Boston Public Library has kept the books in its Rare Book collection and has also digitized them so that scholars may see Adams's marginalia without making a trip to Boston.[27] The library has invested a great deal in the collection. Yet there is some desire on the part of the Quincy City Government to get the books back and to honor Adams's intention that they be preserved in his hometown.

The mayor of Quincy, Thomas Koch, wishes the collection to be housed in the city. In a letter to the Boston Public Library, the mayor outlined his proposal. "My objective is to return this treasure of our local and our national history to the citizens of Quincy and dedicate a presidential library of sorts to John Adams and feature his collection as its centerpiece, among other important displays of our history." He went on to assure David Leonard, president of the Boston Public Library, that the city would do whatever it took to care for the collection. "I fully recognize the importance of this undertaking and am willing to commit the necessary resources to see the proper care of the collection as well as prepare a suitable home for it."[28] Koch made it clear that he wanted to uphold John Adams's wishes and that he was committed to the preservation of the second president's memory. He emphasized the importance of this history to the city. "I trust you can appreciate the spirit and pride that Quincy holds for the Adams' legacy," he wrote to Leonard.[29]

Whether Adams's desire for his books to be preserved in the town will be realized remains to be seen. The Boston Public Library Board discussed the request in executive session in September of 2020, but as of this writing, it has not debated the idea publicly.[30] Still, Koch's inclination to create a presidential library dedicated to John Adams demonstrates his personal investment in the history of the Adams family.

In addition to the deeds in which Adams donated land and funds to the city of Quincy, he also wished to acknowledge his connection to his hometown by commemorating his ancestors. In doing so, John Adams demonstrated his interest in historical memory. In his later years, Adams guaranteed that the town would remember his forebears.

In the center of Quincy, across a new common from the United First Parish Church, sits the Hancock Cemetery.[31] This had been a place of burial from the 1630s, but, according to the guide to the cemetery, "grave markers were often impermanent or non-existent and cattle roamed freely here." It was not until 1809 that a group of citizens purchased the lot and donated it to the town. Among these citizens was President John Adams who had family members buried on the land.[32]

There are many connections to John Adams in this cemetery. Most importantly, this is the graveyard in which he and Abigail were originally laid to rest. A marker on a vault bearing the inscription J Q Adams marks the spot, for John Quincy and his wife, Louisa Catherine, were also originally buried here. The presidents and their wives were moved to the crypt at the United First Parish Church. John and Abigail were moved in 1828; John Quincy and Louisa Catherine in 1852. Yet this vault remains the resting place of numerous family members, including John and Abigail's daughter, Abigail Adams Smith (Nabby). She was the Adamses' oldest child and she died of breast cancer at the age of 48 in 1813.

Adams erected new grave markers for his parents and some of his ancestors. On the new stone built for his great-great-grandfather, Henry Adams, John placed his forebear into a wider context. Henry was the first of John's ancestors to emigrate from England. Adams asserted the reason. Henry Adams came to New England fleeing "from the Dragon persecution in Devonshire in England," and settled near Mount Wollaston. Never one for brevity, John Adams continued his tribute to his ancestor: "This stone and several others have been placed in this yard, by a great-great grandson, from a veneration of the Piety, humility, simplicity, prudence, patience, temperance, frugality, industry and perseverance, of his Ancestors, in hopes of Recommending an imitation of their virtues to their posterity."[33] John Adams also placed new markers on the graves of his great-grandparents as well as his grandparents, Joseph Adams II and Hannah Bass Adams. In an interesting connection to Plymouth history, Hannah was the granddaughter of John Alden and Priscilla Mullins, the famous couple of the Thanksgiving story. John Adams's roots in this region of Massachusetts ran deep and wide. Adams humbled himself by noting on his grandparents' gravestone that the marker was erected by "the lawyer John Adams" in 1823.[34] Finally, Adams honored the memory of his own parents, Deacon John Adams (1691–1761) and Susanna Boylston Adams (1708–1797).

In his retirement and old age, it is clear that Adams was contemplating how he might be remembered. As he was thinking about this, he wished to preserve the memory of those who came before him. Today, the cemetery is an historic site with iron fencing added in 1844. As Adams remembered his forebears, he was also ensuring his own legacy by deeding portions of his landholdings to the city of Quincy. As a result, the town would become a place where John Adams could never be forgotten. Quincy has also contributed to his efforts to be remembered in various ways.

Over the decades, the town of Quincy has embraced its native son by building statues in his honor. There are four extant statues of John Adams in Quincy, although one is in storage at present. The first of the statues, carved by Franco M. Marchini of Barre, Vermont, is a life-size portrait. It depicts Adams during his presidency at approximately 63 years of age. The statue itself was carved from Rhode Island granite, but the base is Quincy's own stone. It stands in Freedom Park, a green space created during the Bicentennial in 1976. At the base of the statue is this inscription: "John Adams: Farmer, Lawyer, Patriot, Diplomat, First Vice-President, Second President of the United States." In addition, there is a quote from John Adams: "There is danger from all men. The only maxim of a free government ought to be to trust no man living with power to endanger the public liberty." This was an interesting choice of quote but given the turmoil of the early- and mid–1970s, it was appropriate. The statue was dedicated in October of 1977.[35]

Another monument connected to John Adams was dedicated in 1980 and commemorates the anniversary of the Massachusetts Constitution. This statue, originally located in the center of town near the United First Parish Church, is abstract in nature. In fact, H. Holly Hobart, writing in 1987 for the *Quincy Historical Society Newsletter*, included a subtle critique of the design. He asserted that the description of the monument, provided on the plaque attached to it, "will give added meaning for some, little to none for others, as is always the case with interpretive art."[36] The monument was designed by Jerome N. Riecher and sculpted by Quincy resident Edward P. Monti. The artwork, which is now located in Freedom Park along with the John Adams statue dedicated in 1977, was commissioned by the city of Quincy. For the town, the writing of the Massachusetts Constitution was the "most important historical event to have taken place here."[37] John Adams scholars have long acknowledged the writing of this constitution and its influence on the drafters of the U.S. Constitution. It is one of the most important contributions John Adams made to the governments of the new nation. While the statue does not depict him, it is part of the homage the town of Quincy pays to its hometown son.

The second statue to Adams in Quincy was sculpted by acclaimed artist Lloyd Lillie and stood in Quincy Center until recently. This bronze, which the *Boston Globe* called "larger than life" because it is taller than Adams was, shows Adams in an interesting stance, as if he is stepping—and looking—forward. His coat seems to move in the sea breeze. The statue was dedicated in 2001 as an accompaniment to the earlier figure of Abigail and a young John Quincy Adams dedicated in 1997. According to the *Boston Globe*, the statue was dedicated with a dinner and a speaker, none other than David McCullough. The *Globe* remarked about John

Adams that "He is the subject of what has been the hottest selling book in the United States for most of this year. He soon may get a memorial in Washington, D.C. Now John Adams finally has a statue in his hometown."[38] Although not actually the first statue of Adams in Quincy, this bronze took on more importance given Lloyd Lillie's name recognition and the presence of David McCullough. Now it and the Abigail statue are in storage, a recent chapter in a long history of the creation and revision of memorials to Adams in his hometown.

In addition to these two life-size statues, there is also a bust of John Adams in the United First Parish Church. According to church historian Bill Westland, the statue does not belong to the church, but rather to the Adams Temple and School Fund.[39] The plate under the bust pays homage to both John and Abigail. The inscription, written by John Quincy Adams, notes that his father was a signer of the Declaration of Independence as well as the peace treaty that ended the Revolutionary War. It also states, "On the fourth of July 1826, he was summoned to the independence of immortality and the judgement of his God." It continues: "This house will bear witness to his piety; This Town, his birth-place to his munificence; History to his patriotism; Posterity to the depth and compass of his mind." Interestingly, there is no mention here of his service as president of the United States. Yet the plaque outside the crypt in this church where Adams is buried does mention his service as president along with his signature on the Declaration of Independence and his authorship of the Constitution for the Commonwealth of Massachusetts. That tablet was erected by the John Adams chapter of the Daughters of the American Revolution in 1900.

One of the newest additions to the commemoration of John Adams in Quincy is the Hancock Adams Common in the center of the city. Spearheaded by Mayor Koch, the Common was dedicated on September 8, 2018, after some ten years of planning. This involved rerouting streets as well as moving water and sewer lines in the center of the city. The project is part of a larger vision for revitalization of Quincy's center, but it also honors two of the city's native sons and Revolutionaries.[40]

Mayor Koch sees the Common as a national monument to two men who contributed to the founding of the nation. In his speech at the dedication ceremony, Koch alluded to the elusive memorial to John Adams in Washington, D.C. "Until that day comes when we have the appropriate memorial to Adams in Washington, I claim these are the two national monuments to Hancock and Adams. Who can argue with me?" asked the mayor.[41] The Common was a collaborative effort, requiring the work of landscape architects, urban planners, and the sculptor of the two statues, Sergey Eylanbekov. Eylanbekov, who has had numerous commissions, including a monument to Dwight D. Eisenhower in Washington, D.C., was one of fifty applicants submitting plans for the bronzes.

The Common unites the Hancock Cemetery, the United First Parish Church as well as Quincy's old City Hall. It includes several water features as well as green space, making it a proper common in the New England sense although it is people who gather there rather than livestock. A long, rectangular green is accented by trees on each side and by the two statues, John Hancock on one end and John Adams on the other. Ironically, it was the creation of this common that sent the Lillie statue of Adams, along with the one of Abigail and John Quincy, into storage.

The newer statue of Adams stands on a pedestal upon which is engraved his signature. He wears his overcoat and hat, looking sideways toward the city hall. While the monument notes his roots in Quincy with an engraving observing that he was born a mile from the site, the statue pictures Adams carrying a walking stick and wearing riding boots, perhaps ready to venture to Philadelphia. At first glance, the sculpture bears some resemblance to Paul Giamatti as John Adams. Whether this is because the sculptor was influenced by the miniseries or because both the statue and Giamatti resemble Adams is difficult to say.[42] The costuming is certainly similar and anyone who has seen the miniseries will recognize the style of coat he is wearing, a fashion typical for the 18th century. This nod to fashion history accuracy is evident in both the statue and the miniseries.

The granite walkway and steps leading to the statue are engraved with Adams's many accomplishments, including his service in the two Continental Congresses as well as his nomination of George Washington to lead the Continental Army. The engravings note his draftsmanship of the Massachusetts Constitution, his role in the peace treaty ending the Revolutionary War in 1783, and his post as the first minister to the Court of St. James's in England. In two places, the monument mentions his role in securing the vote for independence. One engraving calls him a co-author of the Declaration of Independence while another dubs him the Architect of Independence.

The dedication ceremony of the common was an elaborate affair, with music provided by the Quincy Symphony Orchestra and the Quincy Choral Society. Several keynote speakers delivered brief comments on the two Founding Fathers honored at the Common. Among them were Congressman Stephen Lynch, who spoke about the long history of public service among the citizens of Quincy. Governor Charlie Baker addressed the contributions of John Hancock, emphasizing his funding of the Revolution in Massachusetts and his role as governor of the new state. Ben Adams, representing the Adams Family at the ceremony, spoke of Quincy as home.

"Although earlier generations of the Adams Family were often off in Washington or overseas for long stretches of time," he observed, "the Old House and Quincy were always home." For more recent generations, he noted, Quincy was where they came for family gatherings or "just to feel a sense of place in the presence of those who came before us."[43]

Again, the star among the keynote speakers for the dedication was David McCullough. While his biography of John Adams was nearly twenty years old by the 2018 ceremony, McCullough is still given a good deal of credit for putting Quincy on the map in a way that no other writer has. In his remarks, McCullough emphasized Adams's role in the passage of the Declaration of Independence. He used the John Trumbull painting, which hangs in the Rotunda of the Capitol building in Washington, D.C., as an illustration of Adams's importance. While noting correctly that there are many inaccuracies in the painting, McCullough observed that it was important to Trumbull to get the faces correct. Then he moved to the placement of Adams in the artwork. "If you look at the painting with any sense of composition," he remarked, "at the very center of the canvas [John Adams] is the only figure who is portrayed full scale, head to toe." McCullough argued that there was a reason for this. "There is no question that the artist is telling us who, of all these people, mattered most. It's John Adams."

McCullough further observed the rightness of this composition. "John Adams fought for the Declaration of Independence on the floor of the congress in Philadelphia as did no one else, as attributed to not only his determination and his courage but his ferocity in argument—ferocity in speaking for a cause."[44] In Adams's fight for the Declaration itself, this debate was simply a climax to all the work he had done before that time. He worked for months to get state governments in place. He believed that the second day of July—the day the Congress passed the resolution on independence presented by Virginia—was the actual birthdate to commemorate.[45] Yet by placing the emphasis on the Declaration itself, McCullough was able to compare Adams's importance to Jefferson's. "Jefferson by contrast [to Adams] said almost nothing during the whole course of that long summer, but Adams never gave up day after day; as Jefferson himself said, he is the one who made it happen."[46] Comparing the contributions of Jefferson and Adams is not new, but McCullough's remarks in 2018 affirmed to the crowd that their hometown boy deserves the credit for independence as much if not more so than does Jefferson.

For those still waiting for a monument to John Adams in Washington, D.C., the Hancock Adams Common is arguably a model. Adams's contributions to the American Revolution and the new nation are not left to doubt here. This city project, a long time in the making, works better than many people expected, according to Dr. Edward Fitzgerald of the Quincy Historical Society. He credits the mayor with pushing the project forward and wanting to get it right. When it comes to the finished product, Fitzgerald stated, "I just think it's terrific!" He believes the common pulls the city center together. He is, however, still withholding judgment on the latest city project to commemorate its history, The Presidents Trail. This work is still too new to evaluate.

The Presidents Trail is a six-mile tourist path through Quincy which ties together ten historic sites in the city, including all of the sites in the Adams National Historical Park. Since many of these places are spread out through the city, the trail attempts to highlight mainly the colonial and Revolutionary points of interest. Dr. Fitzgerald explained that there had been earlier attempts at historical trails which included every aspect of Quincy history, but they were too unfocused and just did not work the way the town had hoped. What the city wishes for with this new trail is renewed interest in the historic town—and economic stimulus. Since the Adams birthplaces, for example, are located in south Quincy, tourists can take the trail to those sites and eat at one of the restaurants nearby.

The new trail is marked by seals on the sidewalks so that tourists can follow it easily without getting lost. Each stop also has brand new historical signs noting the significance of the place. The city hopes that visitors will take selfies at the signs, post them on social media, and encourage their friends to visit the places. Fitzgerald said that it is too early to tell if the idea will work.[47] One problem is the length of the path. Asking people to commit to six miles to see all the sites may be a stretch. By comparison, the Freedom Trail in Boston, which covers 16 historic sites, is only two and a half miles long. Still, the Presidents Trail demonstrates one more way the city has embraced its history, including the legacy of John Adams. Eight of the ten sites on the trail are connected to Adams in some way.

The public history surrounding John Adams is immense and yet, in many respects, provincial. If the American people are looking for a national monument to John Adams, they need look no further than the city of Quincy. Adams himself helped to guarantee that his hometown would not forget him and in a sense, gave the city permission to use his name in various ways. His children, grandchildren, and great-grandchildren worked to ensure that his legacy would remain in the forefront in Quincy. The mayor of the city has taken the lead in commemorating John Adams.

The one seeming oversight about the Hancock Adams Common is that it has removed Abigail Adams from the picture. With the Lloyd Lillie statue of Abigail in storage at present, her role in John's life is not visible, at least in Quincy Center. This is an oversight that some residents of Quincy protested. Demanding that Abigail be returned to Quincy Center,

Mayor Koch has now promised that a new statue of Abigail, created by Sergei Eylanbekov, will grace the Hancock Adams Common.[48] In the meantime, the memory of John Adams is alive and vivid in Quincy. The future of a John Adams monument in Washington, D.C., remains uncertain—especially in light of the reassessing of all the Founders in the framework of racial and cultural inequities.

It is safe to say, however, that even in the realm of public or collective memory, John Adams has reemerged as a leading figure in the usable past of the American Revolution and the history of Quincy. Moreover, his hometown is finding new ways to use John Adams and his family to boost tourism in their region. As the area plans for its 400th anniversary in 2025, a usable John Adams continues to play a role in the heritage of the town. Separate from the town, but very much a part of that remembrance, is the Adams National Historical Park, the subject of the next chapter.

NINE

The Adams National Historical Park

For travelers planning a trip to the Boston area, the options are endless. Boston itself has enough history to keep a tourist busy for a few days. However, if one wishes to venture beyond the city to other areas of historical interest in the area, the choices are intriguing. Boston is not far from Salem, the home of the notorious witch trials of the 17th century. For the traveler who is more interested in Revolutionary and Presidential history, the Adams National Historical Park is well worth the visit. This opinion is widely shared on the internet; the park has high ratings on both Trip Advisor and Yelp. The evolution of this park is a fascinating story.

Managed by the National Park Service, the Adams National Historical Park encompasses the birthplaces of both John and John Quincy Adams, the Old House—Peacefield, as John Adams named it—bought by John and Abigail upon their return from Europe, and the United First Parish Church where John, John Quincy, Abigail, and Louisa Catherine are buried. While the park receives funding through Congressional approval every year, the church does not.[1]

The park has a long and complicated history that began with the Adams family's gift of Peacefield to the National Park Service.[2] The house itself has a deep connection to Quincy. It was first built in 1731 by Leonard Vassall, owner of a sugar plantation. Vassall had moved to Boston but wanted a home outside the city as a summer residence. Upon Vassall's death, his daughter, Anna, inherited the house. She married John Borland, and the couple moved into the property. However, Borland himself received a substantial inheritance and the couple moved to a new residence in Cambridge, Massachusetts. What would now be known as the Vassall Borland house was leased to tenants, but because the Borlands were Loyalists during the Revolutionary War, the property was confiscated by the government of Massachusetts. Following her husband's death, Anna fled to England for a time.

Upon her return to Massachusetts following the war, Anna got the house back and deeded it to her son, Leonard Vassall Borland. It was from him that John and Abigail bought the estate.[3] The purchase of the house took some creative planning. According to Kelly Cobble, who served as curator of the Adams National Historical Park, when the Adamses attempted to buy the house, the owner, knowing who they were, inflated the price. As a result, John and Abigail had to find some other way to get the house for what it was actually worth. They asked Cotton Tufts, a relation of Abigail's, to act as their agent and it was he who purchased the property for them in 1787.[4]

After John and Abigail moved into the house in 1788, it became the home of four generations of Adamses. Each left their mark on the property through various additions to the house. The 2008 handbook to the park provides a diagram of the floorplan and each renovation.[5] Abigail had remembered a bigger house, but after residence in France and England, found the place too small. She planned additions almost immediately. Every generation after her found ways to improve the house. The last Adams resident was Brooks, who died in 1927. Since he had no children, he left the home to the Adams Memorial Society, a group of family members, which agreed to preserve the property as a museum. With the help of Wilhelmina Sellers Harris, who served as Brooks' social secretary, the family kept the home until 1946.

The house proved too expensive to maintain, however, and in 1946 the Adams Memorial Society donated the home to the people of the United States to be managed by the National Park Service "with the purpose of fostering civic virtue and patriotism."[6] With this statement, it is clear that even as the society was turning the house over to the United States government, family members recognized its place in a usable past and made clear their intention. In 1946, then, the Secretary of the Interior, J.A. Krug, "by means of the authority granted the Secretary of the Interior under section 2 of the Historic Sites Act of August 21, 1935," established the Adams Mansion National Historic Site. In 1950, the Park Service hired Mrs. Harris to serve as superintendent.[7]

The involvement of Harris was noted as a happy occurrence by one of Brooks' nephews, Thomas Boylston Adams. In the foreword to a site pamphlet written by Harris, Adams stated, "It was a rare, good fortune for the people of the United States when Wilhelmina Sellers came to the Old House in Quincy to act as Brooks Adams' private secretary and to assist in the management of his household." Miss Sellers "took quiet charge" of all household arrangements, "leaving Brooks the happy illusion that he was running everything." Following Brooks' death, Sellers married and raised a family, but when the house was turned over to the National Park Service, she returned. "She insisted on working closely with the family," Adams wrote. "To the preservation of the traditions of the place, she brought a knowledge and integrity absolutely unique." Since the Adams family did not care for show but "for what was useful … to the nation," Mrs. Harris made sure the house itself demonstrated the family's wishes.[8]

In her 1983 report on the house and gardens, Superintendent Harris recalled her first visit to the home in 1920 and the pride with which Brooks Adams showed her around. "As we entered the Panelled Room," Harris wrote, "Mr. Brooks Adams remarked that he felt proud but humbled as he recalled the members of his family now gone." He believed that his family and the nation were "richer" because of his famous ancestors. Harris also noted on this first visit that every generation of the family had left furnishings in the house.[9] Yet even more remarkable to her mind were the many distinguished people who had visited the property, including President James Monroe in 1817 and General Lafayette in 1824.[10] Harris used this report to highlight the many artifacts in the mansion and to connect those items with the history of the house. Her focus shifted to the gardens on the estate at the end of her booklet in order to emphasize the site as not only historically significant, but also horticulturally interesting.

In later guides to the park, Peacefield took center stage because of the many items connected to the family which are still *in situ*. The sofa upon which John Adams sat for the painting of his last portrait is pictured in the 2008 handbook, as is his writing desk and his wing chair "where just a few days before his death, he gave his last message to the American People: 'I give you Independence forever.'" In addition, the house boasts the busts of John Adams as well as George Washington. A particularly moving item is an 1826 memorial wreath presented to Louisa Catherine Adams in commemoration of the death of her father-in-law, John Adams.[11] The house today remains a remarkable museum. Visitors can tour the home, the gardens, and visit the carriage house which was added to the estate in 1873. Because of the many artifacts found in the home and the long family traditions associated with it, it is not surprising that Peacefield is the center piece of the Adams National Historical Park. Yet it is not the only home in which John Adams is remembered by the National Park Service in Quincy.

Once the Adams mansion was in the possession of the National Park Service, the site grew incrementally over several decades. In 1952, the Department of the Interior renamed the park the Adams National Historic Site. Yet the National Park Service still did not have possession of the birthplaces of John and John Quincy Adams. Those small saltbox houses had an interesting journey to becoming part of the park.

According to the National Park Service's Park Planner, the two birthplaces associated with the two Adams presidents are the "oldest presidential birth homes still standing." It is remarkable that they have survived. The Adams family retained ownership of both until 1940, but between the years 1784 and 1896, the homes were used as rental properties. Fortunately, in 1896 the Quincy Historical Society and the Daughters of the Revolution[12] began to maintain and manage the properties and opened them to the public.

There was no professional staff during the period that historical society was overseeing the houses. They relied on volunteers and furnished the houses with whatever they could find that might fit the period. The properties were never owned by the historical society, yet it continued to maintain them as best they could.

Then, in 1940, the Adams family gave the houses over to the city of Quincy, insisting that they remain open to the public. The job of providing tours in the homes remained with the Quincy Historical Society. From the 1890s to the 1970s, the Society was in charge of visitorship to the birthplaces. The Society even made a sign, dating to the 1890s, to place outside the cottages at the close of the season. It is badly faded now, but it read, in part, "Clos'd: The 'Cottage' of John & Abigail Adams. Its thrum latch string has been pull'd within—But will be out against the visitations of ye Pilgrims at the __th Mo. A.D. 1893."[13] Through the years, the houses deteriorated, and by the early 1970s even the city of Quincy could no longer afford to maintain them. According to Dr. Edward Fitzgerald, notions of curatorship had changed over the years as well, and the job became too large for the Quincy Historical Society or for the city. At the urging of local politician Paul Harold, the city investigated the possibility of turning the houses over to the National Park Service.[14] Finally, in 1978 Congress passed Public Law 95–625 which made the houses the responsibility of the Department of the Interior. Both the John Adams Birthplace and the John Quincy Adams Birthplace became part of the Adams National Historic Site. The park service then restored them and reopened them to the public in 1984.[15]

The birthplaces today are surrounded by a growing city. They sit at the intersection of two busy streets in South Quincy, and yet they are beautifully preserved. The park service employs preservationists when necessary and they have recently restored the outside of the John Adams birthplace. Unlike Peacefield, the small saltbox cottages are sparsely furnished. None of the furniture in the houses is original to John and Abigail, but the park has selected pieces that are suited to the mid-18th century when John owned the homes. At John Adams's birthplace, the park highlights the great room where John's father would hold meetings and hear arguments relating to the town or the church. John watched all of this as a child and young man. His father's public service influenced him greatly.

In the John Quincy Adams birthplace, visitors see the living area, but also the part of the house that served as John Adams's first law office. In addition, the park staff, for interpretive purposes, displays a copy of the Massachusetts Constitution, which Adams drafted in the home in 1780. Since this is the oldest written constitution still in use, the Park Service emphasizes Adams's role in drafting it as well as its influence on the men who wrote the U.S. Constitution in 1787.

The park guides also discuss here the role of Abigail Adams in keeping the family farm prospering during John's absences. One part of the story that the Park Service tells concerns the dangers Abigail faced while keeping the home fires burning. While it is difficult to perceive today, the cottages are very close to the water. The bay is deep and therefore was navigable for warships. In the early days of the war, before the British evacuated Boston in March of 1776, the danger to the inhabitants of the coastline was real. John knew it and admonished Abigail, "In Case of real Danger, of which you cannot fail to have previous Intimations, fly to the Woods with our Children. Give my tenderest Love to them, and to all."[16]

In addition to maintaining the farm and educating her children, Abigail was in constant fear. In June of 1775, Abigail wrote to John of her concerns. "We now expect our Sea coasts ravaged," she told her husband. "Perhaps, the very next Letter I write will inform you that I am driven away from our, yet quiet cottage. Necessity will oblige Gage to take some desperate steps. We are told for Truth, that he is now Eight thousand strong. We live in continual expectation of alarms."[17]

The other historical event that the Park Service highlights is connected to what is now called the Abigail Adams Cairn, an historic site managed by the city of Quincy. It marks the spot where Abigail and son John Quincy watched the Battle of Bunker Hill and the burning of Charlestown. In a letter to John, Abigail informed him of Joseph Warren's death at the battle. Warren was a longtime friend and a leading voice in the Sons of Liberty. She also related the tension of hearing the battle. "How many have fallen we know not—the constant roar of the cannon is so distressing that we can not Eat, Drink or Sleep."[18] Many years later, in March of 1846, John Quincy Adams recalled climbing Penn's Hill with his mother to observe the battle. The Abigail Adams Cairn marks the spot from which the seven-year-old boy watched the burning of Charlestown with his mother.[19] In June of 2018, Alison M. Kiernan of the National Park Service reenacted Abigail Adams watching the battle from this site.[20]

The park continued to grow over the years. In 1972, "Congress authorized the addition of the neighboring Beale Estate (3.68 acres)" to the site.[21]

Then, in 1980, Congress authorized the addition of the United First Parish Church, the burial place of John, Abigail, John Quincy, and Louisa Catherine Adams to the park. The building, also known as the Church of the Presidents, has a long history of its own.

The town of Boston annexed the area around Mount Wollaston in 1634, meaning that the settlers in the region had to travel to Boston proper to attend church. This was a hardship for the citizens of the area. In 1636, they petitioned the town of Boston, requesting their own congregation or meeting. The Reverend John Wheelwright was called to be the minister of this new congregation, and the town of Boston agreed to the arrangement. The settlers built a small meeting house—dubbed The Chapel of Ease—and the church began holding services. Unfortunately for the citizens in the region, Thomas Wheelwright was caught up in the controversy surrounding his sister-in-law, Anne Hutchinson. In 1637, Hutchinson, Wheelwright, and other followers were banished from Massachusetts Bay. This left the area without a minister once again.[22]

The settlers, however, were not ready to give up on having their own established congregation with a pastor to lead it. In 1639, they sent another petition to the city of Boston, asking for a new pastor to serve the area. The leadership in Boston granted their request, and the Reverend William Thomas led the new independent congregation. In 1666, the old meeting house was replaced by a new stone building, the first stone church in New England. Over the years, this building fell into disrepair and was replaced in 1732 by a wooden structure named in honor of the minister at the time, the Reverend John Hancock. This minister was the father of the famous signer of the Declaration of Independence and was the clergyman who baptized John Adams in 1735.[23] His baptism would mark the first, but by no means the last connection Adams would have with this church building. He worshipped there every Sunday and donated the granite for the current church building, completed shortly after his death.

During Adams's lifetime, the church was part of the Congregational denomination, one of the many iterations of Calvinism. Yet by the late 1700s and into the early 1800s, the church's theology became more liberal. John Adams's own belief system had evolved over his long life, becoming more ecumenical. He reached out to the Episcopal community in Quincy later in his life with a generous offer. In the first deed that John Adams offered to Quincy, he wrote, "[I]f the Episcopalian Society of the said town shall at any time hereafter be about to build a Church for the Worship of God, they shall have liberty to take from the land hereby granted, as much stone, as they may need to use in erecting such Church."[24]

As for John Adams's church, the present building, or the Stone Temple as it is sometimes called, was dedicated in 1828, two years after John

Adams's death. When the Founder died in 1826, John Quincy Adams approached the Adams Temple and Church Fund, requesting the addition of a crypt beneath the unfinished church to house the remains of his father and mother. He offered to pay for the crypt from his own pocket, and the church voted to deed John Quincy Adams fourteen square feet under the front hallway of the church for the crypt. In later years, John Quincy Adams turned over the deed to the Adams Temple and Church Fund for the cost of one dollar. As a result, while the church today organizes tours of the crypt, it does not own the burial sites, expanded by Charles Francis Adams to include John Quincy Adams and his wife.[25]

Because United First Parish is an active congregation and owing to the many entities involved in the historic site and crypt, the church has had an interesting and sometimes uneasy relationship with the city and with the National Park Service. In 1980, according to Bill Westland, the church's current historian,

> Dick Porter from UFPC, Paul Harold of the Quincy City Council and our Congressman, Brian Donnelly, testified before Congress in order to get a bill passed that would allow us to remain completely independent but have the National Park Service responsible for the building restoration and maintenance, seeing as the church had been declared a national historic monument in 1970.[26]

Unfortunately for the church and its expenses, that was not the way the issue was resolved. Instead, the church was added to the Adams National Historic Site by an act of Congress. Public Law 96–435 allowed the Secretary of the Interior, Cecil D. Andrus, to accept conveyance of the church and its property. However, he was also required to describe "the measures which the Secretary intends to take to ensure that in the management of said property there is no violation of the constitutional provisions regarding the separation of church and state."[27] The solution provided to this issue is summed up on the church's website. "While the Church of the Presidents has a cooperative arrangement with the Adams National Historic Park to open the crypt and the church building to visitors, because we are an active congregation we receive no money whatsoever from the Federal Government."[28] "We became part of the Adams National Park in name only," stated Westland. This provision also requires the church to depend on donations to keep the crypt open and provide tours of the church. Adding to the complication is the ownership of the crypt itself since it belongs neither to the church nor the park service.

Despite this complicated arrangement, the United First Parish Church takes its responsibility as the resting place of two presidents seriously and works hard to maintain a visitors' program. This system has evolved over the years and has relied heavily on the work of volunteers as well as donations from the public. The formal visitors' program began in the United States Bicentennial year, 1976. According to Bill Westland, "Longtime church member Dorothy Wrigley started the program and we were open from July 4th to Labor Day, seven days a week. She managed to do this strictly with volunteers, a mind boggling accomplishment. We didn't charge admissions but did have a donation box. The program didn't generate much revenue, but there really weren't any expenses either."

Between 1988 and 1993, the visitors' program was run by various members of the congregation, but it became increasingly difficult to keep the church open seven days a week. Then in 1993, at the urging of the city, the church agreed to be open seven days a week for the same season and hours as the Adams National Historical Park, which operated from April 19 through November 11 at that time. For a while, the church supplemented its volunteer corps with rangers from the National Park Service. In addition, the mayor of Quincy at the time, James Sheets, agreed to find corporate sponsors, allowing the church to hire a full-time coordinator for its visitors' program. According to Westland, the arrangement had limited success. "The first year the City managed to get us $20,000 worth of sponsors, but by 1996 this amount had dropped off to $4,000. Also, the City really wasn't attracting any great number of tourists, and by the end of 1996 the program was $11,260 in debt." The debt mounted until the church was close to shutting down the program altogether.

At this point, the local newspaper, *The Patriot Ledger*, ran a subscription program for the church. They managed to raise close to $44,000 for the visitors' program, demonstrating "how important we were in the eyes of Quincy residents because there were not any corporate contributions involved, only small donations from Quincy and South Shore residents." In addition, the church got a grant from the state to keep its doors open to tourists. By this point, the church was depending on all volunteers to lead tours once again but continued to hire a full-time administrator for the program. One of those hires was Arthur Ducharme and under his leadership, the visitors' program expanded.[29]

Like the other sites connected to John Adams, the church saw a surge in visitors following the publication of the David McCullough biography and the broadcast of the HBO miniseries several years later. This, coupled with additional grant money and some corporate sponsors, kept the visitors' program afloat. According to Bill Westland, the church is due to ask for more sponsorship to fund its efforts and he is hopeful about the future of their endeavors. The city remains dedicated to bringing tourists to see its historic sites, and the United First Parish Church is in a good position to benefit from this.[30]

One major contribution the United First Parish Church makes to the memory of John Adams is the annual wreath-laying ceremony held on his birthday. This tradition began in 1967 and expanded under the leadership of Arthur Ducharme. Each year, the sitting U.S. president honors his deceased predecessors by sending a wreath to the particular president's burial site on his birthday. This is a tradition that has continued to the present day. Some ceremonies are more low-key than others, but United First Parish Church has one of the most elaborate celebrations in July (honoring John Quincy Adams) and October (honoring John Adams). Bill Westland gives credit to the late Arthur Ducharme for turning these events from simple wreath layings to full-blown celebrations. The John Adams ceremony became increasingly popular after author David McCullough spoke at the 2001 event, the first held after the September 11th attacks.[31]

Over the years, a variety of speakers have taken part in the event, including mayors of Quincy, representatives from the Adams National Historical Park, and descendants of John Adams. In addition, the high schools in Quincy as well as the Woodward School for Girls send student speakers chosen for the quality of their essays submitted for the ceremony. Since education was vitally important to John Adams—and to his son—this practice is especially appropriate. Each year, the event coordinator also chooses a theme that the speakers address. The ceremonies have also included music from various groups and musicians who volunteered to participate, including the Quincy Choral Society, choirs from Quincy's high schools, and musicians from the South Shore Conservatory of Music. To cap each ceremony, the church hosts a reception with refreshments and a birthday cake for President John Adams donated by local businesses.[32]

Westland pointed out the one constant in these ceremonies: The United States Navy. It has been involved in these events from the first, held in 1967. This is appropriate given John Adams's connection and advocacy for the Navy. From early on in the Revolution, Adams understood the necessity of a Navy to American defense. It is fitting that the Navy represents the President every year in these observances.[33]

In recent years, the wreath-laying events have been recorded or livestreamed.[34] They demonstrate the respect for John Adams and John Quincy Adams evident in the church and the pride of the organization in its role in preserving Adams's legacy. Given that the church sits on the new Hancock Adams Common, a centerpiece in the city, its profile as an Adams site can only grow.

The final change came to the park in Quincy in 1998, when the Federal Government passed one more law relating to it. The *Adams National Historical Park Act of 1998* changed the name of the site and also called for the acquisition of up to 10 acres "for the development of visitor, administrative, museum, curatorial, and maintenance facilities" for the park. From this point forward, the Adams National Historical Park consisted of the birthplaces, Peacefield (including the stone library built by Charles Francis Adams), the Beale Estate, the United First Parish Church, and the Visitor Center.[35]

Today, the park (not including the United First Parish Church) employs two permanent interpreters and between seven and twelve seasonal workers. The duties of the employees vary. They collect fees, do light cleaning, but also lead tours of the birthplaces and the Old House. Visitors to the site go first to the park's Visitor Center to begin their tour. From there, they go to the birthplaces and then to Peacefield. At each stop, visitors are greeted by interpreters who tell them the history of the homes and guide them through the sites. The interpreters always have in mind the family's wishes for preserving the Adams legacy in these various buildings. They understand the importance of a usable past for the tourists who come to Quincy. Since the Adams National Historical Park is the most prominent of the sites connected to John Adams and his memory, gaining perspective from the people who work there is key to understanding how Adams's legacy is presented.

The park has had two long-term superintendents in its seventy-five year history. The first was Wilhelmina Harris. The second and current superintendent is Marianne Peak. She has served in that capacity since 1987 and was brought into the Park Service by Mrs. Harris. In 2011, she appeared in a C-Span symposium and spoke eloquently of the role of the Park Service in preserving presidential memory. In her appearance, she emphasized the continuing growth of visitorship to the park and the impact that had on the community of Quincy. "They value us. We're relevant, and they really understand that there is an economic impact" to our growing tourism. This, she noted, exploded with the David McCullough biography and the HBO miniseries based on the book. She said that with this book and miniseries—along with the film *Amistad* with its emphasis on John Quincy Adams—"The Adams [park] went Hollywood." She continued, "It changed our world. It has brought audiences to us. And how we serve them now is more relevant than anything else we do. Because their experience is everlasting."[36] Superintendent Peak also noted that "we have outgrown ourselves" because of the rising interest in the Adamses; the Visitor Center was no longer adequate for what the park needed to do.[37] That problem has yet to be resolved, but the park continues to strive to meet the needs of its visitors and has enjoyed the renewed interest in John Adams and four generations of the Adams family.

Superintendent Peak is not the only long-term employee of the park who has witnessed change over time. Curator Kelly Cobble had over thirty years' experience at the Adams National Historical Park before her death in March of 2022. Her passion for her work and the Adamses was contagious. She was also a walking primary source concerning the changing perceptions of John Adams that the park has witnessed. As curator, Cobble was responsible for the homes and everything in them, including the paintings, the furnishings, the sculptures, the books, and all other artifacts that belonged to the Adams family. She approached her job with enthusiasm and felt honored to be a part of the preservation of the family's legacy.

Like Superintendent Peak, Cobble had deep roots in Quincy. She was born and raised in the town and believed that she wanted to leave the city after studying literature and art history in college there. However, she found herself back in Quincy after a short stint in Europe and held various jobs before working temporarily at the Adams National Historical Park. She had spent some time as a teacher, and while classroom work was not for her, she admitted that her teaching took other forms in her job as curator. She loved working with interns, especially those who were willing to do the mundane chores as well as the fun ones. The park is fortunate to have both paid and unpaid interns. Many of them enjoy the work so much that they return year after year. In her first role at the park, Cobble volunteered to do anything that needed to be done, including dusting the books in the library and tracking down primary source material on microfilm to create a "Day in the Life Of" the Adamses. When a position came open for full-time work, she was happy to get it. After some thirty years, she still felt honored to work in an historic space.[38]

Because of her long experience with the site, Cobble was the ideal person to discuss the many changes that have come to the park and how the visitorship has evolved over time. For her own part, she knew little about John Adams before she began working at the park, even though she had been born and raised in Quincy. "I knew he was a president of the United States," Cobble stated. She commented on how nice the property was and how much she loved the daffodils in the spring. "I did know that presidents lived here," she said, and like other schoolchildren in the area, she had gone to the site with her family. She remarked that getting to know more about the place is key to appreciating it. Like many other sites in various places, the hometown people do not always know what is in their own backyard. This was certainly the case for Cobble. Yet once she started working at the park, she was hooked. As a result of her job, she had "fallen in love" with the Adamses and enjoyed living most of her life in the 18th century with John, Abigail, and their family.[39]

Over the years, Cobble had observed the many preconceived notions the public brought to the park. They have changed over time, depending on where John Adams appears in scholarship and in popular culture. In the 1970s, many visitors to the park believed John Adams was the character they saw in the musical *1776*. Cobble thought this is still the biggest perception on the part of the public. This is understandable given that Turner Classic Movies now shows the film of the musical on an annual basis. In addition, people have also seen the stage play in various venues.

In contemplating the scholarship surrounding the Adams family, Cobble remarked, "Much of our history is through the family—Brooks Adams in particular." Wilhelmina Harris shaped the park to reflect Brooks Adams's vision for the public perception of his famous family. In addition, she ensured that the park would pay homage to all four generations who had lived at Peacefield. However, the family placed a moratorium on the Adams papers, and Cobble believed "that kind of wrote them out of the history books." There was some important scholarship done between 1926 and 1983. Both Page Smith and Samuel Flagg Bemis wrote two-volume works on the Adamses, Smith focusing on John Adams and Bemis on John Quincy.[40] Both of these authors, however, had to get special permission to use the Adams papers. As a result, in terms of the park's visibility, Cobble credited one scholar in particular with putting the park on the map. She noted, "We were a sleepy little site" for a long while, and she attributed this to the fact that the Adams papers had been under lock and key for so long.

It was not until Paul C. Nagel published *Descent from Glory: Four Generations of the John Adams Family* in 1983 that the park experienced what Cobble called "the Paul Nagel explosion." Nagel helped to bring the papers out for public consumption. Now people could understand that there was a scholarly back up to *1776* and *The Adams Chronicles* in a way they had never realized. Yet the moratorium on the papers had kept John under the radar for far too long. While Jefferson was "marching along in fanfare," as Cobble phrased it, and Washington, too, John was written out of the story. This is ironic given that both Washington and Jefferson burned many of their papers.[41]

Once Harvard University Press made the papers public and Nagel used them to write his study of the family, people could have a new perspective on John Adams. A cursory glance at his papers reveals a highly transparent John Adams. Still, Cobble was convinced that he was also circumspect in his writing, as was Abigail. Cobble had no doubt that they understood their letters could be stolen and exploited, as in fact they were during John's tenure in the Second Continental Congress. She believed that they were writing in code at times, and nobody has broken it to date. "I think we can't take them at face value all the time," she stated. They were being careful. The other issue is what exists today and why. Even though the Adams Papers collection is massive, it is not complete thanks to the culling done by Charles Francis Adams, John's grandson. Not only did he edit the papers for publication, but he also destroyed all shipping invoices and receipts. Adams's grandson believed that these were unnecessary papers and so they are gone. As a result, we may not have as full a picture of John Adams as we might think.[42]

Despite the gaps that may exist in John Adams's story, people can know more about John Adams than ever before. Now, with the added popularity of David McCullough's biography and especially the miniseries produced for HBO, Adams is, in a sense, an open book as far as public perceptions are concerned. Cobble, however, did not always think this was a good thing. When asked if there was anything she wished people did not know about John Adams, she responded, "I wish people didn't have such a perception of him."[43]

When examining the depiction of John Adams both in *1776* and the miniseries in particular, the audience rarely sees a warm man, capable of deep loyalty and friendship. That lack of depth in these interpretations of Adams also troubles one of the park rangers. Alison M. Kiernan clearly has a soft spot for John Adams. She believes he was a benevolent soul and tells the public so. "John Adams was a marshmallow!" she exclaimed, and she tells her tours that the miniseries did not capture this side of him. He had a zest for life that is not always apparent in the many depictions of him. We never see the John Adams who doted on his grandchildren and encouraged their play.

Park Ranger Richard Shaner echoed these sentiments. He sees in John Adams a special imagination and empathy. He was able to imagine himself in someone else's shoes. Moreover, he married Abigail, which demonstrated excellent judgment. He had a keen respect for women that was unusual for the 18th century. Shaner noted that even when he was arguing with Mercy Otis Warren over her interpretation of the American Revolution, he treated her as a worthy opponent.[44] Joseph Ellis made a point of this as well.[45] Shaner also commented that Adams was eager to find out what "makes people tick" and why things are the way they are.

These important aspects of John Adams's personality are so often missing or overlooked in the popular depictions of him. The people who work at the park are keen to share them with the public.[46] Perhaps this is why Cobble would have liked to have had a chance to educate as many people as possible. "I wish we had a clean slate to teach people about the Adamses. But we don't have one," she lamented. "He's quite an admirable person," she added. "I spend a good deal of time in his brain. I consider myself lucky. He had good people around him that made him a better person."[47]

Cobble admitted that John Adams had his difficulties. He lacked a filter, to be sure. As to the various theories concerning his mental or physical health—such as the theory that he might have suffered from Graves' Disease—she responded, "I don't know! In hindsight, it could be anything." She commented that there were many times when he seemed obsessed, "call it OCD if you like." Yet it is important to note that he "put himself out there so much, when there was a lull and he could take a break…. When he went down, he went DOWN!" Further, if Abigail was not with him, he suffered. She had ways to soothe him and calm him. John himself admitted this, calling Abigail his ballast.[48]

Cobble emphasized the situations in which Adams found himself and the fact that there was no precedent for him to follow. The contributions and sacrifices he made for his new country came from his own personal courage. He believed he was doing what was right and once he determined that course, he never wavered. As Cobble contemplated his role in the movement toward independence, she viewed Adams, out in the lead, with the other members of Congress saying, "yeah, go ahead John. We've got your back."[49]

In addition, Cobble admired Adams's capacity for friendship. She believed that people still underestimate his relationship with Thomas Jefferson. They were very close in Europe and when the friendship faltered, John was devastated. When discussing the manipulations of the election of 1800, she asserted, "John would never do that to anybody!" He did not even campaign, but Jefferson played dirty, and he was motivated by ego. She admitted that she "could be sugar coating" her view of Adams in that situation, but her loyalty is clear.

Cobble would have liked to see Adams placed in a broader—even global—context more often. There is an increasing academic foundation for Cobble's vision. Jeanne E. Abrams's recently published work, *A View from Abroad: The Story of John and Abigail Adams in Europe*, provides scholarly scaffolding for discussing Adams's influence on, and attitudes about, other parts of the world.[50] In addition, the John Adams Institute in Amsterdam honors his memory and "provides an independent podium for American culture in the Netherlands." On the institute's website, it recognizes Adams as "a great lover of culture and scholarship." The webpage notes that, as envoy from the United States to the Netherlands, Adams "actively sought contact with the social and economic elite, befriending bankers, politicians and other influential persons who could support the fledgling republic in its war of independence. Adams laid an enduring foundation for Dutch-American friendship by signing the Treaty of Amity and Commerce with the Dutch in 1782."[51] The year 2005 was designated "John Adams Year" by the institute to mark the 225th anniversary of "our honorable namesake's arrival as America's first envoy to the Netherlands."[52] Beyond the scholarly works which have focused on Adams outside of the United States and the continuing work of the John Adams Institute, there is at least one more commemoration of Adams abroad.

In the center city of Bilbao, in the province of Biscay, Spain, stands a statue of John Adams. This seems an unlikely place to find him, but Adams visited the city in 1780 to learn about its system of government. He later wrote about what he gleaned from his visit in his *A Defence of the Constitutions of Government of the United States of America*. In letter IV, he wrote, "...this extraordinary people have preserved their ancient language, genius, laws, government and manners, without innovation, longer than any other nation in Europe." This quotation is inscribed on the statue, unveiled in the city in 2011.[53]

Cobble did not know what challenges the Park would face in light of the ongoing debates surrounding who we remember and how we remember them.[54] Yet she did want people to appreciate the significance of what John Adams did to bring us forward in human rights as he fought for independence and helped to create the United States. She remained dedicated to his and his family's history. The other staff members of the park share that commitment. Their enthusiasm is evident. They also see that the community supports their efforts. Richard Shaner saw this movingly demonstrated when a family who lived near Peacefield delivered a birthday card to John Adams. Addressed to "President John Adams," the card thanked him for his service to the country and for the beautiful home he left the family to enjoy in Quincy.[55]

With all that Quincy and the National Park Service have done to preserve the memory of John Adams and bring him to the forefront of American history, their reach is still somewhat limited. One way that John Adams is reaching a broader audience is through John Adams reenactors. Three people in particular have taken center stage with Mr. Adams.

Peyton Dixon works through his website called Historic Experience and brings to life both John Adams and Theodore Roosevelt. He is available for events and has done a number of YouTube videos. In two of these, he reads and responds to the reviews of the Adams National Historical Park—as John Adams. While they are highly amusing, they are also extraordinary in their accuracy. Dixon is able to capture Adams reading 21st-century English and adds commentary on Adams's life and career.[56] Dixon has done several presentations of this nature, many of them accessible through YouTube.[57]

Sam Goodyear is another prominent John Adams reenactor who has done work for Public Broadcasting and on stage. He has lived as John Adams for more than twenty years and has written a one-man show called

John Adams: The Man from Massachusetts that he has performed in various venues. He also appears annually with the Colonial Williamsburg Foundation along with long-time Jefferson reenactor Bill Barker. The two, as Adams and Jefferson respectively, address various topics from their years as collaborators, friends, and rivals. In addition, they both appeared in a filmed play made for the Colonial Williamsburg Foundation entitled *Jefferson and Adams* that was released in 2004.[58] They have performed this piece, in which Abigail also plays a prominent role, several times at the Adams National Historical Park.

Finally, Michael Lepage does the duty of playing John Adams at the Adams National Historical Park. He has appeared as John Adams numerous times at the park to answer visitor questions on various topics.[59] Unfortunately, it is difficult to comment on his interpretation of Adams since none of his performances have been recorded. Which of these reenactors comes closest to the real John Adams is open for debate and does not really matter. These actors find a way to embody the spirit of their subject for myriad purposes, both entertaining and educating as they do so. In the process, they keep John Adams in the public eye.

The Adams National Historical Park, with its long history, is central to the commemoration of John Adams in Quincy. The staff members at the park value the opportunities they have to educate the public about this remarkable family. Working in partnership with the city, they have kept the memory of John Adams alive, and they provide the closest thing to a national monument that Adams currently has. Adams would scarcely recognize what he called his "Sweet little farm" today.[60] Yet he could take comfort in knowing that his birthplace, the small cottage he shared with Abigail, and the home in which he spent the last years of his life are still lovingly preserved, along with his memory. The story that the Adams National Historical Park relates to the public is one of respect for and acceptance of the man who is so often depicted as difficult. The park employees who work at all levels understand the importance of the Adams family and they approach their responsibilities with respect. They meet the challenges each year brings by creatively adding to their programming and social media presence. The staff tells the most complete story possible and hopes to continue to do so in the future.

Conclusion

On "To Tell the Truth," a popular game show televised between 1956 and 1968, one noteworthy individual along with two imposters attempted to fool a panel of celebrities. By asking a series of questions, the panelists had to discover which person was the actual individual. The climax of each episode was the reveal. The host would ask, "Will the real _____ please stand up?" In many respects, any study of history and memory asks the same question. In this case, it is: "Will the real John Adams please stand up?" The problem is, even after examining all the biographies and artistic works, the possibility of finding the *real* John Adams may be beyond our capabilities. Who was he, really? More important, does how we remember him reflect who he was? Or does it change who he was? Does our perception of the man create a new version of him?

In order to tell the truth of John Adams, it is vital to peel back the interpretations and see the man in his many dimensions. Biographers have attempted to do this in various ways, some trying to correct what they believe are unfair assessments of him. Others have endeavored to truly understand who he was. Even in his lifetime, Adams observed the revision of his own history. He railed against the mythology surrounding the American Revolution while at the same time despairing of his place in its story. His need to set the record straight exacerbated the problem, for in trying to explain himself, he left behind the writings of a bitter man. Yet when he finally found some peace within himself, when he renewed bonds with former colleagues and let the record stand, his warmth and capacity for closeness shone through. By the time he died, he felt the love of his family, the warmth of renewed friendships, and the gratitude of his community.

In the 19th century, however, John Adams's narrative was largely overlooked in favor of others. Even one of his eulogists acknowledged how difficult it was for Adams to walk in the footsteps of the great George Washington. When bookended by Washington and Jefferson, Adams appeared not to measure up. The history written in the first hundred years of the United States demonstrates this principle. While his son and grandson attempted to bring his work to the public, they did so in a highly edited fashion. Even his own great-grandson felt he did not know much about John Adams. In the autobiographical *The Education of Henry Adams*, this descendant of John Adams, writing his narrative in third person, noted, "He knew as yet nothing about his great-grandfather, who had died a dozen years before his own birth: he took for granted that any great-grandfather of his must have always been good, and his enemies wicked; but he divined his great-grandfather's character from his own."[1]

It would not be until the early 20th century that biographers outside of the family reinserted Adams into the narrative of the nation's founding. These early writers were handicapped by the lack of sources. While the *Works* of John Adams were available to scholars, they did not provide a full portrait. This left historians to build on what they had and—in one case—even create a John Adams who never died. The watershed moment for Adams scholarship was yet to come.

With the editing and publication of the Adams Papers, a new John Adams emerged in scholarly works. With all the evidence at their fingertips, scholars wrote massive two-volume works, psychological studies, family histories, and philosophical analyses of Adams. Some of these books created a perception of Adams as an unhealthy man, with mental health issues that made him difficult to love. He still could not be remembered in the same glowing light as Washington, Jefferson, or Franklin, a Founding Father who, it would seem, could do no wrong.

Given the careful way in which these other Founders protected their papers, the accuracy of their portrayals is questionable as well. Historians and biographers have long abandoned the mythical aura surrounding the figures of the American Revolution. Yet even when all these individuals were put under scholarly microscopes, Adams still stood out as the difficult Founding Father. When historians of the 1990s and early 2000s approached Adams, they did so with an intense desire to understand him better than their predecessors had. In some cases, they grew to admire him and defend him against the criticism of earlier scholars. These biographers walked a tightrope in writing about Adams.

In sharing his experience as a biographer in *Writing Lives Is the Devil! Essays of a Biographer at Work*, scholar Gale E. Christianson discussed the perils of writing biography. "Historians are trained not to engage their subjects on a first name basis," he noted.[2] In other words, they should not like the people they are writing about *too* much. In an effort to make the case for John Adams standing in the pantheon of the Founders, some scholars have crossed this line, overlooking some of his more problematic traits in an attempt to make him likable. In an effort to place him into the

usable past they saw in their own times, they often were too quick to forgive or excuse his foibles and mistakes.

However, when looking at scholarly biographies, there is another
dilemma that arises, one that plagues experienced writers of other people's lives. "Weighing the thoughts and deeds of other human beings out
of the context of their times is both dangerous and unfair," Christianson observed. "By the same token, when motives and actions are regarded
primarily within their historical setting, critical evaluation is at a dis-
count, rendering history useless as a moral as well as an intellectual pursuit."[3] Some scholars writing biographies of John Adams understood these
difficulties better than others. In an effort to make John Adams useful
and relevant in his own time as well as for later generations, scholars have
worked to understand him and explain him to their readers. In the process, they sometimes crossed the line from so-called objective historian to
advocate.

Yet scholars were not the only people attempting to construct a past
that would be applicable for the present, nor were they alone in finding
John Adams a useful tool with which to do so. According to historians
Nancy Isenberg and Andrew Burstein, "It is the persistence of the Adamses in popular culture, not their omission, that best explains their popularity in the twenty-first century."[4] There is no denying that John Adams
in particular has graced many genres of culture over the years. Any argument that he has been neglected or forgotten is no longer credible. What is
interesting is *how* he has been remembered.

The public, outside of scholarly circles, found John Adams in different places and the man they discovered, while admirable, often lacked
nuance. He frequently became a caricature of himself, with the crusty
New Englander more apparent than any other trait. Part of this happened
because of the nature of the genres involved. As professor of English Linda
Hutcheon has observed, telling a written story of any kind, including an
historical event, allows the narrator to "describe, explain, summarize,
expand; the narrator has a point of view and great power to leap through
time and space and sometimes venture inside the minds of characters."[5]

Building on Hutcheon's perspective, it seems likely that the literary
genre offers the best place to look for a complete portrait of John Adams
in popular culture. From the poetry of Ezra Pound to the novels of the
early 21st century, the many qualities of John Adams's personality shine
through. In this category, he appears as a loving husband, loyal friend,
ambitious lawyer, tortured father, and dedicated patriot. In addition, all
of the writers discussed in Chapter Four put John Adams to use in ways
that advanced their own narratives. The fictionalized biographies by Samuel McCoy and Catherine Drinker Bowen emphasized Adams's ego and

passion while giving readers a sense of his accomplishments. To create their version of a usable John Adams, both authors imagined scenes and dialog to advance their points of view about him. For Ezra Pound, John Adams represented the poet's view of good government and balance. While Pound included incidents in Adams's life, what mattered most to him was Adams's attachment to balance.

Novelists such as Irving Stone, Barbara Hamilton, and Jodi Daynard, as well as playwright William Gibson, used John Adams to advance their plots. The nature of this literature allowed these writers to delve into the thinking and feeling of their characters, seeking to depict the workings of the inner mind in a way that the performing arts could not. The exception here is Gibson's *American Primitive*. Unfortunately, the play is so seldom staged that the only way to experience Gibson's interpretation of John Adams is to read the work. The fictionalized accounts of John Adams in popular literature have more in common with historiography than with most of those on the stage or screen. It would seem that to experience John Adams as a multidimensional person, the public is required to read rather than to watch.

According to Hutcheon, once an event or person moves into a film, musical, play or opera, the audience experiences the event in real time.[6] It is up to the writer or actor, then, to stage the character's thoughts and feelings. Even the finest actor would struggle with this. Many performers approached Adams as a role in a script, resisting the temptation to do further research on the historical Founder. As a result, in many instances of popular culture, the same John Adams emerges. Who is this one-dimensional figure and where did he come from? Not from scholarship or literature but from the stage.

The irritable, loud, annoying John Adams of *1776* fame is consciously or unconsciously played by actors and written by screenwriters. Again and again, the "obnoxious and disliked" trope becomes the starting point. Yet this characterization of Adams throughout his life is not entirely accurate. The musical drama *1776* captured Adams at a moment in time, a particularly intense one for him. Yet when this image of him is projected through the rest of his life, the multifaceted man gets lost. He is then dismissed as a person who was always cranky, never reasonable. This assessment may lead people to dismiss him out of hand; ignore his contributions; and look for other, more charming figures to take his place. The shrill impatience captured by the scriptwriter mirrored Adams's own writings from that period. It is also important to remember the timing of the show. The late 1960s was a period of division and turmoil in the United States, and the Founding Fathers offered an escape from that. However, the writers of *1776* did not create an instant observable unity. Their audiences needed to see the struggle that took place to get to a unanimous vote on independence. John Adams provided the consistent voice in that fight, but in order for him to achieve that goal, he became annoying, irritating, "obnoxious and disliked." Even beyond this musical, too often, this is as far as the depiction of Adams goes. One need look no further than his appearances on television to see this trend, albeit with some interesting variations on the theme.

In the years before *1776*, the television appearances of John Adams were limited to two episodes of *Profiles in Courage*. The usable John Adams in these episodes was a man of bravery in one case and a person with regrets in another. The personality traits that will become so much a part of his later depictions are present in both shows, but they are understated. John Adams is neither shrill nor particularly passionate. Yet by 1976 and *The Adams Chronicles*, the viewing audience saw an emphasis on his vanity and his unending struggle with his inner demons. The John Adams of *The Rebels* served as a sounding board for various issues that arose during the summer of 1776. Yet this portrayal offered a touch of respect in the words Philip Kent spoke to Adams—even as Adams was being self-deprecating. The documentaries on John and Abigail offered history with dramatic touches and Beale's performance in particular stands out.

Yet even these works do not present a complete image of John Adams. *Liberty's Kids* recognized his many achievements during the Revolution, but it also put other people's words into Adams's mouth and ignored historical accuracy in other ways. Finally, by 2015, and the airing of *Sons of Liberty*, John Adams is hardly recognizable. His purpose in that series was to offer a responsible adult character that would counter the teen-angst depiction of Samuel Adams. Each one of these portraits presents the man in part, and none of them address his entire life. In fact, no complete biography exists on the television screen. The closest candidate came from HBO and its adaptation of a popular historian's work.

The John Adams in popular memory received a huge boost from David McCullough. Although some scholars and a few critics have not wholly embraced his biography of Adams, it is clear that the public has. The sales figures and the time the book spent on the *New York Times* best-seller list attest to its popularity. Furthermore, McCullough became a dedicated booster for John Adams, speaking in favor of a monument in Washington, D.C., and serving as a keynote speaker at two separate statue dedications in Quincy. Interestingly, while there was a statue to Adams in Quincy's freedom park as of 1977, no statue of Adams existed in the city center until 2001, the year that McCullough's biography was published. The author was the guest speaker at the dedication ceremony for the Lloyd Lillie statue, just as he would be 17 years later for the Hancock Adams Common celebration. In addition, he lent his voice to documentaries on Adams and spoke to the media on a number of occasions, explaining his take on the Founder. Despite the criticism that McCullough's biography has received from some scholars, he captured the many sides of John Adams. Unfortunately, the miniseries based upon this work was not always successful in this.

Once again, the differences between a written narrative and a story told on the screen can account for the distinctions between McCullough's work and the HBO series. Few question Paul Giamatti's acting skills, but the scripts from which he worked did not always provide the nuance that scholars of John Adams would have liked. Historians have been critical of the series, some even unnecessarily harsh. Yet it is true that once again, the public experienced—if not a one-dimensional Adams—then an incomplete one. It is safe to say that finding a depiction of John Adams that would satisfy everyone who investigates him, either as a scholarly exercise or as part of a public history initiative, is difficult.

Many of the portrayals of John Adams on stage and screen are one-dimensional caricatures of the man. These are the issues that frustrate many staff members at the Adams National Historical Park. These people, who know John Adams as well as anyone can two hundred years later, wish the public to understand as much about John Adams as possible. For curator Kelly Cobble, in an ideal world, people would come to the park with no preconceived notions, with open minds. The question is, without the depictions in popular culture, would tourists go to the park at all? Cobble herself admitted that the park was a quiet site until the 1980s, when Paul C. Nagel brought the family to the forefront of scholarship. However, the evidence also suggests that the *1776* John Adams is so prevalent in the popular mind, escaping it is difficult. HBO's miniseries simply reinforced this image. Still, both of these pieces have brought visitors to Quincy.

In Adams's hometown, the public has the benefit of those who have studied John Adams and have also presented his legacy. For the interpreters at the Adams National Historical Park, their roles are ever changing, depending on the popular culture dominating at any given time. As Kelly Cobble asserted, the task ahead for the park is how to place Adams in the broader context of history. How does a park that tells the story of a white Founding Father navigate the emerging and necessary need for the reassessment of those who created the United States? Further, how will the reconstruction of the past, history that is relevant to all U.S. citizens, affect the image of John Adams in the public's memory? This is an ongoing opportunity for the Adams National Historical Park and its subject, a task that the staff is honored to embrace. It is also a struggle for all such sites in the National Park Service as well as those supported by private foundations whose job it is to preserve the history of the United States.

Who the public remembers and how they commemorate those people is under close scrutiny in the 21st century. How does a nation come to terms with white men and women who lived in the 18th and 19th centuries? When addressing the popular memory of John Adams, is it enough to assert, as David McCullough did on a number of occasions, that he never owned an enslaved person? Adams visited the topic of slavery several times in his later life, writing twice that "I never owned a slave."[7] On the other hand, he also wrote that he did not believe in reproaching his contemporaries who were slaveowners. "They have given proofs of dispositions favourable to the gradual abolition of Slavery, more explicit than could have been expected," he reasoned. "All Nations civil and Savage have practiced Slavery and time must be allowed to eradicate an Evil that has infected the whole Earth."[8]

Adams was clearly disturbed by the subject of slavery and did not know how to solve the problem. This perceived ambiguity toward the practice is troubling to scholars, as is the fact that, in his defense of the British soldiers in 1770, he included racist remarks that 21st-century Americans find offensive. This means that 21st-century observers require more than the mere absence of slaves in his household. Adams thought slavery an evil but did little to eradicate it. Therefore, his aversion to owning slaves is little comfort to people who expect more of their Founders. John Adams, along with the entire Revolutionary generation, is once again under scrutiny for his views in scholarly circles, even as a new production of *1776* offers a fresh perspective on the summer of independence. What does all this mean for the public memory of the American Revolution and those who participated in it?

In the 250 or so years since the beginning of the imperial crisis with England, scholars and the public alike have attempted to find meaning in the American Revolution. In many ways, it has been a keystone for the usable past of various generations. As historian Michael Kammen asserted, the American Revolution "stands as the single most important source for our national sense of tradition—such as it is, and insofar as we can be said to possess one."[9] This rather conditional statement demonstrates the dilemma faced by scholars and the public in attempting to interpret the past in the face of diverse perspectives. This, in turn, leads to discomfort in assessing the role of the Founding Fathers. Even though he was writing in the late 1970s, Kammen sensed this uneasiness. He wrote, "So we have been uncertain how properly to praise the character of our Founding Fathers without enshrining them uncritically as demigods. On the other hand, we do not quite know how to humanize them without either demeaning or stripping them of their exemplary qualities."[10]

In this sense, John Adams stands out as an unusual example amongst the Founders. He has rarely, if ever been seen as a demigod. If anything, he has, to an inordinate degree, been humanized both in scholarship and popular culture. However, in examining artistic works, John Adams has also been used as a counter to those Founders who have achieved something closer to demigod status. Even as he was praised for his courage, his honesty, and his commitment, he was also remembered as irritable, arrogant, vain, and difficult. His humor and his loyalty to his friends were rarely useful to artists as they constructed his image for their purposes. There are exceptions and they provide the most well-rounded depictions of Adams, but the qualities that made him endearing to his friends were more often than not downplayed or absent. While not a demigod, John Adams is equally one-dimensional and therefore not fully human in popular culture.

In March of 1797, after delivering his Presidential Inaugural Address, John Adams turned introspective while writing to Abigail concerning the occasion. He wrote, "I have been So Strangely Used in this Country, so belied and so undefended—that I was determined to say some Things, as an Appeal to Posterity. Foreign nations and future times will understand them better than my Ennemies, or friends will own they do."[11] Even during his lifetime, John Adams knew he was being interpreted and adapted, often to meet the needs of his political opponents. Yet he hoped that generations in the future would understand him better than his contemporaries did. However, discerning who John Adams really was is difficult. All scholars can do is dive into his papers to find his innermost thoughts. The public depends upon the popular culture put before it. If those images cause people to investigate further, to pick up a biography of John Adams or to read his letters to his family and friends, then those of us in "future times" might develop a better understanding of him.

Whether more public attention to Adams will lead to a monument in Washington, D.C., is difficult to say. It has not thus far, and it may be an idea whose time has passed—especially given the current reassessment of who and what we commemorate in this way. According to Michael Kammen, "we have not always been comfortable about the suitability of monuments and memorials in a society whose stated ethos, at least is egalitarian."[12] This statement, published in 1978, still rings true. In the end, the question of monument or no monument is less important than the realization that there are many ways to remember an event and those who participated in it. Moreover, people do find value in remembering the past, but it is a complex practice. According to Catharine R. Stimpson, human beings are *driven* to remember and ask questions of history. "We wonder what of the past remains for us.... We wonder, too, what the past has denied us; what is irretrievably gone. We query the framework and content of our own reconstructions. We are aware that because of faulty records, wavering memories, nostalgia, or ideology, we regard history with one blurred eye."[13]

John Adams understood the complexity that Stimpson described. In one of the last letters he wrote, he declined an invitation to attend the celebration of the 50th anniversary of independence. He asserted the importance of the occasion by calling it "A Memorable epoch in the annals of the human race." Yet Adams warned that the meaning of the day would forever be subject to interpretation. He said the anniversary of American independence was "destined, in future history, to form the brightest or the blackest page, according to the use or the abuse of those political institutions by which they shall, in time to come, be shaped, by the *human mind.*"[14] Adams clearly understood the concept of historical interpretation and of a usable past. Of how *he* should be used in that history, John Adams had nothing left to say.

Chapter Notes

Introduction

1. For the Jonathan Sewall story, see David McCullough, *John Adams* (New York: Simon and Schuster, 2001), 71; 348–350.

2. Evan Thomas, "Founders Chic: Live from Philadelphia," *Newsweek,* July 9, 2001, 48.

3. Gregory H. Nobles, "Historians Extend the Reach of the American Revolution," *Whose American Revolution Was It? Historians Interpret the Founding,* edited by Alfred F. Young and Gregory H. Nobles (New York: New York University Press, 2011), 137, n2. For the connection to *Hamilton,* see for example, Ken Owens, "Historians and Hamilton: Founders Chic and the Cult of Personality," *The Junto: A Group Blog on The American Revolution,* April 21, 2016, Accessed December 11, 2021. https://earlyamericanists.com/2016/04/21/historians-and-hamilton-founders-chic-and-the-cult-of-personality/; Andrew M. Schocket, "The Founders Chic of *Hamilton,*" *NYU Press Blog,* October 9, 2015, Accessed December 11, 2021. https://www.fromthesquare.org/the-founders-chic-of-hamilton/.

4. Catharine R. Stimpson, Preface to *Past Meets Present: Essays about Historic Interpretation and Public Audiences,* edited by Jo Blatti (Washington, D.C.: Smithsonian Institution Press: 1986), ix.

5. Van Wyck Brooks, "On Creating a Usable Past," *The Dial: A Fortnightly Journal of Criticism and Discussion of Literature and the Arts,* Volume LXIV (Chicago: The Dial Publishing Company, January 3 to June 6, 1918): 337–341. Quotes on page 339.

6. For some examples of scholars' use of the term "usable past," see Casey Nelson Blake, "The Usable Past, the Comfortable Past, and the Civic Past: Memory in Contemporary America," *Cultural Anthropology,* Volume 14, No. 3 (August 1999): 423–435; Colin Gordon, "Crafting a Usable Past: Consensus, Ideology, and Historians of the American Revolution," *The William and Mary Quarterly,* Volume 46, No. 4 (October, 1989): 671–695; J.V. Matthews, "'Whig History': The New England Whigs and a Usable Past," *The New England Quarterly,* Volume 51, No. 2 (June 1978): 193–208.

7. Peter C. Rollins, Ed., *Hollywood As Historian: American Film in a Cultural Context,* Revised Edition (Lexington, Kentucky: The University of Kentucky Press, 1983), 1.

8. See Thomas L. Connelly, *The Marble Man: Robert E. Lee and His Image in American Society* (Baton Rouge, LA: Louisiana State University Press, 1977); William Garrett Piston, *Lee's Tarnished Lieutenant: James Longstreet and His Place in Southern History* (Athens, GA: The University of Georgia Press, 1987).

9. Michael Kammen, *A Season of Youth: The American Revolution and the Historical Imagination* (Ithaca and London: Cornell University Press, 1978), 3; xv.

10. See François Furstenberg, *In the Name of The Father: Washington's Legacy, Slavery, and the Making of a Nation* (New York: Penguin Books, 2006).

11. Andrew M. Schocket, *Fighting Over the Founders: How We Remember the American Revolution* (New York: New York University Press, 2015), 4.

12. Michael D. Hattem, *Past and Prologue: Politics and Memory in the American Revolution* (New Haven: Yale University Press, 2020), 3.

13. Keith Beutler, *George Washington's Hair: How Early Americans Remembered the Founders* (Charlottesville: University of Virginia Press, 2021).

14. Edith B. Gelles, "The Abigail Industry," *The William and Mary Quarterly*, Volume 45, No 4. (October 1988): 656–683.

15. Alfred F. Young, *The Shoemaker and The Tea Party: Memory and the American Revolution* (Boston: Beacon Press, 1999), vii.

16. Mitch Kachun, *First Martyr of Liberty: Crispus Attucks in American Memory* (Oxford: Oxford University Press, 2017), 5.

17. The author's term.

18. John Adams to William Sumner, March 28, 1809, Founders Online, National Archives, Accessed August 5, 2019, https://founders.archives.gov/documents/Adams/99-02-02-5328.

19. Robert Rosenstone, *History on Film/Film on History* (New York: Pearson Longman, 2006), 9; 2.

Chapter One

1. Since I am using information from various biographies and from Adams's own words for this chapter, I will keep the endnotes to a minimum.

2. For the history of this find, see L.H. Butterfield, "Introduction," *The Earliest Diary of John Adams* (Cambridge: The Belknap Press of Harvard University Press, 1966), 2.

3. John Adams, June 8, 1755, *The Earliest Diary of John Adams*, 43. The editor explained in a footnote that Powers was Peter Powers, a classmate of John Adams.

4. For John Quincy's attitudes toward his father's autobiography, see Joseph Ellis, *Passionate Sage: The Character and Legacy of John Adams* (New York: W.W. Norton and Company, 1993), 59.

5. On September 2, 1752, the English Parliament voted to adopt the Gregorian Calendar to replace the Julian Calendar. As result of the shift in calendars, September 2nd was followed immediately by September 14th. Therefore, John Adams's birthday moved from October 19th to October 30th, the day it is commemorated now. For an interesting overview of this calendar change and the reactions to it, see Richard Cavendish, "The Gregorian Calendar Adopted in England, September 2nd, 1752," *History Today*, Volume 52, Issue 9 (September 2002): 54.

6. John Adams, *Diary and Autobiography of John Adams*, Volume 3: Diary 1782–1804, Autobiography Through 1776 (Cambridge: Harvard University Press, 1962), 256. For the full genealogy Adams provided, see 254–257. Hereafter cited as *Diary and Autobiography*.

7. *Ibid.*, 257.

8. *Ibid.*, 262.

9. John Adams, March 15, 1756, *Diary and Autobiography*, Volume 1, Diary 1755–1770 (Cambridge: Harvard University Press, 1962), 13–14.

10. *Ibid.*, August 23, 1756, 44.

11. Understandably, Adams was distraught by this. See his diary entry on the subject, John Adams, Friday, December 29, 1758 in *Diary and Autobiography*, Volume 1, 64–65.

12. See Joseph Ellis, *First Family: Abigail and John Adams* (New York: Alfred A. Knopt, 2010), 3–7.

13. Abigail Adams to John Adams, March 31, 1776, *Adams Family Correspondence,* Volume 1, Adams Family Papers Digital Edition, Accessed on June 28, 2019. https://www.masshist.org/publications/adams-papers/index.php/view/ADMS-04-01-02-0241#sn=0.

14. John Adams to Abigail Adams, April 14, 1776, *Adams Family Correspondence,* Volume 1, Adams Family Papers Digital Edition, Accessed on June 28, 2019. https://www.masshist.org/publications/adams-papers/index.php/view/ADMS-04-01-02-0248.

15. For an excellent analysis of Abigail's "Remember the Ladies" letter, see Woody Holton, *Abigail Adams* (New York: Free Press, 2009), 99–105.

16. Colin Nicolson and Owen Dudley Edwards, *Imaginary Friendship in the American Revolution: John Adams and Jonathan Sewall* (New York: Routledge, 2019), 22; 30.

17. For the mystery surrounding the identity of *Massachusettensis*, see *Ibid.*, 13–14.

18. Page Smith, *John Adams*, Volume 1, The Library of the Presidents, Collector's Edition (Norwalk, Connecticut: The Easton Press, 1963), 100–101.

19. Nicolson and Edwards, 111.

20. John Adams, *Diary and Autobiography* Volume 2 (Cambridge: Harvard University Press, 1962), 121. For an example of his note-taking skills in the meetings of the Congress see 124–126. Here he quotes Patrick Henry asserting that "I am not a Virginian, but an American." How Adams felt about this statement, he did not record. Quotation on 125.

21. *Ibid.*, 150.

22. For an interesting study on John Adams's memory of the events of 1776, see Robert E. McGlone, "Deciphering Memory: John Adams and the Authorship of the Declaration of Independence," *The Journal of American History*, Volume 85, No. 2 (September 1998): 411–438.

23. John Adams, *Diary and Autobiography*, Volume 2, 276–77.

24. *Ibid.*, 286; For Butterfield's information on Adams's follow-up to Barron's death, see 287, n 4.

25. For Adams's description of the infighting see *Ibid.*, 304.

26. *Ibid.*, 305.

27. Massachusetts Court System, "Guide to John Adams and the Massachusetts Constitution," Mass. gov, Accessed October 15, 2021. https://www.mass.gov/guides/john-adams-the-massachusetts-constitution.

28. For Adams's feelings about Franklin and how they affected his diplomatic efforts, see Chapter Three on the recent historiography of Adams.

29. For an insightful look into Abigail's feelings concerning John's diplomatic work and his ambition, see Ellis, *First Family*, 103–107.

30. *The Massachusetts Centinel*, June 18, 1788, quoted in *Diary and Autobiography*, Volume 3, 216, n 7.

31. *Ibid.* In this very long footnote, Butterfield describes in detail Adams's homecoming up to and including his purchase of the John Borland house, now Peacefield.

32. John Adams to Abigail Adams, December 19, 1793, Adams Family Correspondence, Volume 9, *Adams Papers*, Digital Edition. Accessed October 18, 2021. https://www.masshist.org/publications/adams-papers/index.php/view/ADMS-04-09-02-0278#sn=0.

33. John R. Howe Jr., *The Changing Political Thought of John Adams* (Prince-

ton: Princeton University Press, 1966), 194–195.

34. For a thorough discussion of this split in the Federalist Party, see Manning J. Dauer, *The Adams Federalists* (Baltimore: John Hopkins University Press, 1953). Dauer concentrated on the Adams Presidency while Howe investigated Adams's political thought through the Revolution, his presidency, and his retirement years.

35. Howe, 199–200.

36. Dauer, 265.

37. Howe, *The Changing Political Thought of John Adams,* 211.

38. For John Adams blaming Hamilton for the acts see John Adams to Benjamin Rush, July 25, 1808, *John Adams: Writings from the New Nation, 1784–1826*, edited by Gordon Wood (New York: The Library of America, 2016), 501. For quotation, see John Adams to Benjamin Rush, December 25, 1811, *John Adams: Writings from the New Nation, 1784–1826*, 529.

39. John Adams to Abigail Adams, May 19, 1794, *Adams Family Papers: An Electronic Archive*, Accessed October 19, 2021. https://www.masshist.org/digitaladams/archive/doc?id=L17940519jasecond.

40. Ellis, *First Family*, 210–11.

41. John Adams to Thomas Boylston Adams, December 18, 1800, quoted in *Ibid.*, 209. Ellis noted that Adams had renounced Charles in life, but that his love for him still ran deep.

42. *Ibid.*, 213.

43. John Adams to Abigail Adams, November 2, 1800, *Adams Family Papers: An Electronic Archive*. Accessed October 19, 2021. https://www.masshist.org/digitaladams/archive/doc?id=L18001102ja.

44. For the history of the quotation's carving, see "State Dining Room," *The White House Historical Association*. Accessed October 19, 2021. https://www.whitehousehistory.org/white-house-tour/state-dining-room.

45. John Adams to Thomas Jefferson, October 20, 1818, *John Adams: Writings from the New Nation, 1784–1826*, 642.

46. Thomas Jefferson to John Adams, November 13, 1818, *Collections Online*, Massachusetts Historical Society. Accessed October 19, 2021. https://www.masshist.org/database/viewer.php?item_id=1746&pid=36.

47. L.H. Butterfield, "The Jubilee of

Independence: July 4, 1826," *The Virginia Magazine of History and Biography*, Volume 6, No. 2 (April 1953): 119–21. Quotation on page 119.

48. John Adams, quoted in Ellis, *First Family*, 254.

49. John Quincy Adams, quoted in Smith, *John Adams*, Volume 2, 1137.

50. Nathaniel Bowditch, quoted in Ellis, *Passionate Sage*, 210.

51. John A. Shaw, *Eulogy on John Adams and Thomas Jefferson, Delivered August 2, 1826 by Request of the Inhabitants of Bridgewater* (Taunton, MA., S.W. Mortimer, 1826), 7.

52. *Ibid.*, 8.

53. *Ibid.*, 10.

54. *Ibid.*, 17; 20.

55. Daniel Webster, *A Discourse in Commemoration of the Lives and Services of John Adams and Thomas Jefferson, Delivered in Faneuil Hall, Boston, August 2, 1826*, reprinted in *A Selectin of Eulogies: Pronounced in the Several States in Honor of Those Illustrious Patriots and Statesmen, John Adams and Thomas Jefferson*, Kindle (Hartford, Connecticut: D.F. Robinson & Co., 1826; edition: HardPress, 2018), 3656–3657.

56. J.V. Matthews, "'Whig History': The New England Whigs and a Usable Past," *The New England Quarterly*, volume 51, No. 2 (June 1978): 193 for all quotes.

57. *Ibid.*, 199.

58. *Ibid.*

59. *Ibid.*, 201; 202.

60. *Ibid.*, 206.

Chapter Two

1. The two works are Samuel McCoy's *This Man Adams: The Man Who Never Died* and Catherine Drinker Bowen's *John Adams and the American Revolution*. Both writers used Adams's own works and other primary sources to write their narratives. Yet they also engaged literary strategies, invented dialog, and created scenes much as a novelist would. Therefore, I have made the decision to include them in the literature chapter.

2. John Quincy Adams and Charles Francis Adams, *John Adams, 2 Volumes* (Philadelphia: Lippincott, 1871); American Statesmen Series, Arthur M. Schlesinger, Jr. General Editor, reprint 1980.

3. *Ibid.*, quotation on back cover.

4. See for example, his discussion of Adams's absence from Thomas Jefferson's inauguration. *Ibid.*, Volume 2, 353–354.

5. Theodore Parker, *Historic Americans* (United Kingdom: H.B. Fuller, 1871), 201; 211–212; 216.

6. *Ibid.*, 231. Capitalization is as published.

7. Gilbert Chinard, *Honest John Adams* (Boston: Little, Brown, and Company, 1933), v.

8. *Ibid.*

9. *Ibid.*, 346.

10. *Ibid.*, 23.

11. *Ibid.*

12. *Ibid.*, 32–33.

13. *Ibid.*, 76; 88.

14. *Ibid.*, 70–71.

15. *Ibid.*, 282–3.

16. See Chinard, 333–335.

17. See John Adams, *The Works of John Adams, Second President of the United States: With a Life of the Author*, edited by Charles Francis Adams (Boston: Little Brown, and Company, 1850–56).

18. A discussion of this appears later in this chapter.

19. Zoltán Haraszti, *John Adams and The Prophets of Progress: A Study in the Intellectual and Political History of the Eighteenth Century* (New York: Grosset & Dunlap, 1952), vi.

20. *Ibid.*, 9.

21. Dena Kleiman, "Lyman H. Butterfield, Editor of The Adams Papers," *New York Times*, April 26, 1982, Section B., page 14. Accessed October 12, 2021. https://www.nytimes.com/1982/04/26/obituaries/lyman-h-butterfield-editor-of-the-adams-papers.html.

22. Lyman H. Butterfield, "The Papers of the Adams Family: Some Account of Their History," *Proceedings of the Massachusetts Historical Society*, Third Series, Volume 71 (October 1953-May 1957): 328–356. Quotation on page 352.

23. *Ibid.*, 355; 356.

24. "John Adams and America's Birthday: Behind the Scenes of History—New Series on The Adams Papers," *Life*, June 30, 1961, 79.

25. Lyman Butterfield, quoted in *Ibid.*

26. "Private Thoughts of a Founding Father," *Life*, June 30, 1961, 81.

27. John F. Kennedy, "Review of *The*

Adams Papers, Series I, Diaries. Diary and Autobiography of John Adams," *The American Historical Review*, Volume 68, No. 2 (January 1963): 478–480. Quotations on 479.

28. Edmund S. Morgan, "John Adams and the Puritan Tradition," *The New England Quarterly*, Volume 34, No. 4 (December 1961): 519.

29. *Ibid.*, 520–21.

30. *Ibid.* For comparison of Winthrop and Adams see page 527. For quotation, see page 529.

31. Bernard Bailyn is known for many works, but his most famous is *The Ideological Origins of The American Revolution*, published in 1967. Bernard Bailyn, *The Ideological Origins of the American Revolution* (Cambridge: Harvard University Press, 1967).

32. Bernard Bailyn, "Butterfield's Adams: Notes for a Sketch," *The William and Mary Quarterly*, Volume 19, No. 2 (April 1962): 244.

33. *Ibid.*, 246.

34. *Ibid.* For Chinard's assessment of Adams, the writer, see discussion of Chinard, earlier in this chapter.

35. Bailyn, "Butterfield's Adams" 250.

36. *Ibid.*

37. Page Smith, *John Adams: Volume I 1735–1784; Volume II 1784–1826*, The Library of the Presidents, Collector's Edition (Norwalk, Connecticut: The Easton Press, 1963), vii.

38. Smith, Volume II, 1139.

39. *Ibid.*

40. *Ibid.*

41. *Ibid.*

42. Smith, Volume I, vii.

43. *Ibid.*, viii.

44. *Ibid.* 1.

45. See John Adams, *Diary*, Volume 3, *Adams Papers*, Digital Edition, Massachusetts Historical Society, Accessed June 10, 2020. https://www.masshist.org/publications/adams-papers/index.php/view/ADMS-01-03-02-0016-0002#sn=0.

46. Smith, Volume I, 13.

47. *Ibid.*, 70–71.

48. Smith also covers this revelation in depth. See Smith, Volume II, 952–965.

49. The name of the party founded by Jefferson can be confusing. It is often listed as the Democratic-Republican Party but gets shorten to simply the Republican Party. It, however, is not the same party that was founded in 1855, the Republican Party still in existence today.

50. The Sedition Act, "Transcript of the Alien and Sedition Acts, 1798," www.Ourdocuments.gov, Accessed 10 July 2020. https://www.ourdocuments.gov/doc.php?flash=false&doc=16&page=transcript#no-3.

51. Smith, 976.

52. *Ibid.*, 977.

53. *Ibid.*

54. *Ibid.*

55. *Ibid.*

56. *Ibid.*, 978.

57. See, for example, Chinard's treatment of the acts in which he quotes Adams blaming Alexander Hamilton for them. Chinard, 275–276; David McCullough called the acts "infamous and claimed them to be "rightly judged by history as the most reprehensible acts of his presidency." Yet, he, too emphasized putting them in the context of "tumult and fear." David McCullough, *John Adams* (New York: Simon and Schuster, 2001), 504.

58. Anne Husted Burleigh, *John Adams* (New Brunswick: Transaction Publishers, 1969), 340.

59. Smith, 1056.

60. *Ibid.*, 1058.

61. *Ibid.*, 1070,1078, 1087.

62. *Ibid.*, 1082

63. *Ibid.*, 1138.

64. Burleigh, *John Adams*, 1.

65. Burleigh, Introduction to the Transaction Edition, ix.

66. *Ibid.*

67. See Bernard Bailyn, *The Ideological Origins of the American Revolution*; Gordon S. Wood, *The Creation of the American Republic, 1776–1787* (Chapel Hill and London: Published for the Omohundro Institute of Early American History and Culture at Williamsburg, Virginia, by The University of North Carolina Press, 1969).

68. Burleigh, Introduction to the Transaction Edition, xi.

69. Burleigh, 143.

Chapter Three

1. Tammy S. Gordon, *The Spirit of 1976: Commerce, Community, and the Politics of*

Commemoration (Amherst: University of
Massachusetts Press, 2013), 1.
  2. *Ibid.*, 6.
  3. *Ibid.*, 9.
  4. For a list of the Bicentennial Minutes, see https://www.imdb.com/title/tt0224835/. For a critique, see Eric Sterner, May 18, 2021, "Bicentennial Minutes" *Emerging Revolutionary War Era*, Accessed August 27, 2021. https://emergingrevolutionarywar.org/2021/05/18/bicentennial-minutes/. For *The Adams Chronicles*, See Chapter Five, "John Adams on the Small Screen."
  5. See Thomas Wendel, "The Character of John Adams," *The American Historical Review*, Volume 84, No. 2 (April 1979): 541–542; Robert M. Calhoon, "John Adams and the Psychology of Power," *Reviews in American History*, Volume 4, No. 4 (December 1976): 520–525.
  6. Peter Shaw, *The Character of John Adams* (Chapel Hill: The University of North Carolina Press, Published for the Institute of Early American History and Culture, Williamsburg, Virginia, 1976), vii.
  7. *Ibid.* For a discussion of Pound's depiction of John Adams in the *Cantos*, see Chapter Four of this book.
  8. Shaw, viii.
  9. *Ibid.* Interestingly, in a jab to certain academic terms, Shaw added, "If the word 'interdisciplinary' had not come to connote the avoidance of all disciplines rather than the use of more than one, I would have subtitled this work 'an interdisciplinary study.'"
  10. Shaw, 15.
  11. *Ibid.*, 162.
  12. *Ibid.*, 279.
  13. *Ibid.*
  14. The public sometimes forgets that Franklin, too, was raised in Massachusetts by a Puritan father. See Edmund S. Morgan, *Benjamin Franklin* (New Haven: Yale University Press, 2002), 16–17.
  15. Shaw, 281.
  16. *Ibid.*
  17. *Ibid.*, 314.
  18. For a brief overview of some of the fighting that occurred amongst the founders, see Paul Aron, *Founding Feuds: The Rivalries, Clashes, and Conflicts That Forged a Nation* (Williamsburg, VA: Sourcebooks, 2016).

  19. The author's term.
  20. Stephen Floyd, "The Best Biographies of John Adams," My Journey Through the Best Presidential Biographies, Word Press.com, March 9, 2013, Accessed July 24, 2021. https://bestpresidentialbios.com/2013/03/09/the-best-biographies-of-john-adams/.
  21. See John Ferling, "'Oh That I was a soldier': John Adams and the Anguish of War," *American Quarterly*, Volume 36, No. 2 (Summer, 1984): 258–275; John Ferling, "John Adams: Diplomat," *The William and Mary Quarterly*, Volume 51, No. 2 (April 1994): 227–252; John Ferling and Lewis E. Braverman, "John Adams' Health Reconsidered," *The William and Mary Quarterly*, Volume 55, No. 1 (January 1998): 83–104.
  22. John Ferling, *John Adams: A Life* (New York: Henry Holt and Company, 1992), vii.
  23. *Ibid.*, 3.
  24. For all of the quotations and comparisons in this paragraph, see *Ibid.*, 3–4.
  25. *Ibid.*, 30.
  26. *Ibid.*, 5.
  27. John Adams to François Adriaan Van der Kemp, 29 January 1807, *Founders Online*, National Archives, Accessed September 17, 2021. https://founders.archives.gov/documents/Adams/99-02-02-5164.
  28. *Ibid.*
  29. Ferling, *John Adams*, 449–450.
  30. *Ibid.*, 450.
  31. *Ibid.*, 451.
  32. *Ibid.*, 453–454. Quotation on 454.
  33. John Ferling, "John Adams, Diplomat," 227.
  34. *Ibid.*, 228.
  35. *Ibid.*
  36. Here, Ferling was countering the earlier work of historian William C. Stinchcombe, who believed that the Model Treaty was really nothing new. See William C. Stinchcombe, "John Adams and the Model Treaty" in *The American Revolution and 'A Candid World*,' edited by Lawrence S. Kaplan (Kent, Ohio: Kent State University Press, 1977), 69–84.
  37. *Ibid.*, 229. Ferling quoted James H. Hutson, *John Adams and the Diplomacy of the American Revolution* (Lexington, KY., 1980), 37–44.
  38. *Ibid.*
  39. *Ibid.*
  40. *Ibid.*, 230.

41. *Ibid.*, 235; 244–45.

42. *Ibid.*, 249.

43. *Ibid.*

44. *Ibid.*, 251.

45. *Ibid.*, 251–252.

46. The portion of Braintree in which Adams was born and raised was set off in 1792 and renamed Quincy in honor of Colonel John Quincy.

47. Benjamin Franklin to Robert R. Livingston quoted in "John Adams's Health Reconsidered," 83.

48. *Ibid.*, 84.

49. *Ibid.*

50. *Ibid.*

51. *Ibid.*

52. *Ibid.*, 88.

53. *Ibid.*, 104.

54. Joseph J. Ellis, *Passionate Sage: The Character and Legacy of John Adams* (New York: W.W. Norton, 1993), 11–12.

55. Donald H. Stewart and George P. Clark, "Misanthrope or Humanitarian" John Adams in Retirement," *The New England Quarterly.* Volume 28., No. 2 (June 1955): 236.

56. Ellis, *Passionate Sage,* 12.

57. *Ibid.*, 60–61. Ellis discussed all three of these attempts to set the record straight in great detail. See Ellis, Chapter 3, "History and Heroes."

58. *Ibid.*, 100.

59. John Adams to Hezekiah Niles, February 13, 1818, *John Adams: Writings from the New Nation, 1784–1826*, Edited by Gordon S. Wood (New York: The Library of America, 2016), 629.

60. Ellis, *Passionate Sage*, 105.

61. *Ibid.*, 107. For Adams quotation, see John Adams to Benjamin Rush, October 22, 1812, *Founders Online*, National Archives, Accessed October 8, 2021. https://founders.archives.gov/documents/Adams/99-02-02-5883.

62. The entire correspondence between Adams and Jefferson was originally edited and published by Lester J. Cappon in 1959. *The Adams-Jefferson Letters: The Complete Correspondence Between Thomas Jefferson and Abigail and John Adams*, 2 Volumes (Chapel Hill: University of North Carolina Press, 1959). For the most recent discussion of the Adams-Jefferson friendship, see Gordon S. Wood, *Friends Divided: John Adams and Thomas Jefferson* (New York: Penguin Press, 2017).

63. Ellis, *Passionate Sage*, 135. In a long footnote on these ideas, Ellis explained the historical debate concerning Jefferson's ties to liberalism and Adams's to conservatism as well as radicalism. See Ellis, notes from pages 132–136, note 42 on page 258.

64. *Ibid.*, 179–180.

65. *Ibid.*, 185.

66. *Ibid.*

67. *Ibid.*, 185–186. For a contrast of Adams's and Jefferson's views on women, see page 187.

68. For a thorough discussion of this development see *Ibid.*, 216–224.

69. *Ibid.*, 242.

70. Richard D. Brown, "The Apotheosis of John Adams," *The William and Mary Quarterly* Volume 59, No. 1 (January 2002): 305; 314. In this review, Brown discussed C. Bradley Thompson, *John Adams and the Spirit of Liberty*; John Ferling, *Setting the World Ablaze: Washington, Adams, Jefferson, and the American Revolution*; David McCullough, *John Adams.*

71. James Grant, *John Adams: Party of One* (New York: Farrar, Straus and Giroux, 2005), 39.

72. *Ibid.*, 4.

73. *Ibid.*, 268–269.

74. John Adams to Abigail Adams, July 1, 1782 in *Adams Family Correspondence* volume 4, *Adams Papers* Digital Edition, Massachusetts Historical Society, Accessed August 26, 2021. https://www.masshist.org/publications/adams-papers/index.php/view/ADMS-04-04-02-0224#sn=0.

75. *Ibid.*

76. John Adams to Josiah Quincy, October 6th, 1775 in *Papers of John Adams*, Volume 3, Digital Edition, Massachusetts Historical Society, Accessed August 23, 2021. https://www.masshist.org/publications/adams-papers/index.php/view/ADMS-06-03-02-0095#sn=0.

77. Grant, 157.

78. John R. Howe, Jr., *The Changing Political Thought of John Adams* (Princeton: Princeton University Press, 1966), xiii.

79. *Ibid.*, 318.

80. For quotations from the original Massachusetts Constitution, see John Adams, *The Report of a Constitution or Form of Government for the Common-*

wealth of Massachusetts in *John Adams: Revolutionary Writings, 1775–1783* edited by Gordon Wood (New York: The Library of America, 2011), 250, 260, 262, 264, 269. All caps in original. For Grant's assertion on the Protestant faith, see Grant, 446.

81. Grant, 446.

82. See Arthur Scherr, "John Adams, Political Moderation, and the 1820 Massachusetts Constitutional Convention: A Reappraisal" in *Historical Journal of Massachusetts*, Volume 46, No. 1 (Winter 2018): 114–159. In this article, Scherr cites this error in Chinard's *Honest John Adams* as well as in McCullough's biography. To his credit, he also acknowledged that he, too, in earlier writings, had made this assertion.

83. Grant, 450.

84. *Ibid.*, 222.

85. *Ibid.*, 164.

86. Edith B. Gelles, *Abigail and John: Portrait of A Marriage* (New York: Harper Perennial, 2009), xi.

87. Joseph J. Ellis, *First Family: Abigail and John Adams* (New York: Alfred A. Knopf, 2010), x.

88. Sara Georgini, *Household Gods: The Religious Lives of The Adams Family* (Oxford: Oxford University Press, 2019).

89. Jeanne E. Abrams, *A View from Abroad: The Story of John and Abigail Adams in Europe* (New York: New York University Press, 2021).

90. Ronald Angelo Johnson, *Diplomacy in Black and White: John Adams, Toussaint Louverture, and Their Atlantic World Alliance* (Athens: The University of Georgia Press, 2014); Arthur Scherr, *John Adams, Slavery, and Race: Ideas, Politics, and Diplomacy in an Age of Crisis* (Santa Barbara, California: Praeger, 2018).

91. R.B. Bernstein, *The Education of John Adams* (Oxford: Oxford University Press, 2020).

92. Dan Abrams and David Fisher, *John Adams Under Fire: The Founding Father's Fight for Justice in The Boston Massacre Murder Trial* (Toronto: Hanover Square Press, 2020).

93. The author's term.

94. Scherr, "John Adams, Political Moderation, and the 1820 Massachusetts Constitutional Convention: A Reappraisal," 117.

Chapter Four

1. Fanny Butcher, "The Literary Spotlight," *The Chicago Tribune*, May 14, 1950, 194.

2. Samuel McCoy, *This Man Adams: The Man Who Never Died* (New York: Brentano's, 1928), 15.

3. *Ibid.*, 16.

4. *Ibid.*, 29. Italics in the original.

5. *Ibid.*, 31. Italics in the original. Capitalization as it appears in the original.

6. *Ibid.*, 175. Italics in the original.

7. *Ibid.*, 183.

8. For the entire argument, see *Ibid.*, 175–211.

9. McCoy, 227.

10. *Ibid.*, 214–15. Italics in original.

11. *Ibid.*, 278.

12. John Adams to John Quincy Adams, May 14, 1781, *Adams Family Correspondence,* Volume 4, Adams Papers, Digital Edition, Accessed February 19, 2020. https://www.masshist.org/publications/adams-papers/index.php/view/ADMS-04-04-02-0078.

13. Alec Marsh, *Ezra Pound* (London, England: Reaktion Books, Limited, 2011), 14.

14. David Ten Eyck, *Ezra Pound's Adams Cantos* (London: Bloomsbury, 2012), 14.

15. *Ibid.*, 15. This is the spelling of "principle" that the author used.

16. *Ibid.*, 16.

17. Marsh, 124.

18. *Ibid.*, 125.

19. *Ibid.*, 125–126. For Marsh's full argument concerning fascism, Mussolini, and Pound, see 124–126.

20. Marsh provided a detailed description of Pound's work in the period of the 1930s and the connections Pound was making between Italy and the American Revolution. See *Ibid.*, 129–134.

21. See Marsh, Chapter Ten, "Madman or Political Prisoner?" for details of the case against Pound and the outcome.

22. Ten Eyck, 1.

23. *Ibid.*

24. Frederick K. Sanders, *John Adams Speaking: Pound's Sources For the Adams Cantos* (Orono, Maine: University of Maine Press, 1975), 2.

25. *Ibid.*, 3.

26. *Ibid.*, 4.

27. For Sanders's overview of the ne-

glect of the "Adams Cantos" see *Ibid.*, 7–15.

28. *Ibid.*, 15.

29. Clinton Rossiter, "The Legacy of John Adams," *The Yale Review*, 46 (1957): 529. Quoted in *Ibid.*, 16.

30. Sanders, 18.

31. Ten Eyck, 17.

32. *Ibid.*, 18.

33. Ten Eyck, 65.

34. *Ibid.*

35. Sanders, 20–21.

36. Because quoting works of poetry is problematic, I will simply be restructuring Pound's themes. Readers who are interested in the "Adams Cantos," can find them within *The Cantos of Ezra Pound*. They are Cantos LXII through LXXI. For my reading, I used Ezra Pound, *The Cantos of Ezra Pound* (New York: A New Directions Book, 1934–1972).

37. Sanders, 120.

38. *Ibid.*, 456.

39. For a thorough discussion of this and other connections Pound made to history and law, see Ten Eyck, Chapter 4, "The Representation of History and Law in the Adams Cantos," 85–109.

40. For the translation and attribution, see Sanders, 506.

41. Ten Eyck, 56.

42. Both quotations in Prologue to Sanders (no page number listed).

43. Sanders, 523–524.

44. *Ibid.*, 6.

45. Last page of prologue to Sanders (no page number listed) fn.

46. Page Smith called her work on John Adams "novelized biography," but acknowledged her role in helping to humanize Adams. Page Smith, *John Adams* Volume II, Collector's Edition (Norwalk, Connecticut: The Easton Press, 1963), 1139.

47. Catherine Drinker Bowen, *John Adams and the American Revolution* (Boston: Little, Brown, and Company, 1950), 642.

48. Catherine Drinker Bowen, quoted in Paul Jorden-Smith, "Scholar John Adams Helps Found Nation," *The Los Angeles Times,* June 11, 1950, 117.

49. Bowen, Prologue.

50. Bowen, 13.

51. *Ibid.*, 56.

52. For Putnam's fictionalized thoughts on John Adams see Bowen, 148–149.

53. John Adams, *Diary and Autobiography of John Adams*, Volume 1, Diary 1755–1770, January 1759 (Cambridge, Massachusetts: The Belknap Press of Harvard University Press, 1962), 67.

54. Bowen, 189.

55. *Ibid.*, 263. For the line in John Adams's papers, see John Adams, *The Works of John Adams, Second President of the United States*, Volume 4, Preface to the edition of 1819 (Boston: Little, Brown, and Company, 1851), 6, Accessed October 23, 2020. https://oll.libertyfund.org/titles/adams-the-works-of-john-adams-vol-4.

56. Bowen, 455–6.

57. *Ibid.*, 456.

58. *Ibid.*, 456–57.

59. *Ibid.*, 457.

60. *Ibid.*, 591.

61. *Ibid.*, 607.

62. On her Notes page, Bowen wrote, "These notes are designed to be read all at once, either before or after the narrative—or skipped entirely. To look them up each time is to risk fatal interruption." Bowen, 609.

63. Julian P. Boyd to Catherine Drinker Bowen, September 29, 1966, Finding Aid, Catherine Drinker Bowen Papers, Library of Congress, Accessed May 12, 2021. https://findingaids.loc.gov/db/search/xq/searchMfer02.xq?_id=loc.mss.eadmss.ms011156&_faSection=overview&_faSubsection=scopecontent&_dmdid=d8949e19#ref1.

64. John Adams to Abigail Adams, February 10, 1795, Adams Family Correspondence, Volume 10, Adams Papers, Digital Edition, Massachusetts Historical Society, Accessed May 26, 2020. https://www.masshist.org/digitaladams/archive/doc?id=L17950210ja.

65. For the scene, see Irving Stone, *Those Who Love: A Biographical Novel of Abigail and John Adams* (Garden City, New York: Doubleday and Company, Inc., 1965), 8; For the reference to Abigail's life beginning with this scene, see Stone, 647.

66. Joseph J. Ellis, *First Family: Abigail and John Adams* (New York: Alfred A. Knopf, 2010), 3.

67. *Ibid.*, 4.

68. Stone, 71.

69. For the date range for the correspondence between Abigail and John see "About the Correspondence between John and Abigail Adams" on the Adams Family

Papers Guide from the Massachusetts Historical Society, Accessed May 26, 2020. https://www.masshist.org/digitaladams/archive/letter/.

70. William D. Hoyt, Jr., "Life of Abigail Adams: Good View of the Late Eighteenth Century" in *The Boston Globe*, November 28,1965, 135.

71. Marcus Cunliffe, "John and Abigail's Road to the White House," *New York Times*, November 7, 1965, 56.

72. John Barkham, "Fact and Fancy," *Tucson Daily Citizen*, November 13,1965, 30.

73. Lorraine Youngquist, "Life: For 'Those Who Love,'" *The Marysville Advocate*, February 19, 1976, 14.

74. Hedda Hopper, "The Adamses in Hollywood," *The Daily News*, December 24, 1965, 237.

75. See, for example, Abigail's reflection on her inclusion into her husband's life and her comparison of John to George Washington. Stone, 208, 306.

76. Stone, 455.

77. *Ibid.*, 644.

78. Albin Krebs, "Irving Stone, Author of 'Lust for Life,' Dies at 86," *New York Times*, August 28, 1989, Section B, page 6.

79. William Gibson, *American Primitive (John & Abigail)* (New York: Dramatists Play Service, Inc., 1971), front cover.

80. *Ibid.*, 4.

81. Elyse Sommer, Review of *American Primitive (Abigail and John)* produced by The Berkshire Theatre Festival's Unicorn Theatre, directed by Gary English, *Curtain Up: The Internet Theater Magazine of Reviews, Features, Annotated Listings*, May 2003, Accessed November 16th, 2020. http://www.curtainup.com/american primitive.html.

82. Gibson, 3. All caps in original.

83. *Ibid.*, 6.

84. *Ibid.*, 8.

85. *Ibid.*, 11.

86. *Ibid.*, 20.

87. Abigail Adams to John Adams, July 16, 1775, *Adams Family Correspondence*, Volume 1, Adams Papers, Digital Edition, Massachusetts Historical Society, Accessed December 28, 2020. https://www.masshist.org/publications/adams-papers/index.php/view/ADMS-04-01-02-0162#sn=0.

88. John Adams to Abigail Adams, May 22, 1776, *Adams Family Correspondence*, Volume 1, Adams Papers, Digital Edition, Massachusetts Historical Society, Accessed December 28, 2020. https://www.masshist.org/publications/adams-papers/index.php/view/ADMS-04-01-02-0267#sn=0.

89. *Ibid.*

90. John Adams to Abigail Adams, February 10, 1777, *Adams Family Correspondence*, Volume 2, Adams Papers, Digital Edition, Massachusetts Historical Society, Accessed December 28, 2020. https://www.masshist.org/publications/adams-papers/index.php/view/ADMS-04-02-02-0115#sn=1. In his play, Gibson used the later transcription of this letter by Charles Francis Adams in which he changed "N.J.C. and T." to "my children." See note on this letter in the Adams Family Correspondence Digital Edition.

91. Gibson, 46–47.

92. *Ibid.*, 47.

93. Ellis, *First Family*, 91.

94. *Ibid.*, 94.

95. The scene is played out over several pages as John is preoccupied with the progress of the war. See Gibson, 48–51.

96. Michael Kammen, *A Season of Youth: The American Revolution and the Historical Imagination* (Ithaca: Cornell University Press, 1978), 141.

97. *Jefferson and Adams: A Stage Play*, DVD, Dir. Douglas Anderson, Written by Howard Ginsberg, Perf. Bill Barker, Sam Goodyear, Abigail Schumann (Colonial Williamsburg Foundation in Association with The Jefferson Legacy Foundation, 2004).

98. *Ibid.*

99. John Jakes, *The Rebels* (New York: Signet 1975; 2003), xi.

100. Jakes, 136. The content of this conversation was related by Adams many years after the fact and while Jefferson did not recall the conversation, the story has appeared in biographies of Adams and in several dramatizations of the writing of the document. For Adams's version of the conversation, see John Adams to Timothy Pickering, 6 August 1822, *Founders Online*, National Archives, Accessed December 30, 2020. https://founders.archives.gov/documents/Adams/99-02-02-7674.

101. Jakes, 155–6.

102. *Ibid.*, xiii.

103. Aaron Sorkin and Patrick Caddell, "The West Wing," Season 2, Episode 8, "Shibboleth," DVD, directed by Laura Innes, Warner Brothers, August 28, 2007.

104. "Historical Mystery Fiction" website, Last modified April 20, 2021, Accessed May 13, 2021. https://brerfox.tripod.com/historicalmystery.html. For the list of the Benjamin Franklin mysteries, see the list under "Regency" mysteries at https://brerfox.tripod.com/regency.html.

105. See Barbara Hamilton, *The Ninth Daughter* (New York: The Berkley Publishing Group, 2009), 3.

106. *Ibid.*

107. See, for example, John Adams to Mercy Otis Warren, August [26], 1775. *Papers of John Adams*, Volume 3, Adams Papers, Digital Edition, Massachusetts Historical Society, Accessed February 11, 2021. https://www.masshist.org/publications/adams-papers/index.php/view/ADMS-06-03-02-0071#sn=17.

108. Barbara Hamilton, *A Marked Man* (New York: Berkley Prime Crime, 2010), 1–4.

109. Jodi Daynard, *The Midwife's Revolt* (Seattle: Lake Union Publishing, 2015), 392–398.

110. Daynard, *Our Own Country* (Seattle: Lake Union Publishing, 2016), 374.

111. *Ibid.*, 379–381; 412–414.

112. Daynard, *A More Perfect Union* (Seattle: Lake Union Publishing, 2017), 33–34.

113. *Ibid.*, "Author's Note," 420; 422.

Chapter Five

1. Greg Evans, "Broadway-Bound '1776' Musical Revival Announces Female, Non-Binary and Trans Cast," Deadline.com. (April 8, 2022). Accessed June 8, 2022. https://deadline.com/2022/04/broadway-bound-1776-revival-female-non-binary-trans-cast-1234997377/.

2. For insight into the creative approach to this production and reviews, see American Repertory Theater's website at https://americanrepertorytheater.org/shows-events/1776-revival/.

3. Biography of Sherman Edwards can be found at Allmusic.com, Accessed July 24, 2019. https://www.allmusic.com/artist/sherman-edwards-mn0000026459/biography.

4. John Reddy, "*1776*: The Idea that Would Not let Go," *Reader's Digest*, February 1970, 199–200.

5. *Ibid.*, 202.

6. *Ibid.*

7. William Daniels, *There I Go Again: How I Came to Be Mr. Feeny, John Adams, Dr. Craig, KITT, & Many Others* (Lincoln, Nebraska: Potomac Books, an Imprint of the University of Nebraska Press, 2017), 133–34.

8. Peter Hunt, in an interview with Ron Fassler in Ron Fassler, *Up in the Cheap Seats: A Historical Memoir of Broadway* (Santa Monica, California: Griffin Moon, 2017), 68.

9. Jeffrey Kare, "The Making of America's Musical—1776: The Story Behind the Story," *Broadway World* online, July 4, 2016, Accessed on July 24, 2019. https://www.broadwayworld.com/article/The-Making-of-Americas-Musical--1776-The-Story-Behind-the-Story-20160704.

10. Daniels, 157.

11. Daniels, 134–35.

12. Reddy, 204; Daniels, 139.

13. Daniels, 139.

14. Reddy, 204.

15. Peter Hunt, quoted in Fassler, 67.

16. Fassler, 84.

17. Daniels, 141.

18. *Ibid.*, 142.

19. For the complete story of the White House command performance, see Daniels 141–143.

20. William Daniels, in an interview with Jeremy Binckes, "1776" star William Daniels opens up about performing for Richard Nixon, meeting "Hamilton" creator Lin-Manuel Miranda, on becoming John Adams in "1776," "Daniels Acted First and Asked questions Later," *Salon*, March 13, 2017, Video produced by Peter Cooper, Accessed July 24, 2019. https://www.salon.com/2017/03/13/watch-1776-star-william-daniels-opens-up-about-performing-for-richard-nixon-meeting-hamilton-creator-lin-manuel-miranda/.

21. *Ibid.*

22. Daniels, 136.

23. *Ibid.*

24. For the story of the extraordinary complexity of Tony nominations and how they affected Daniels, see *Ibid.*, 140; Eric

Grode, "The 1969 Tonys Was a Night to Remember. Just Ask James Earl Jones. It was the season of 'Hair' vs. '1776' and the arrival of a young actor named Al Pacino," *New York Times Online*, June 5, 2019.

25. Clive Barnes, "Spirited 1776: Founding Fathers' Tale is a Happy Musical," *New York Times*, March 17, 1969, 46.

26. Alessandra Stanley, "Blowhard, Patriot, President," March 14, 2008, *New York Times*.

27. Peter Filichia, "1776: IT'S A MASTERPIECE, I SAY," *Masterworks Broadway*, August 5, 2014, Accessed July 24, 2019. https://masterworksbroadway.com/blog/1776-its-a-masterpiece-i-say/. Also quoted in Fassler, 72.

28. Julie Newell, Comment posted on Facebook, June 28, 2019. Permission to quote given by Julie Newell.

29. Daniels, 140.

30. Richard Stockton, quoted in Page Smith, *John Adams*, Volume 1, 1735–1784, Collector's Edition (Norwalk, Connecticut: The Easton Press, 1963), 268–69.

31. Thomas Jefferson to James Madison, August 30, 1823, National Archives, *Founders Online*, Accessed July 23, 2019. https://founders.archives.gov/documents/Jefferson/98-01-02-3728.

32. Thomas Jefferson, quoted in a letter from William P. Gardner to John Adams, May 19, 1818, National Archives, *Founders Online*, Accessed July 23, 2019. https://founders.archives.gov/documents/Adams/99-02-02-6895.

33. Peter Stone and Sherman Edwards, *1776: A Musical Play*, Historical Notes (New York: The Penguin Group, 1976), 169.

34. *Ibid.*

35. I have discovered no evidence that Samuel Adams said or wrote these words. I continue to search for the primary source.

36. Stone and Edwards, script, 126.

37. Smith, 241.

38. John Adams, *Thoughts on Government*, in Gordon Wood, ed., *John Adams: Revolutionary Writings, 1775–1783* (New York: The Library of America, 2011), 56.

39. Smith, 261.

40. John Adams to William Cushing, June 9, 1776, Papers of John Adams, Volume 4, Adams Papers, Digital Edition, Massachusetts Historical Society. Accessed July 28, 2019. https://www.masshist.org/publications/adams-papers/index.php/view/ADMS-06-04-02-0109#sn=0.

41. *Ibid.*

42. Smith, 256.

43. Stone and Edwards, 1. This quotation was thought to be taken from John Adams's own words, but there is no evidence that he ever said or wrote anything close to it, regardless of countless attributions on the internet.

44. *Ibid.*

45. Daniels, 136.

46. Stone and Edwards, 5–6. Emphasis as it appears in the script.

47. Smith, 263.

48. Stone and Edwards, xiii.

49. Abigail Adams to John Adams, 27 May 1776, *Adams Family Correspondence,* Volume 1, *Adams Papers*, Digital Edition, Accessed July 28, 2019. https://www.masshist.org/publications/adams-papers/index.php/view/ADMS-04-01-02-0269#sn=0.

50. Stone and Edwards, 6.

51. *Ibid.*, 12.

52. For the lyrics to the song "But Mr. Adams" in which Adams described himself as obnoxious and disliked, see *Ibid.*, 58–65.

53. *Ibid.*, Historical Notes, 157.

54. John Adams to Timothy Pickering, 6 August 1822, *Founders Online*, Accessed July 29, 2019. https://founders.archives.gov/documents/Adams/99-02-02-7674.

55. Smith, 253.

56. David McCullough, *John Adams* (New York: Simon and Schuster, 2001), 119–20.

57. For Dickinson's reputation for colonial rights, especially his "Letter from a Farmer," see Thomas P. Slaughter, *Independence: The Tangled Roots of The American Revolution* (New York: Hill and Wang: A Division of Farrar, Straus and Giroux, 2014), 255–56; for "The Liberty Song," see Todd Andrlik, "John Dickinson's Hit Single: Liberty Song," in *The Journal of the American Revolution*, March 12, 2014, Accessed July 30, 2019. https://allthingsliberty.com/2014/03/the-liberty-song/.

58. John Adams to James Warren, July 24, 1775, *Papers of John Adams, Volume 3*, Adams Papers Digital Edition, Accessed July 30, 2019. https://www.masshist.org/publications/adams-papers/index.php/view/ADMS-06-03-02-0052#sn=1.

59. Stone and Edwards, 25; *1776* Director's Cut, Blue-Ray, Directed by Peter Hunt, Performers, Jonathan Moore and Donald Madden (Columbia Pictures, 1972, Blue-Ray distributed by Sony Pictures Home Entertainment, 2007).

60. Stone and Edwards, 43.

61. John Adams, *Diary of John Adams*, Volume 3, July 1, 1776, Adams Papers Digital Edition, Accessed July 30, 2019. https://www.masshist.org/publications/adams-papers/index.php/view/ADMS-01-03-02-0016-0142#sn=54.

62. Smith, 268.

63. John Adams to Samuel Chase, July 1, 1776, *Founders Online*, National Archives. Accessed January 15, 2022. https://founders.archives.gov/?q=John%20Adams%20to%20Samuel%20Chase%20July%201%2C%201776%20Author%3A%22Adams%2C%20John%22%20Recipient%3A%22Chase%2C%20Samuel%22&s=1111311111&r=2.

64. Stone and Edwards, 140–41.

65. For John Dickinson's army service and later public life, see Jack Rakove, "The Patriot Who Refused to Sign the Declaration of Independence," HistoryNet, Accessed September 9, 2019. https://www.historynet.com/the-patriot-who-refused-to-sign-the-declaration-of-independence.htm.

66. Thomas Jefferson, *The Papers of Thomas Jefferson*, Vol. 1, 1760–1776. Edited by Julian P. Boyd (Princeton: Princeton University Press, 1950), 243–247.

67. For the entire scene surrounding the slavery clause, see Stone and Edwards, 115–124.

68. John Adams to Timothy Pickering, August 6, 1822, *Founders Online*, National Archives, Accessed December 2, 2021. https://founders.archives.gov/documents/Adams/99-02-02-7674.

69. Arthur Scherr, *John Adams, Slavery, and Race: Ideas, Politics, and Diplomacy in an Age of Crisis* (Santa Barbara, California: Praeger, 2018), 14.

70. Stone and Edwards, 126–7.

71. John Adams to Abigail Adams, 3, July 1776, Adams Family Correspondence, Volume 2, Adams Papers Digital Edition, Accessed July 30, 2019. https://www.masshist.org/publications/adams-papers/index.php/view/ADMS-04-02-02-0016#sn=0. It is a shame that it is so difficult to quote song lyrics, for Edwards's incorporation of this letter and Adams's 1774 conversation with his Tory friend Jonathan Sewall is quite effective. For the song lyrics see, Edwards and Stone, 130–32.

72. Stone and Edwards, 145.

73. Release date and box office numbers comes from IMDB website. Accessed July 31, 2019. https://www.imdb.com/title/tt0068156/.

74. Roger Ebert, review of "1776," December 26, 1972, on Roger Ebert.com. Accessed July 31, 2019. https://www.rogerebert.com/reviews/1776-1972; For the blogger's rebuttal, see "Roger Ebert's Worst Reviews" 42. "1776," Accessed July 31, 2019. https://rogersworst.blogspot.com/2011/01/42-1776-1772.html.

75. Cotton Seiler, "The American Revolution," in *The Columbia Companion to American History on Film: How the Movies have Portrayed the American Past*, edited by Peter C. Rollins (New York: Columbia University Press, 2003); Vincent Canby, "Film View; Once More 1776 Taxes Filmgoers," *New York Times,* January 12, 1986, section 2, page 1.

76. For full lyrics, see Stone and Edwards, 92–97.

77. Susan King, "With restored version out, '1776' director recalls politics behind cuts," *Lost Angeles Times*, July 9, 2015.

78. For William Daniels's reaction to the film, see Daniels, 147.

79. For the opening sequence, see *1776* Director's Cut, Blue-Ray, Performers, William Duell and William Daniels.

80. The author is grateful to James Beaman who graciously allowed sharing of his blog here, "with his blessing." Email from Beaman to author, December 2, 2021.

81. James Beaman, "Post One," Becoming John Adams, James Beaman, June 2, 2014, https://www.youtube.com/watch?v=IwY-MzraWU8&list=PLjYaFvkEvRlUXnTD4eBNcRgiYDdNMQqhX&index=1&t=13s.

82. James Beaman, "Post Two," Becoming John Adams, James Beaman, June 5, 2014, Accessed December 3, 2021. https://www.youtube.com/watch?v=BFfOG275Cbw&list=PLjYaFvkEvRlUXnTD4eBNcRgiYDdNMQqhX&index=2. For the Pinterest Board, see https://www.pinterest.com/jamesbeaman581/john-adams-and-1776/.

83. James Beaman, "Post Three," Becoming John Adams, James Beaman, June 9, 2014, Accessed December 3, 2021. https://www.youtube.com/watch?v=do-4w20lsQ4&list=PLjYaFvkEvRlUXnTD4eBNcRgiYDdNMQqhX&index=3; James Beaman, "Post Four," Becoming John Adams, James Beaman, June 12, 2014, Accessed December 3, 2021. https://www.youtube.com/watch?v=y9zbaA6xCTU&list=PLjYaFvkEvRlUXnTD4eBNcRgiYDdNMQqhX&index=4; James Beaman, "Post Five," Becoming John Adams, James Beaman, June 16, 2014, Accessed December 3, 2021. https://www.youtube.com/watch?v=dZ2Qp8fVTmI&list=PLjYaFvkEvRlUXnTD4eBNcRgiYDdNMQqhX&index=5; James Beaman, "Post Six," Becoming John Adams, James Beaman, June 19, 2014, Accessed December 3, 2021. https://www.youtube.com/watch?v=BRfi_0R0c54&list=PLjYaFvkEvRlUXnTD4eBNcRgiYDdNMQqhX&index=6; James Beaman, "Post Seven," Becoming John Adams, James Beaman, June 22, 2014, Accessed December 3, 2021. https://www.youtube.com/watch?v=OwM-f6KsCBE&list=PLjYaFvkEvRlUXnTD4eBNcRgiYDdNMQqhX&index=7.

84. See James Beaman, "James Beaman," https://www.jamesbeaman.com/.

85. Matt Weinstock, "The Legacy of *1776*: A Conversation with William Daniels and Lin-Manuel Miranda," *Playbill*, reprinted in Daniels, 201–207. Quoted conversation on 203.

86. Diane Paulus, "Artistic Director's Welcome," American Repertory Theater. org. Accessed June 10, 2022. https://americanrepertorytheater.org/explore/art-guide-spring-2022/.

Chapter Six

1. I would like to thank Dr. Edward Fitzgerald, Executive Director of the Quincy Historical Society for alerting me to this series. In addition, I am most grateful to Thomas Film Classics for making this series available on DVD.

2. *Profiles in Courage*, Episode 7, "John Adams," directed by Michael Ritchie, written by Andy Lewis, Produced by Robert Saudek Associates, 1964, converted to DVD by Thomas Film Classics.

3. For a fascinating reassessment of the relationship between Bostonians and the soldiers, see Serena Zabin, *The Boston Massacre: A Family History* (Boston: Houghton Mifflin Harcourt, 2020).

4. John Adams, *Diary and Autobiography of John Adams*, Volume 3 (Cambridge, MA: The Belknap Press of Harvard University Press, 1962), 293.

5. Zabin, 191.

6. John Ferling, *John Adams: A Life* (New York: Henry Holt and Company, 1992), 67. Ferling referenced Hiller Zobel's study of the Boston Massacre in his discussion of Adams's motives. See Hiller B. Zobel, *The Boston Massacre* (New York: W.W. Norton, 1970).

7. Zabin, 216.

8. There were in fact two trials, one of Captain Preston who led the troops and one of the soldiers. In dramatizations, the trials are either combined or, as is the case with this television depiction, Preston simply becomes one of the soldiers on trial.

9. For the quotation from the trial, see John Adams, *Legal Papers of John Adams*, Volume 3, "Adams' Argument for the Defense," 266, Adams Papers, Digital Edition, Accessed November 30, 2021. https://www.masshist.org/publications/adams-papers/index.php/view/LJA03p242. For all quotes and references to the episode, see *Profiles in Courage*, episode 7, "John Adams," directed by Robert Stevens, written by Walter Bernstein, perf. David McCallum, Torin Thatcher, Gene Lyons, Andrew Prine, Produced by Robert Saudek Associates, 1964, converted to DVD by Thomas Film Classics, 2021.

10. For all quotations and references to the episode, see *Profiles in Courage*, episode 22, "John Quincy Adams," directed by Michael Ritchie, written by Andy Lewis, perf. Douglas Campbell, Laurence Naismith, Nancy Wickwire, Produced by Robert Saudek Associates, 1965, converted to DVD by Thomas Film Classics, 2021.

11. *The Adams Chronicles*, DVD, Directed by Paul Bogart, Fred Coe, Barry Davis, Bill Glenn, James Cellen Jones, and Anthony Page, Educational Broadcasting Corporation and Acorn Media, 2008.

12. James Truslow Adams, *The Adams Family* (Boston: Little, Brown, and Company, 1930), 3.

13. *Ibid.*

14. *Ibid.*, 8.

15. John Adams, *Autobiography* in *Diary and Autobiography of John Adams* Volume 3, edited by L.H. Butterfield (Cambridge, Massachusetts: The Belknap Press of Harvard University Press, 1962), 256.

16. *Ibid.*, 8; 3.

17. Francis Russell, *Adams: An American Dynasty* (New York: American Heritage Publishing Co., Inc., Book Trade Distribution by McGraw-Hill Book Company, 1976), 16.

18. Paul C. Nagel, *Descent from Glory: Four Generations of the John Adams Family* (New York, Oxford: Oxford University Press, 1983), vii. This lack of citation is frustrating in this work and despite Nagel's explanation, one scholar in particular took issue with it. Edith Gelles, in writing about the many depictions of Abigail in historiography, gave Nagel credit for what he had accomplished, noting, "Nagel's great forte is storytelling. Furthermore, he is a virtuoso with the Adams sources. The combination should make for superlative history or biography." However, she questioned Nagel's methods, asking, "But is this history? Or biography?" She noted that without proper citations, "the story is freed from accountability." Gelles made clear that she did not care for Nagel's interpretation of Abigail, and this fed her criticism of his works. She concluded her discussion of Nagel's books by contending, "Storytelling and free use of sources reinforce Nagel's negative view of Abigail. The continued exposition of private issues, secrets, and gossip begun in *Descent from Glory* makes *The Adams Women* a sensational tale, but perhaps the low point of the Abigail industry." See Edith B. Gelles, "The Abigail Industry," *The William and Mary Quarterly*, Volume 45, No. 4 (October 1988): 679; 680.

19. Nagel, 3.

20. *Ibid.*, 6.

21. *Ibid.*

22. *Ibid.*, 7.

23. Richard Brookhiser, *American's First Dynasty: The Adamses, 1735–1918* (New York: The Free Press, 2002), 5–6.

24. See *Ibid.*, 181–219.

25. *Ibid.*, 211.

26. *Ibid.*, 212.

27. "From 'Adams' Struggle to Nash-ville Romance," *The Tennessean* (Nashville, Tennessee), March 21, 1976, 97.

28. *Ibid.*

29. *Ibid.*

30. Quotation from George Grizzard, "George Grizzard: Living, Dying in PBS Series," *Democrat and Chronicle* (Rochester, New York), January 19, 1976, 148.

31. "Opening Season of Fall Treats," *Muncie Evening Press* (Muncie, Indiana), September 18, 1976, 17.

32. "And here are Peabody Winners," *Daily News* (New York, New York), April 19, 1977, 469; Emmy Awards are listed at https://www.emmys.com/shows/adams-chronicles.

33. Jay Sharbutt, "'Adams Chronicles' A $6.7 Million Series," *Lincoln Journal Star* (Lincoln, Nebraska), January 25, 1976, 68.

34. George Grizzard to Harry Harris, "George Grizzard Settles for the Presidency," *The Philadelphia Inquirer* (Philadelphia, Pennsylvania), January 18, 1976, 223.

35. Daniel Boorstin, quoted in Jack Shepherd, *The Adams Chronicles: Four Generations of Greatness*, Introduction by Daniel J. Boorstin (Boston: Little, Brown, and Company, 1975), xii.

36. John Adams, *Diary and Autobiography of John Adams*, Volume 3, Diary 1782–1804; Autobiography Through 1776 (Cambridge, MA: The Belknap Press of Harvard University Press, 1961, 1962), 253–254; For Grizzard voice-over, see *The Adams Chronicles* (1976), Disc 1, DVD, Directed by Paul Bogart and James Cellan Jones, Perf. George Grizzard (DVD B0013NAMLD: Educational Broadcasting Corporation and Acorn Media, 2008).

37. Nancy Isenberg and Andrew Burstein, "The Adamses on Screen," *A Companion to John Adams and John Quincy Adams*, First Edition, edited by David Waldstreicher (Hoboken, New Jersey: John Wiley & Sons, Ltd., 2013), 498.

38. For Adams's recollections of this time, see John Adams, *Diary and Autobiography of John Adams*, Volume 3, Diary 1782–1804; Autobiography Through 1776 (Cambridge, MA: The Belknap Press of Harvard University Press, 1961, 1962), 270–271.

39. *The Adams Chronicles* (1976), Disc 1, DVD, Directed by Paul Bogart and James Cellan Jones, Perf. George Grizzard,

Kathryn Walker (DVD B0013NAMLD: Educational Broadcasting Corporation and Acorn Media, 2008).

40. *The Adams Chronicles* (1976), Disc 3, DVD, Dir. Bill Glenn and Fred Coe, Perf. George Grizzard, William Daniels (DVD B0013NAMLD: Educational Broadcasting Corporation and Acorn Media, 2008).

41. George Grizzard, quoted in William A. Raidy, "Versatile Star has Best of Two Worlds," *The Morning Call* (Allentown, Pennsylvania), December 26, 1976, 132.

42. George Grizzard, quoted in Betty Utterback, "George Grizzard: Living, Dying in PBS Series," *Democrat and Chronicle* (Rochester, New York), January 18, 1976, 146.

43. *Ibid.*

44. "Front Matter." *American Libraries* 7, no. 1 (1976).

45. Richard W. Smith, "Educational Television is Not Educating," *Change*, Dec. 1978–Jan. 1979, Volume 10, No. 11 (Dec. 1978–Jan. 1979): 63.

46. Richard Rollins, "Review of *The Adams Chronicles: Four Generations of Greatness* by Jack Shepard; *The World of the Adams Chronicles: Forging Our Nation* Edited by David J. Rothman; *The Adams Chronicles: A Student Guide* by Regina Janes," *The History Teacher*, Volume 10, No. 3 (Society for History Education: May 1977): 453;455.

47. John O'Connor, "'The Adams Chronicles': American Television at Its Best," *New York Times*, January 20, 1976. No page given.

48. Clifford S. Griffin, "TV Viewing Guide: The Adams Chronicles," *American Studies*, Volume 19, No. 2, A New Look at Old Masters (Mid-America American Studies Association: Fall 1978): 82.

49. Operation Primetime was a television production and distribution company designed to compete with network television. For a description and production history see "Operation Primetime" Accessed June 30, 2021. http://tviv.org/Operation_Prime_Time; Peter J. Boyer, "TV Movie 'The Rebels' Making Debut," *The Central New Jersey Home News* (New Brunswick, New Jersey), May 14, 1979, 18.

50. For Hardy Boys quotation, see Dick Shippy, "A Revolutionary Winter for Doug

McClure," *The Akron Beacon Journal* (Akron, Ohio), May 13, 1979, 177; Other quotation from Peter J. Boyer, "TV Movie 'The Rebels' Making Debut," *The Central New Jersey Home News* (New Brunswick, New Jersey), May 14, 1979, 18.

51. *The Rebels*, Directed by Russ Mayberry, DVD (Universal Studios, 2019).

52. *The Rebels*, DVD, Perf. Tom Bosley, Don Johnson, Kevin Tighe, William Daniels.

53. *Ibid.*, Perf. William Daniels, Kevin Tighe.

54. For a summary of Jefferson's role in the Second Continental Congress in 1775 and 1776, see Page Smith, *John Adams Volume I, 1735–1784* Collector's Edition (Norwalk, Connecticut: The Easton Press, 1962), 266.

55. *The Rebels*, DVD, Perf. William Daniels, Andrew Stevens.

56. *The Rebels*, DVD, perf. William Daniels, Don Johnson, Kevin Tighe, Tom Bosley.

57. For the deletion of the Slave Trade clause, see Smith, Volume I, 272 and David McCullough, *John Adams* (New York: Simon & Schuster, 2001), 134.

58. *The Rebels*, DVD, Perf. William Daniels, Andrew Stevens, Marc Vahanian.

59. See Diary entry, John Adams, January 24, 1776, reprinted in *John Adams: Revolutionary Writings, 1775–1783*, edited by Gordon Wood (New York: Library of America, 2011), 40–41.

60. John Adams, *Thoughts on Government*, reprinted in *Ibid.*, 49–56; quotation on page 50.

61. John Adams to Horatio Gates, March 23, 1776, reprinted in *Ibid.*, 47–48.

62. *Biography*, "John and Abigail Adams: Love and Liberty" DVD (A&E Television Networks, 2002), back cover.

63. Elizabeth Deane, speaking at the Boston Public Library, recorded for the GBH Forum Network on YouTube (2005), Accessed July 5, 2021. https://www.youtube.com/watch?v=TrTWEAeJ-Jk&t=604s.

64. For comments from Cobble and Chu, see *Ibid.*

65. ArchitectureChicago Plus Blogspot, "Tonight on WYIN—Founding Father Rescued from the Waxworks—Simon Russell Beale as John Adams," February 6, 2006, Accessed July 5, 2021.http://archchicago.blogspot.com/2006/02/tonight-on-wyin-founding-father.html.

66. "John & Abigail Adams" on *American Experience*, front cover, DVD, Directed by Peter Jones, PBS Home Video (2006).

67. *Ibid.*, perf. Simon Russell Beale and Linda Emond.

68. Simon Russell Beale, DVD Special Features, Behind the Scenes, "John and Abigail Adams on the Set," PBS Home Video (2006).

69. Verne Gay, "Time to pay A Call on the Adams Family," *Newsday* (Nassau Edition, Hempstead, New York, January 23, 2006), 69.

70. David McCullough, transcript of "John & Abigail Adams," *American Experience*, Accessed, July 5th, 2021. https://www.pbs.org/wgbh/americanexperience/films/adams/#transcript.

71. For the broadcast history, see Andrew M. Schocket, "Little Founders on the Small Screen: Interpreting a Multicultural American Revolution for Children's Television," *Journal of American Studies*, February 2011, Volume 45, No. 1 (February 2011): 145–146.

72. John Adams, *The Adams Papers: Diary and Autobiography of John Adams*, Volume 2: Diary 1771–1781 edited by L.H. Butterfield (Cambridge, MA: The Belknap Press of Harvard University Press, 1962), 125. John Adams took copious notes at the meeting of the First Continental Congress and included many of them in his diary.

73. *Liberty's Kids*, Episode 103, "United We Stand," Directed by Judith Reilly, Perf. Billy Crystal, 2002, Accessed on YouTube, August 5, 2021. https://www.youtube.com/watch?v=oAbMPt1vXpU&list=PLHeaIWvdbER3Ic90BzhPsH2aJ5KI3UtmM&index=3.

74. For Adams's own words from the Massachusetts Constitution, see John Adams, "The Report of a Constitution or Form of Government for the Commonwealth of Massachusetts" reprinted in *John Adams: Revolutionary Writings 1775–1783* edited by Gordon Wood (New York: The Library of America, 2011), 276.

75. For the full episode, see *Liberty's Kids*, Episode 131, "Bostonians," Directed by Judith Reilly, Perf. Billy Crystal, Annette Benning, 2002, Accessed on Youtube, August 5, 2021. https://www.youtube.com/watch?v=eqJ9PLGzvLc.

76. Andrew M. Schocket, "Little Founders on the Small Screen: Interpreting a Multicultral American Revolution for Children's Television," 146.

77. About the series, http://www.history.com/shows/sons-of-liberty/about. Accessed October 27, 2016. This was the original content on the website. It has since been updated to read: "Men who dubbed themselves Sons of Liberty helped spark the American Revolution; the young rebels from varied backgrounds struggled to find purpose in their lives but eventually became legends. The men started by seeking equality, but they found something even better—Independence. The featured firebrands in the historical drama miniseries include charismatic leader Sam Adams, artisan/militia-man Paul Revere, conservative lawyer John Adams, Gen. George Washington, and brilliant-but-mischievous diplomat Ben Franklin." The disclaimer has disappeared from the web site. Accessed July 9, 2021. https://www.history.com/shows/sons-of-liberty.

78. Stephen David, quoted in George Dickie, "Series Follows Young Dissidents in 'Sons of Liberty,'" *The Daily Oklahoman* (Oklahoma City, Oklahoma January 23, 2015), 55.

79. Stephen David, executive producer/co-writer, *Sons of Liberty*, Blue-Ray, Blu-Ray Bonus Features, "Men of Independence," (Lionsgate Films, History, 2015).

80. Henry Thomas, quoted in Dickie, "Series Follows Young Dissidents."

81. "Men of Independence," *Sons of Liberty*.

82. Peter Shaw, *The Character of John Adams* (Chapel Hill: The University of North Carolina Press, Published for the Institute of Early American History and Culture, Williamsburg, Virginia, 1976), 33.

83. James Grant, *John Adams: Party of One* (New York: Farrar, Straus and Giroux, 2005), 65.

84. For the story of Adams's selection to argue this case with Otis and Gridley, see *Ibid.*, 68.

85. *Sons of Liberty*, episode one, "A Dangerous Game," Blue-Ray, directed by Kari Skogland, perf. Henry Thomas, Ryan Eggold.

86. *Ibid.*, perf. Henry Thomas, Ben Barnes.

87. *Ibid.*

88. John Adams, *The Adams Papers: Diary and Autobiography of John Adams*, Volume 1: Diary 1755–1770 edited by L.H. Butterfield (Cambridge, MA: The Belknap Press of Harvard University Press, 1962), 271.

89. This phrase came from former Governor Shirley in 1771. John Adams recorded the words in his diary in February 1772. The Governor had asked about certain men prominent in Boston politics and was given the names of some of the leaders there including "Mr. Cushing, Mr. Hancock, Mr. Adams and Mr. Adams." Governor Shirley replied, 'Mr. Cushing I know…and Mr. Hancock I know, but where the Devil this Brace of Adams's came from, I cant conceive." *The Adams Papers: Diary and Autobiography of John Adams*, Volume 2: Diary 1771–1781, edited by L.H. Butterfield (Cambridge, MA: The Belknap Press of Harvard University Press, 1962), 54–55.

90. *Ibid.*, 55.

91. For Gage's threats to John Adams, see *Sons of Liberty*, Episode 2, "Uprising," Blue-Ray, directed by Kari Skogland, perf. Henry Thomas, Marton Csokas.

92. *Sons of Liberty*, Episode 3, "Independence," Blue-Ray, directed by Kari Skogland, perf. Henry Thomas, Ben Barnes.

93. Alessandra Stanley, "Ale and Muskets Frame Revolt," *New York Times* (January 23, 2015).

94. Mary McNamara, "Never Let Facts Get in the Way: 'Sons' miniseries takes too many liberties on History about the American Revolution," *The Los Angeles Times* (January 24, 2015), 21;23.

95. *Ibid.*

Chapter Seven

1. Barry Gewen, "Forget the Founding Fathers," *New York Times*, Section 7, pg. 30, June 5, 2005.

2. Simon and Schuster, Official website, Accessed June 29, 2019. https://www.simonandschuster.com/books/John-Adams/David-McCullough/9780743223133.

3. Heinz-D Fischer, Ed. *The Pulitzer Prize Archive Part G: Supplements Volume 20: Chronicle for the Pulitzer Prizes for Biography*. K.G. Saur Münch, 2006.

4. *New York Times*, Editor's Choice, December 2, 2001.

5. *Ibid.*

6. Gordon Wood, "In the American Grain," *The New York Review of Books*, June 1, 2001, Accessed June 30, 2019. https://www.nybooks.com/articles/2001/06/21/in-the-american-grain/.

7. Robert Middlekauff, "*John Adams* by David McCullough," *The New England Quarterly* Volume 75, No. 1 (March 2002): 141.

8. Lance Banning, "Popularizing the Founding: A Review Essay," *The Register of The Kentucky Historical Society*, Volume 99, No. 2 (Spring 2001): 155.

9. John Howe, "*John Adams* by David McCullough," *The Journal of American History* Volume 90, No. 1 (June 2003): 211.

10. Pauline Maier, "Plain Speaking: In David McCullough's telling, the second president is reminiscent of the 33rd (Harry Truman)," *New York Times*, May 27, 2001, Section seven, 9.

11. Jean Edward Smith, "*John Adams* by David McCullough," *Political Science Quarterly*, Volume 117, No. 1 (Spring, 2002): 131 and 132.

12. Nancy Isenberg and Andrew Burstein, "America's Worst Historians," *Salon*. August 19, 2012, Accessed June 29, 2019. https://www.salon.com/2012/08/19/americas_worst_historians/.

13. Sean Wilentz, "America Made Easy: McCullough, Adams, and the Decline of Popular History," *The New Republic*, July 2, 2001, Accessed June 30, 2019. https://newrepublic.com/article/62368/tnrs-founding-fathers-spectacular.

14. Brooke Allen, "John Adams: Realist of the Revolution," *The Hudson Review*, Volume 55, No. 1 (Spring, 2002): 50.

15. See Chapter Eight on the dedication of the Hancock Adams Common in Quincy, Massachusetts.

16. David McCullough discusses his biography, "John Adams," the story of the nation's second president who died on July 4, 1826, PBS NewsHour, July 4, 2002, Accessed June 25, 2019. https://www.pbs.org/newshour/show/david-mccullough-discusses-his-book-john-adams.

17. *Ibid.*

18. Linda Hutcheon, *A Theory of Adaptation* (New York: Routledge, 2006), 6.

19. David McCullough, *John Adams* (New York: Simon and Schuster, 2001), 17.

20. *Ibid.*, 18.

21. *Ibid.*, 18–19.

22. Paul Lieberman, "Paul Giamatti Is So Imperfect for the Role," *Los Angeles Times*, April 13, 2008.

23. *Ibid.*

24. *Ibid.*

25. Paul Giamatti, quoted in "Paul Giamatti Plays Really Weird John Adams" by Fred Topel, Rotten Tomatoes, August 24, 2007, Accessed June 29, 2019. https://editorial.rottentomatoes.com/article/paul-giamatti-plays-really-weird-john-adams/.

26. For examples, see McCullough, *John Adams*, 244–59; 261–73.

27. "Paul Giamatti is so Imperfect for the Role."

28. For Paul Giamatti's complete comments in 2018, see Paul Giamatti, "Full Q&A, Oxford Union," *Oxford Union*, YouTube, 25:10–28:45.

29. Alessandra Stanley, "Blowhard, Patriot, President," TV Review: "John Adams," *New York Times*, March 14, 2008. See extended comments in the *1776* chapter.

30. Benji Wilson, "Laura Linney in John Adams: Closest to Tears When She Is Smiling," *The Telegraph*, December 8, 2008.

31. John Quincy Adams and Charles Francis Adams, *John Adams*, Volume 1 (New York: Chelsea House, 1871, reprint 1980), 159.

32. For the ages of the Adams children, see the Massachusetts Historical Society, Adams Papers, Digital Edition, Accessed on Jun 27, 2019.https://www.masshist.org/publications/adams-papers/. Abigail had one more pregnancy in 1777, but the baby girl was stillborn. See Woody Holton, *Abigail Adams* (New York: Free Press, 2009), 124–125.

33. John Adams, Sep. 11, 1774, *Diary and Autobiography of John Adams*, Volume 2, L.H. Butterfield, Editor (Cambridge, MA, The Belknap Press of Harvard University Press, 1962), 131.

34. *Ibid.*, August 31, 1774, 117.

35. See Željko Ivanek's portrayal of John Dickinson in *John Adams*, DVD, Directed by Thomas Hooper (HBO Films, 2008).

36. John Adams to Abigail Adams, October 9th, 1774, *Adams Family Correspondence*, Volume 1, Adams Family Papers Digital Edition, Accessed June 29, 2019. https://www.masshist.org/publications/adams-papers/index.php/view/ADMS-04-01-02-0111.

37. *Journals of the Continental Congress, 1774–1789*, Edited from the Original Records in the Library of Congress by Worthington Chauncy Ford, Chief, Division of Manuscripts, Vol. 5 1776, June 5–October 8 (Washington: Government Printing Office, 1909), 504. Digitized by Google, Accessed on June 29, 2019. https://babel.hathitrust.org/cgi/pt?id=mdp.39015068528697&view=1up&seq=96.

38. *John Adams*. Episode Two, "Independence," DVD, Directed by Thomas Hooper, Perf. Paul Giamatti (HBO Films, 2008).

39. McCullough, 71.

40. *John Adams*, Episode One, "Join or Die," DVD, Directed by Thomas Hooper, Perf. Paul Giamatti, Guy Henry (HBO Films, 2008).

41. Page Smith, *John Adams* Volume 2, Collector's Edition (Norwalk, Connecticut: The Easton Press,1963), 645.

42. McCullough, *John Adams*, 47.

43. See, for example, Eliot Gorn, et al, *Constructing the American Past*, Volume 1 (Oxford University Press, 2017).

44. McCullough, 104–105.

45. *John Adams*, Episode 2, "Independence," DVD, directed by Thomas Hooper, perf. Paul Giamatti, Laura Linney (HBO Films, 2008).

46. Jeremy Stern, "What's Wrong with HBO's Dramatization of John Adams's Story," History News Network, GW Columbian College of Arts and Sciences, Accessed June 30, 2019. https://historynewsnetwork.org/article/56155.

47. McCullough, *John Adams*, 170.

48. *Ibid.*, 220; 225.

49. John Adams to Benjamin Rush, October 25, 1809, *Founders Online*, National Archives, Accessed December 10, 2021. https://founders.archives.gov/documents/Adams/99-02-02-5454.

50. John Adams to Benjamin Rush, February 10, 1812, *Founders Online*, National Archives, Accessed December 10, 2021. https://founders.archives.gov/documents/Adams/99-02-02-5753.

51. Benjamin Rush to John Adams, February 17, 1812, *Founders Online*, National Archives, Accessed December 10, 2021. https://founders.archives.gov/documents/Adams/99-02-02-5758.

52. Stern, "What's Wrong with HBO's Dramatization of John Adams's Story."

53. John Adams to Abigail Adams, April 26, 1777, *Adams Family Correspondence*, Volume 2, Adams Family Papers Digital Edition, Accessed June 29, 2019. https://www.masshist.org/publications/adams-papers/index.php/view/ADMS-04-02-02-0169.

54. Stern, "What's Wrong with HBO's Dramatization of John Adams's Story."

55. James T. Kloppenberg, "*John Adams* by Tom Hooper, David Coastworth and Steve Shareshian," *The Journal of American History*, Volume 95, No. 3 (December 2008): 939.

56. *Ibid.*, 940.

57. Andrew Schocket, *Fighting over the Founders: How We Remember the American Revolution* (New York: New York University Press, 2015), 4.

58. *Ibid.*, 5.

59. *Ibid.*, 156.

60. *Ibid.*, 155.

61. *Ibid.*, 160.

62. Nancy Isenberg and Andrew Burstein, "The Adamses on Screen," *A Companion to John Adams and John Quincy Adams*, First Edition (Hoboken, New Jersey: John Wiley & Sons, Ltd., 2013), 504–505; 507.

63. *Ibid.*, 156.

64. See Chapter Nine for the comments of staff members at the Adams National Historical Park.

65. Robert A. Rosenstone, *History on Film/Film on History* (Harlow, UK: Pearson Longman, 2006), 37.

66. David McCullough on How to Write Biography, Interview with John Avlon at the Charleston Library Society, April 15, 2015, YouTube. https://www.youtube.com/watch?v=U-iWlND7DII.

Chapter Eight

1. Katherine Tully-McManus, "House Backs Plan for John Adams Memorial," *Roll Call*, July 23, 2018, Accessed July 15, 2021. https://rollcall.com/2018/07/23/house-backs-plan-for-john-adams-memorial/.

2. *Ibid.*

3. The statue in Spain is discussed in Chapter Nine.

4. Visit Rapid City, "John Adams," 2021, Accessed November 19, 2021, https://www.visitrapidcity.com/things-to-do/all-things/attractions/city-presidents/john-adams.

5. Dr. Edward Fitzgerald, Executive Director of the Quincy Historical Society, Interview with author, Quincy Historical Society, Quincy, Massachusetts, October 28, 2021.

6. John Adams to Abigail Adams, August 15, 1782, The Adams Papers, Digital Edition, Accessed November 8, 2021. https://www.masshist.org/publications/adams-papers/index.php/view/ADMS-04-02-0236#sn=0.

7. *Ibid.*

8. Charles Francis Adams, Jr., *The New English Canaan of Thomas Morton with Introductory Matter and Notes* (Project Gutenberg: Free eBooks, 1883), 15–16.

9. *Ibid.*

10. For a succinct early history of the region, see Nina Sankovitch, *American Rebels: How the Hancock, Adams, and Quincy Families Fanned the Flames of Revolution* (New York: St. Martin's Press, 2020), 9–15.

11. *Ibid.*, 12.

12. For a good but succinct history of Anne Hutchinson and her arguments with Winthrop, see Edmund S. Morgan, *The Puritan Dilemma: The Story of John Winthrop* (New York: Pearson Longman, 3rd edition, 2006). For a biography of Anne Hutchinson, see Eve LaPlante, *American Jezebel: The Uncommon Life of Anne Hutchinson, The Woman Who Defied the Puritans* (New York and San Francisco: HarperSanFrancisco, 2004).

13. Sankovitch, 14.

14. Further evidence of this is discussed in the history of United First Parish Church covered in the next chapter.

15. Sankovitch, 15.

16. John Adams, *Autobiography of John Adams* (Cambridge, MA: Harvard University Press, 1961), 254 n 3. The churchyard to which Adams referred is now the Hancock Cemetery in Quincy Center.

17. Both Dr. Fitzgerald and Bill West-

land, historian of the First United Parish Church, have explained that the town using funds to build a church was acceptable because in 1822, there was still no formal separation of church and state in the Commonwealth of Massachusetts. Dr. Edward Fitzgerald, Interview with author, Quincy Historical Society, Quincy, Massachusetts, October 28, 2021; Bill Westland, Historian of First United Parish Church, "Adams Temple and School Fund" vignette, sent to the author by Mr. Westland, November 2, 2021.

18. For the quotations, see From John Adams to MA Town of Quincy, June 29, 1822, in John Adams, *Deeds and Other Documents Relating to the Several Pieces of Land and to the Library Presented to the Town of Quincy, by President Adams, Together with a Catalogue of the Books* (Cambridge: Printed by Hilliard and Metcalf, 1823, Reprinted in London: Forgotten Books, FB&Ltd, Dalton House, 2018), 3–4. The name of the fund and the trustees is taken from Bill Westland, Historian of First United Parish Church, "Adams Temple and School Fund" vignette, sent to the author by Mr. Westland, November 2, 2021.

19. John Adams, *Deeds and Other Documents*, 4.

20. The Selectmen of the Town of Quincy, *At a Meeting of the Inhabitants of the Town of Quincy, Holden on the 8th Day of July, A.D. 1822*, in *Ibid.*, 6–7.

21. John Adams to the Town of Quincy, in *Ibid.*, 10.

22. From John Adams to MA Town of Quincy, July 27, 1822, in *Ibid.*, 7–9.

23. Dr. Edward Fitzgerald, Interview with author, Quincy Historical Society, Quincy, Massachusetts, October 28, 2021.

24. The catalog was done and is found in John Adams, *Deeds and Other Documents*, 15–67.

25. From John Adams to MA Town of Quincy, August 10, 1822, in John Adams, *Deeds and Other Documents*, 12.

26. *Ibid.*, 12–13.

27. Boston Public Library, "Adams, John (1735–1826) Library," last modified 2021, Accessed November 9, 2021. https://www.bpl.org/archival_post/adams-john-1735-1826-library/.

28. Mayor Thomas Koch to David Leonard, President, Boston Public Library,

quoted in Mary Whitfill, "Quincy takes first step toward Potential John Adams Presidential library," *The Patriot Ledger*, August 14, 2020.

29. *Ibid.*

30. Mary Whitfill, "Boston library board discusses Quincy Request for John Adams Collection," *The Patriot Ledger*, September 30, 2020.

31. The author would like to thank Kelly Cobble of the Adams National Historical Park for alerting her to the importance of this cemetery to John Adams. Kelly Cobble, phone interview with the author, January 8, 2020.

32. Quincy Historical Society, "Quincy's Historic Hancock Cemetery: An Introduction and Guide" (Quincy, Massachusetts: Quincy Historical Society, Massachusetts Cultural Council, and the Quincy Arts Council, 2002), 1.

33. Gravestone of Henry Adams (1583–1646), Hancock Cemetery, Quincy, Massachusetts.

34. Gravestone of Joseph Adams II (1654–1736) and Hannah Bass Adams (1667–1705), Hancock Cemetery, Quincy, Massachusetts.

35. My sincere gratitude goes to Alexandra Elliot and Corinne Waite of the Quincy Historical Society for their diligent search to find information about this statue. The details come from two newspaper clippings, both with the same title. "John Adams Statue to be Unveiled Sunday in Freedom Park," *The Quincy Sun*, October 13, 1977, 17; "John Adams Statue to be Unveiled at Freedom Park," *The Quincy Patriot Ledger*, October 7, 1977, no page listed.

36. H. Hobart Holly, "Quincy and the Constitution," *Quincy History*, Quincy Historical Society (Fall, 1987): 8.

37. H. Hobart Holly, "The 'Most Important Historical Event,'" *Quincy History*, Quincy Historical Society (Fall, 1980): 2.

38. *The Boston Globe*, "John Adams Gets Statue at City Hall," Boston, Massachusetts, November 4, 2001, 246.

39. Bill Westland, "Adams Temple and School Fund," vignette shared with author, November 2021.

40. Daniel Windsor, AICP, PP, Practice Leader, Urban Revitalization, Woodward and Curran, "Hancock Adams Common: Quincy's Vision Four Decades in the

Making," 2021, Accessed November 22, 2021, https://www.woodardcurran.com/blog/hancock-adams-common.

41. Mayor Thomas Koch, Speech given at the dedication of the Hancock Adams Common, Quincy, Massachusetts, September 8, 2018, quoted in "Gov. Baker, Historian McCullough Keynote Hancock-Adams Common Dedication," *The Quincy Sun, Historic Quincy: 2019 Visitor Guide*, Thursday, May 16, 2019, 45A.

42. I am also willing to concede that the resemblance to Giamatti may only be in the eye of this beholder (the author). Others may not see it. This was my first impression.

43. For Lynch's remarks, see "Gov. Baker, Historian McCullough Keynote Hancock-Adams Common Dedication," 47A. For Baker's remarks, see 46A. For Ben Adams's remarks see 47A.

44. For McCullough's comments, see *Ibid.*, 46A–47A.

45. For Adams's thoughts on the importance of the establishment of State governments, see John Adams to Abigail Adams, May 17, 1776, in *John Adams: Revolutionary Writings, 1775–1783*, edited by Gordon Wood (New York: Library of America, 2011), 70; For Adams's famous observation concerning the anniversary celebration of the United States, see John Adams to Abigail Adams, July 3, 1776, in *John Adams: Revolutionary Writings, 1775-1783*, 93.

46. David McCullough, Speech at the Dedication of the Hancock Adams Common, "Gov. Baker, Historian McCullough Keynote Hancock-Adams Common Dedication," *The Quincy Sun, Historic Quincy: 2019 Visitor Guide*, Thursday, May 16, 2019, 46A.

47. Dr. Edward Fitzgerald, Interview with author, Quincy Historical Society, Quincy, Massachusetts, October 28, 2021.

48. For the full story of the saga of Abigail's statue, see Mary Whitfill, "'The most important woman of her generation': Abigail Adams to get downtown Quincy statue," *The Patriot Ledger*, April 14, 2022, Accessed April 18, 2022. https://www.patriotledger.com/story/news/2022/04/14/abigail-adams-get-downtown-quincy-statue-section-hancock-adams-common/7311895001/.

Chapter Nine

1. For the relationship between the National Park Service and the United First Parish Church, see "Visitor's Program" on the church's website. Accessed October 22, 2021.https://ufpc.org/visitors-program-1.

2. This house has gone by a number of names. John Adams named it "Peacefield" to commemorate the peace Treaty of 1783 which granted the American colonies their independence, a treaty that he helped to negotiate. He also referred to it as "Montezillo" or Little Hill to contrast it with Jefferson's "Monticello" or Little Mountain. It is also referred to at times as "Peace Field" and more generally as "The Old House."

3. Caroline Keinath, *Adams National Historical Park* (Lawrenceburg, IN: R.L. Ruehrwein, The Creative Company, 2008), 10.

4. Kelly Cobble, Curator, Adams National Historical Park, Interview with author, October 27, 2021.

5. See Keinath, 11.

6. Wilhelmina S. Harris, *Adams National Historic Site: A Family's Legacy to America* (Washington, D.C.: U.S. Department of the Interior, National Park Service, 1983),1.

7. For Krug's authorization quotation, see United States Congress, *Adams National Historical Park Act of* 1998, Public Law 105–342, Section 2,105th Congress, 1998. This act outlined the history of the site from 1946 to 1998. For this early history, see National Park Planner, "Adams National Historical Park: Park at a Glance," Park Overview. https://npplan.com/parks-by-state/massachusetts-national-parks/adams-national-historical-park-park-at-a-glance/. Information on the involvement of Wilhelmina Harris came from a phone interview with Kelly Cobble, conducted by the author, August 11, 2021.

8. Thomas Boylston Adams, Foreword, in Harris, vii–viii.

9. Harris, 2.

10. *Ibid.*, 4–5.

11. Keinath, 13; 20. For a description of the wreath, see page 19. Curator Kelly Cobble mentioned that the wreath was her favorite artifact in the house in an interview for "Revolution 250 Podcast: Adams

National Historical Park." Host: Bob Allison, August 10, 2021.

12. According to Dr. Edward Fitzgerald, Executive Director of the Quincy Historical Society, the Daughters of the Revolution was a similar but distinct organization from the Daughters of the American Revolution. It was the sister organization to the Sons of the Revolution. The latter is still in existence today.

13. Thanks to Dr. Edward Fitzgerald for sharing the sign with the author. Also, thanks to Alexandra Elliott for the transcription. The sign used the 18th-century style of "s" appearing as "f," which I have modernized and the month of reopening is too badly faded to read.

14. Dr. Edward Fitzgerald, Interview with author, Quincy Historical Society, Quincy, Massachusetts, October 28, 2021.

15. For the history of the birthplaces, see "Adams National Historical Park: Park at A Glance," Park Overview. https://npplan.com/parks-by-state/massachusetts-national-parks/adams-national-historical-park-park-at-a-glance/. For the conveyance of the birthplaces to the National Park service, see United States Congress, *National Park and Recreation Act of 1978*, Public Law 95–625, Section 312, 95th Congress, 1978.

16. John Adams to Abigail Adams, May 2, 1775, *Adams Family Correspondence*, Volume 1, Adams Papers Digital Edition, Accessed November 12, 2021. https://www.masshist.org/publications/adams-papers/index.php/view/ADMS-04-01-02-0128.

17. Abigail Adams to John Adams, June 16 [?] 1775, *Adams Family Correspondence*, Volume 1, Adams Papers Digital Edition, Accessed November 12, 2021. https://www.masshist.org/publications/adams-papers/index.php/view/ADMS-04-01-02-0147.

18. Abigail Adams to John Adams, June [17], 1775, *Adams Family Correspondence*, Volume 1, Adams Papers Digital Edition, Accessed November 12, 2021. https://www.masshist.org/publications/adams-papers/index.php/view/ADMS-04-01-02-0150. There is some confusion about the date of this letter. It is dated the 18th of June, but we know the battle took place on the 17th. She is clearly writing as the battle was taking place.

19. John Quincy Adams to James Sturge,

March 1846, *Adams Family Papers*, Massachusetts Historical Society Collections Online, Accessed November 12, 2021. http://www.masshist.org/database/405.

20. *Patriot Ledger*, "Abigail Adams at Penn's Hill on Bunker Hill Day," YouTube Video, 2:42, June 17, 2018, https://www.youtube.com/watch?v=777PpMyYRgM&list=PL6LRlnIInytB0a6L49RArSiLN3NMVLbNt&index=15.

21. U.S. Department of the Interior, National Park Service, *Foundation Document Overview, Adams National Historical Park, Massachusetts* (Washington, D.C., Department of the Interior, no date given), 4.

22. Bill Westland, Visitor Program Vignettes, "Three Hundred and Eighty-One Years," shared with the author on October 7, 2020; United First Parish Church Website, "History of Our Church," Last modified 2020, Accessed November 15, 2021. https://ufpc.org/ufpc-history. The author is deeply indebted to Mr. Westland for sharing his encyclopedic knowledge of his church's history with her and answering any and all questions she had.

23. Westland, "Three Hundred and Eighty-One Years."

24. *Ibid.*; Quotation from John Adams, *Deeds and Other Documents relating to the Several Pieces of Land And to the Library presented to the Town of Quincy, by President Adams, Together With a Catalogue of The Books* (Cambridge: Printed By Hilliard and Metcalf, 1823, Reprinted in London: Forgotten Books, FB&Ltd, Dalton House, 2018), 5.

25. Bill Westland, Visitor Program Vignettes, "Church Building Dedication," shared with the author on November 10, 2021.

26. Bill Westland, Visitor Program Vignettes, "History of the Visitor's Program," shared with the author on November 4, 2021.

27. United States Congress, *Authorizing the Secretary of the Interior to accept the conveyance of the United First Parish Church in Quincy, Massachusetts, and authorizing the Secretary to administer the United First Parish Church as a National Historic Site, and for other purposes*, Public Law 96–435, 96th Congress, October 10, 1980.

28. United First Parish Church,

"Visitors Program," Accessed October 22, 2021, https://ufpc.org/visitors-program-1.

29. For the history and figures listed, see Westland, "History of the Visitor's Program."

30. *Ibid.*

31. Bill Westland, Visitor Program Vignettes, "Wreath Laying," shared with the author on September 21, 2021.

32. *Ibid.* Many of these traditions were suspended due to the pandemic, but Westland is working to reinstate them.

33. *Ibid.*

34. For the 2021 John Adams event, see Quincy Access Television, "John Adams Presidential Wreath Laying Ceremony, October 29, 2021," YouTube, Accessed November 16, 2021. https://www.youtube.com/watch?v=P12fVbRWHLw&list=PL6LRlnIInytB0a6L49RArSiLN3NMVLbNt&index=5&t=773s.

35. United States Congress, *Adams National Historical Park Act of 1998*, Public Law 105–342, 105th Congress, November 2, 1998.

36. Marianne Peak, "The Presidency: Presidential Libraries Symposium," C-Span, February 28, 2011, 2:13:39, Time stamp: 2:06:55, Accessed November 17, 2021. https://www.c-span.org/video/?-298234-1/presidential-libraries-symposium.

37. *Ibid.*

38. Kelly Cobble, Interview with the author, Quincy, Massachusetts, October 27, 2021.

39. *Ibid.*

40. See Page Smith, *John Adams*, 2 volumes, The Library of the Presidents, Collector's Edition (Norwalk, CT: The Easton Press, 1963); Samuel Flagg Bemis, *John Quincy Adams and The Foundations of American Foreign Policy & the Union* 2 Volumes (New York: Alfred A. Knopf, 1949).

41. Kelly Cobble, Interview with the author, Quincy, Massachusetts, October 27, 2021.

42. *Ibid.*

43. *Ibid.*

44. Alison Kiernan, Richard Shaner informal interviews with the author, Peacefield Carriage House, October 28, 2021.

45. See Joseph Ellis, *Passionate Sage: The Character and Legacy of John Adams* (New York: W.W. Norton & Company,

1993), 183–185. Ellis's book is popular with the staff at the Adams National Historical Park. Cobble loved the book.

46. Alison Kiernan, Richard Shaner informal interviews with the author, Peacefield Carriage House, October 28, 2021.

47. Kelly Cobble, Interview with the author, Quincy, Massachusetts, October 27, 2021.

48. *Ibid.*

49. *Ibid.*

50. Jeanne E. Abrams, *A View from Abroad: The Story of John and Abigail Adams in Europe* (New York: New York University Press, 2021).

51. The John Adams Institute, "About Us: Mission," Accessed November 19, 2021. https://www.john-adams.nl/about-us/mission/.

52. The John Adams Institute, "John Adams Year 2005 Celebration," Accessed November 19,2021. https://www.john-adams.nl/john-adams-year-2005-celebration/.

53. For quotation, see John Adams, *A Defence of the Constitutions of Government of the United States of America, Volume 1, letter IV* (Philadelphia: Budd and Bartran, 1797 orig. printing; Quincy, MA: Liberty's Lamp Books, 2015 repr.), 16; For statue, see Anne-Marie Chiramberro, *Hella Basque*, "How John Adams Drew Inspiration from the Basque Country in Drafting the U.S. Constitution," February 18, 2019, Accessed November 19, 2021. https://www.hellabasque.org/johnadams/.

54. Kelly Cobble, Interview with the author, Quincy, Massachusetts, October 27, 2021.

55. A picture of this card was shared with the author via email by Richard Shaner.

56. For information on Peyton Dixon, see Peyton Dixon, "Historic Experience," 2021, Accessed November 24, 2021. https://www.historicexperience.com/. For Dixon's reading reviews of the park, see Historic Experience, "John Adams Reviews the Reviews, Part 1," YouTube Video, 5:36, June 2, 2021, https://www.youtube.com/watch?v=9SNtyyWP0_c&list=PL6LRlnIInytB0a6L49RArSiLN3NMVLbNt&index=10. Historic Experience, "John Adams Reviews the Reviews, Part 2," YouTube Video, 5:33, September 3, 2021, https://www.youtube.com/watch?v=hs9wG-mvdr

U&list=PL6LRlnIInytB0a6L49RArSiLN3NMVLbNt&index=10.

57. I have reached out to Mr. Dixon, but as of this writing, he has not responded to my request for an interview.

58. There are various places to spot Sam Goodyear on the Internet. His one-man play is available as an audio book and a Kindle book on Amazon. Sam Goodyear, *John Adams: The Man From Massachusetts*, Kindle Edition (Campton, NH: Simply Magazine, 2014); For *Jefferson and Adams* production details, see IMDb, "Jefferson and Adams" 2021, Accessed November 24, 2021. https://www.imdb.com/title/tt1239367/?ref_=nm_knf_t1. See a longer discussion of the play mentioned here in Chapter Four.

59. Most recently, Lepage appeared on July 3, 2022 at the Hancock Adams Common. See Adams National Historical Park Facebook Page, July 3, 2022.

60. John Adams to Abigail Adams, February 27, 1793, The Adams Papers, Digital Edition, Accessed January 25, 2022. https://www.masshist.org/publications/adams-papers/index.php/view/ADMS-04-09-02-0237#sn=0.

Conclusion

1. Henry Adams, *The Education of Henry Adams* (Boston: Houghton Mifflin Company, 1918), 9–10.

2. Gale E. Christianson, *Writing Lives Is the Devil! Essays of a Biographer at Work* (Hamden, Connecticut: Archon Books, 1993), xv.

3. *Ibid.*, 10.

4. Nancy Isenberg and Andrew Burstein, "The Adamses on Screen," *A Companion to John Adams and John Quincy Adams*, First Edition (Hoboken, New Jersey: John Wiley & Sons, Ltd., 2013), 488.

5. Linda Hutcheon, *A Theory of Adaptation* (New York: Routledge, 2006), 13.

6. *Ibid.*

7. See, for example, John Adams to Richard Rush, November 20, 1813, *John Adams: Writings from the New Nation, 1784–1826* edited by Gordon S. Wood (New York: The Library of America, 2016). 576; John Adams to Robert J. Evans, *Writings from the New Nation*, 647.

8. John Adams to Henry Colman in *Ibid.*, 621.

9. Michael Kammen, *A Season of Youth: The American Revolution and the Historical Imagination* (Ithaca: Cornell University Press, 1978), 256.

10. *Ibid.*, 222.

11. John Adams to Abigail Adams, March 9, 1797, Adams Family Correspondence, Volume 12, *Adams Papers Digital Edition*. Accessed June 27, 2022. https://www.masshist.org/publications/adams-papers/index.php/view/ADMS-04-12-02-0009#sn=0.

12. Kammen, 222.

13. Catharine R. Stimpson, Preface, *Past Meets Present: Essays about Historic Interpretation and Public Audiences*, edited by Jo Blatti (Washington D.C.: Smithsonian Institution Press, 1986), ix.

14. John Adams to John Whitney, June 7, 1826, in *John Adams: Writings from the New Nation, 1784–1826*, edited by Gordon S. Wood (New York: The Library of America, 2016), 675. Italics in original.

Bibliography

Abrams, Dan and Fisher, David. *John Adams Under Fire: The Founding Father's Fight for Justice in the Boston Massacre Murder Trial.* Toronto: Hanover Square Press, 2020.

Abrams, Jeanne E. *A View from Abroad: The Story of John and Abigail Adams in Europe.* New York: New York University Press, 2021.

Adams, Charles Francis, Jr. *The New English Canaan of Thomas Morton with Introductory Matter and Notes.* Project Gutenberg: Free eBooks, 1883. Release date: February 14, 2017 [eBook # 541627].

Adams, Henry. *The Education of Henry Adams.* Boston: Houghton Mifflin Company, 1918.

Adams, James Truslow. *The Adams Family.* Boston: Little, Brown, and Company, 1903.

Adams, John. *Deeds and Other Documents Relating to The Several Pieces of Land and to the Library Presented to the Town of Quincy, By President Adams, Together with a Catalogue of The Books.* Cambridge: Printed by Hilliard and Metcalf, 1823, Reprinted in London: Forgotten Books, FB&Ltd, Dalton House, 2018.

_____. *A Defence of the Constitutions of Government of the United States of America,* Volume 1, Letter IV. Philadelphia: Bud and Bartram, 1797 original printing. Reprint Quincy, MA: Liberty's Lamp Books, 2015.

_____. *Diary and Autobiography,* Volumes 1–4, edited by L.H. Butterfield. Cambridge: Harvard University Press, 1962.

_____. *The Earliest Diary of John Adams,* edited by L.H. Butterfield. Cambridge: The Belknap Press of Harvard University Press, 1966.

_____. *John Adams: Revolutionary Writings, 1775–1783,* edited by Gordon Wood. New York: The Library of America, 2011.

_____. *John Adams: Writings from the New Nation, 1784–1826,* edited by Gordon Wood. New York: The Library of America, 2016.

_____. *The Works of John Adams, Second President of the United States: With a Life of the Author,* edited by Charles Francis Adams. Boston: Little, Brown, and Company, 1850–56.

Adams, John Quincy and Charles Francis Adams. *John Adams, 2 Volumes.* Philadelphia: Lippincott, 1871. Reprint American Statesmen Series, edited by Arthur M. Schlesinger. New York: Chelsea House, 1980.

Adams, Val. "And Here Are Peabody Winners." *Daily News,* April 19, 1977.

The Adams Chronicles. DVD. Directed by Paul Bogart, Fred Coe, Barry Davis, Bill Glenn, James Cellen Jones, and Anthony Page. Educational Broadcasting Corporation and Acorn Media, 2008.

Allen, Brooke. "John Adams: Realist of the Revolution." *The Hudson Review,* Volume 55, No. 1. (Spring 2002): 45–54.

Allmusic.com. "Biography of Sherman Edwards." Accessed July 25, 2019. https://www.allmusic.com/artist/sherman-edwards-mn0000026459/biography.

American Experience. "John & Abigail Adams." DVD. Directed by Peter Jones. PBS Home Video, 2006.

American Repertory Theater. Website. https://americanrepertorytheater.org/shows-events/1776-revival/.

Andrlik, Todd. "John Dickinson's Hit Single: Liberty Song." *The Journal of the*

American Revolution, March 12, 2014. Accessed July 30, 2019, https://allthings liberty.com/2014/03/the-liberty-song/.

Ann-Marie. *Hella Basque.* "How John Adams Drew Inspiration from the Basque Country in Drafting the U.S. Constitution." February 18, 2019. Accessed November 19,2021. https://www.hellabasque.org/johnadams/.

ArchitectureChigago Plus Blogspot. "Tonight on WYIN-Founding Father Rescued from the Waxworks- Simon Russell Beale as John Adams." February 6, 2006. Accessed July 5, 2021. http://arcchicago.blogspot.com/2006/02/tonight-on-wyin-founding-father.html.

Aron, Paul. *Founding Feuds: The Rivalries, Clashes, and Conflicts That Forged a Nation.* Williamsburg, VA: Sourcebooks, 2016.

Bailyn, Bernard. "Butterfield's Adams: Notes for a Sketch." *The William and Mary Quarterly,* Volume 19, No. 2 (April, 1962): 238–256.

_____. *The Ideological Origins of the American Revolution.* Cambridge: Harvard University Press, 1967.

Banning, Lance. "Popularizing the Founding: A Review Essay." *The Register of The Kentucky Historical Society,* Volume 99, No. 2 (Spring 2001): 153–157.

Barkham, John. "Fact and Fancy." *Tucson Daily Citizen,* November 13, 1965.

Barnes, Clive. "Spirited 1776: Founding Fathers' Tale is a Happy Musical." *New York Times,* March 17, 1969.

Beaman, James. "Becoming John Adams: A Video Blog Series. Seven Posts." *James Beaman.* Jamesbeaman.com. https://www.jamesbeaman.com/video.

Bernstein, R.B. *The Education of John Adams.* Oxford: Oxford University Press, 2020.

Beutler, Keith. *George Washington's Hair: How Early Americans Remembered the Founders.* Charlottesville: University of Virginia Press, 2021.

Binckes, Jeremy. Interview with William Daniels. "*1776* Star William Daniels opens up about performing for Richard Nixon, meeting *Hamilton* creator Lin-Manuel Miranda." *Salon,* March 13, 2017. Video produced by Peter Cooper. Accessed July 24, 2019. https://www.salon.com/2017/03/13/watch-1776-star-william-daniels-opens-up-about-performing-for-richard-nixon-meeting-hamilton-creator-lin-manuel-miranda/.

Biography. "John and Abigail Adams: Love and Liberty." DVD. A&E Television Networks, 2002.

Blake, Casey Nelson. "The Usable Past, The Comfortable Past, and The Civic Past: Memory in Contemporary America." *Cultural Anthropology,* Volume 14, No. 3 (August 1999): 423–435.

Blatti, Jo, Ed. *Past Meets Present: Essays about Historic Interpretation and Public Audiences.* Washington, D.C.: Smithsonian Institution Press, 1986.

The Boston Globe. "John Adams Gets Statue at City Hall." Boston, Massachusetts, November 4, 2001.

Boston Public Library. "Adams, John (1735–1826) Library." Last modified 2021. Accessed November 9, 2021. https://www.bpl.org/archival_post/adams-john-1735-1826-library/.

Bowen, Catherine Drinker. *John Adams and the American Revolution.* Boston: Little, Brown, and Company, 1950.

Boyer, Peter J. "TV Movie 'The Rebels' Making Debut." *The Central New Jersey Home News* (New Brunswick, New Jersey). May 14, 1979.

Brookhiser, Richard. *America's First Dynasty: The Adamses, 1735–1918.* New York: The Free Press, 2002.

Brooks, Van Wyck. "On Creating a Usable Past." *The Dial: A Fortnightly Journal of Criticism and Discussion of Literature and The Arts,* Volume LXIV. January 3 to June 6, 1918: 337–341.

Brown, Richard D. "The Apotheosis of John Adams." *The William and Mary Quarterly,* Volume 59, No.1 (January 2002): 305–314.

Burleigh, Anne Husted. *John Adams.* New Brunswick: Transaction Publishers, 1969.

Butcher, Fanny. "The Literary Spotlight." *The Chicago Tribune,* May 14, 1950.

Butterfield, L.H. "The Jubilee of Independence: July 4, 1826." *The Virginia Magazine of History and Biography,* Volume 6, No. 2 (April 1953): 119–140.

_____. "The Papers of the Adams Family: Some Account of Their History." *Proceedings of the Massachusetts Historical Society,* Third Series, Vol. 71. (October 1953-May 1957): 328–356.

Calhoon, Robert. "John Adams and the Psychology of Power." *Reviews in American History*, Volume 4, No.4 (December 1976): 520–525.

Cappon, Lester J., ed. *The Adams-Jefferson Letters: The Complete Correspondence Between Thomas Jefferson and Abigail and John Adams*, 2 Volumes. Chapel Hill: University of North Carolina Press, 1959.

Cavendish, Richard. "The Gregorian Calendar Adopted in England, September 2nd, 1752." 54. *History Today*, Volume 52, Issue 9, September 2002.

The Charleston Library Society. "How to Write Biography." John Avlon Interview with David McCullough, Jun 4, 2015. Accessed June 30, 2019. https://www.youtube.com/watch?v=U-iWlND7DII.

Chinard, Gilbert. *Honest John Adams*. Boston: Little, Brown, 1933.

Christianson, Gale E. *Writing Lives Is the Devil! Essays of a Biographer at Work*. Hamden, CT: Archon Books, 1993.

Chu, Jonathan, Cobble, Kelly, and Deane, Elizabeth. GBH Forum Network on YouTube. 2005. Accessed July 5, 2021. https://www.youtube.com/watch?v=TrTWEAeJ-Jk&t=604s.

Cobble, Kelly. Interview with the author, John Adams and John Quincy Adams birthplaces, Quincy, Massachusetts, October 27, 2021.

Connelly, Thomas L. *The Marble Man: Robert E. Lee and His Image in American Society*. Baton Rouge: Louisiana State University Press, 1977.

Cunliffe, Marcus. "John and Abigail's Road to the White House." *New York Times*, November 7, 1965.

Daniels, William. *There I Go Again: How I Came to Be Mr. Feeny, John Adams, Dr. Craig, KITT, & Many Others*. Lincoln: Potomac Books, an Imprint of University of Nebraska Press, 2017.

Dauer, Manning J. *The Adams Federalists*. Baltimore: Johns Hopkins University Press, 1953.

David, Louise. "From 'Adams' Struggle to Nashville Romance." *The Tennessean* (Nashville, Tennessee). March 21, 1976.

Daynard, Jodi. *The Midwife's Revolt*. Seattle: Lake Union Publishing, 2015.

———. *A More Perfect Union*. Seattle: Lake Union Publishing, 2017.

———. *Our Own Country*. Seattle: Lake Union Publishing, 2016.

Dickie, George. "Series Follows Young dissidents in 'Sons of Liberty.'" *The Daily Oklahoman* (Oklahoma City, Oklahoma). January 23, 2015.

Dixon, Payton. "John Adams Reviews the Reviews, Part 1 and 2. YouTube Videos. June 2 and September 3, 2021. Accessed November 5, 2021. https://www.youtube.com/watch?v=9SNtyyWP0_c&list=PL6LRlnIInytB0a6L49RArSiLN3NMVLbNt&index=10. https://www.youtube.com/watch?v=hs9wG-mvdrU&list=PL6LRlnIInytB0a6L49RArSiLN3NMVLbNt&index=10.

Ebert, Roger. "Review of *1776*." Roger Ebert.com. December 26, 1972. Accessed July 31, 2019, https://www.rogerebert.com/reviews/1776-1972.

Editor, *New York Times*. "Editor's Choice." December 2, 2001.

Ellis, Joseph. *First Family: Abigail and John Adams*. New York: Alfred A. Knopf, 2010.

———. *Passionate Sage: The Character and Legacy of John Adams*. New York: W.W. Norton, 1993.

Evans, Greg. "Broadway-Bound '1776' Musical Revival Announces Female, Non-Binary And Trans Cast." Deadline.com. April 8, 2022. Accessed June 25, 2022. https://deadline.com/2022/04/broadway-bound-1776-revival-female-non-binary-trans-cast-1234997377/.

Fassler, Ron. *Up in the Cheap Seats: A Historical Memoir of Broadway*. Santa Monica, California: Griffin Moon, 2017.

Ferling, John. *John Adams: A Life*. New York: Henry Holt and Company, 1992.

———. "John Adams, Diplomat." *The William and Mary Quarterly*, Volume 51, No. 2 (April 1994): 227–252.

———, and Braverman, Lewis E. "John Adams' Health Reconsidered." *The William and Mary Quarterly*, Volume 55, No. 1 (January 1998): 83–104.

Filichia, Peter. "*1776*: IT'S A MASTERPIECE, I SAY." *Masterworks Broadway*, August 5, 2014. Accessed July 24, 2019, https://masterworksbroadway.com/blog/1776-its-a-masterpiece-i-say/.

Fischer, Heinz-D., Ed. The Pulitzer Prize Archive Part G: Supplements Volume 20: Chronicle for the Pulitzer Prizes for Biography. K.G.Saur Münch, 2006.

Fitzgerald, Edward. Interview with the author, Quincy Historical Society, Quincy, Massachusetts, October 28, 2021.

Floyd, Stephen. "The Best Biographies of John Adams." *My Journey Through the Best Presidential Biographies.* WordPress.com, March 9, 2013. Accessed July 24, 2021.https://bestpresidentialbios. com/2013/03/09/the-best-biographies-of-john-adams/.

"Front Matter." *American Libraries,* 7, No. 1. 1976.

Furstenberg, François. *In the Name of the Father: Washington's Legacy, Slavery, and the Making of a Nation.* New York: The Penguin Press, 2006.

Gelles, Edith B. *Abigail and John: Portrait of a Marriage.* New York: Harper Perennial, 2009.

_____. "The Abigail Industry." *The William and Mary Quarterly,* Volume 45, No. 4. October, 1988: 656–683.

Georgini, Sara. *Household Gods: The Religious Lives of the Adams Family.* Oxford: Oxford University Press, 2019.

Gewen, Barry. "Forget the Founding Fathers." *New York Times,* June 5, 2005.

Giamaitti, Paul. "Paul Giamatti, Full Q & A." *Oxford Union.* YouTube. 38:02. June 11, 2018. Accessed December 15, 2021. https://www.youtube.com/watch?v=Ouz-_VzanOA.

Gibson, William. *American Primitive (John & Abigail).* New York: Dramatists Play Service, Inc., 1971.

Ginsberg, Howard. *Jefferson and Adams: A Stage Play.* DVD. Directed by Douglas Anderson. Colonial Williamsburg Foundation in Association with the Jefferson Legacy Foundation, 2004. DVD.

Goodyear, Sam. *John Adams: The Man from Massachusetts.* Kindle. Campton, NH: Simply Magazine, 2014.

Gordon, Colin. "Crafting a Usable Past: Consensus, Ideology, and Historians of the American Revolution." *The William and Mary Quarterly,* Volume 46, No. 4. (October 1989): 671–695.

Gordon, Tammy S. *The Spirit of 1976: Commerce, Community, and the Politics of Commemoration.* Amherst: University of Massachusetts Press, 2013.

Grant, James. *John Adams: Party of One.* New York: Farrar, Straus and Giroux, 2005.

Griffin, Clifford S. "TV Viewing Guide: *The Adams Chronicles.*" *American Studies,* Volume 19, No. 2, A New Look at Old Masters. Mid-America American Studies Association (Fall 1978): 75–84.

Grode, Eric. "The 1969 Tonys Was a Night to Remember." *New York Times,* June 5, 2019.

Hamilton, Barbara. *A Marked Man.* New York: Berkley Prime Crime, 2010.

_____. *The Ninth Daughter.* New York: The Berkley Publishing Group, 2009.

_____. *Sup with the Devil.* New York: The Berkley Publishing Group, 2011.

Haraszti, Zoltán. *John Adams and the Prophets of Progress: A Study in the Intellectual and Political History of the Eighteenth Century.* New York: Grosset & Dunlap, 1952.

Harris, Harry. "George Grizzard Settles for the Presidency." *The Philadelphia Inquirer.* January 18, 1976.

Harris, Wilhelmina S. *Adams National Historic Site: A Family's Legacy to America.* Washington, D.C.: U.S. Department of the Interior, National Park Service, 1983.

Hattem, Michael. *Past and Prologue: Politics and Memory in the American Revolution.* New Haven: Yale University Press, 2020.

History.Com. "Sons of Liberty." Accessed October 27, 2016. http://www.history.com/shows/sons-of-liberty/about.

Holly, Hobart. "The 'Most Important Historical Event.'" *Quincy History,* Quincy Historical Society (Fall, 1980).

_____. "Quincy and the Constitution." *Quincy History,* Quincy Historical Society (Fall, 1987).

Holton, Woody. *Abigail Adams.* New York: Free Press, 2009.

Hopper, Hedda. "The Adamses in Hollywood." *The Daily News,* December 24, 1965.

Howe, John. *The Changing Political Thought of John Adams.* Princeton: Princeton University Press, 1966.

_____. "*John Adams* by David McCullough." *The Journal of American History,* Volume 90, No. 1. (June 2003): 210–211.

Hoyt, William D., Jr. "Life of Abigail Adams: Good View of the Late Eighteenth Century." *The Boston Globe,* November 28, 1965.

Hurt, N.S. "Historical Mystery Fiction." Last modified October 12, 2021. Accessed May 13, 2021. https://brerfox.tripod.com/historicalmystery.html.

Hutcheon, Linda. *A Theory of Adaptation.* New York: Routledge, 2006.

Isenberg, Nancy, and Burstein, Andrew. "The Adamses on Screen." *A Companion to John Adams and John Quincy Adams,* First Edition. Hoboken, New Jersey: John Wiley & Sons, Ltd., 2013.

_____. "America's Worst Historians." *Salon,* August 19th, 2012. Accessed June 29, 2019. https://www.salon.com/2012/08/19/americas_worst_historians/.

Jack (no last name given). "Roger Ebert's Worst Reviews" *Rogersworst Blogspot.* Accessed July 31, 2019. https://rogersworst.blogspot.com/2011/01/42-1776-1772.html.

Jakes, John. *The Rebels.* New York: Signet, 1975; 2003.

Jefferson, Thomas. *The Papers of Thomas Jefferson,* Volume 1, 1760–1776. Edited by Julian P. Boyd. Princeton: Princeton University Press, 1950.

John Adams. DVD. Directed by Thomas Hooper. HBO Films, 2008.

"John Adams and America's Birthday: Behind the Scenes of History—New Series on The Adams Papers." *Life.* June 30, 1961.

The John Adams Institute. Website Accessed November 19, 2021. https://www.john-adams.nl/.

Johnson, Ronald Angelo. *Diplomacy in Black and White: John Adams, Toussaint Louverture, and Their Atlantic World Alliance.* Athens: The University of Georgia Press, 2014.

Jorden-Smith, Paul. "Scholar John Adams Helps Found Nation." *The Los Angeles Times,* June 11, 1950.

Kachun, Mitch. *First Martyr of Liberty: Crispus Attucks in American Memory.* Oxford: Oxford University Press, 2017.

Kammen, Michael. *A Season of Youth: The American Revolution and the Historical Imagination.* Ithaca and London: Cornell University Press, 1978.

Kare, Jeffrey. "The Making of America's Musical—*1776*: The Story Behind the Story." *Broadway World Online,* July 4, 2016. Accessed on July 24, 2019. https://www.broadwayworld.com/article/The-Making-of-Americas-Musical--1776-The-Story-Behind-the-Story-20160704.

Keinath, Caroline. *Adams National Historical Park.* Lawrenceburg, IN: R.L. Ruehrwein, The Creative Company, 2008.

Kennedy, John F. "Review of *The Adams Papers, Series I, Diaries. Diary and Autobiography of John Adams.*" *The American Historical Review,* Volume 68, No.2. (January 1963): 478–480.

Kiernan, Alison M. Informal interview with the author. Peacefield Carriage House, Adams National Historical Park, Quincy, MA, October 28, 2021.

King, Susan. "With Restored Version Out, '1776' Director Recalls Politics Behind Cuts." *Los Angeles Times,* July 9, 2015.

Kleiman, Dena. "Lyman H. Butterfield, Editor of The Adams Papers." *New York Times,* April 26, 1982.

Kloppenberg, James T. "*John Adams* by Tom Hooper, David Coatsworth and Steve Shareshian," *The Journal of American History,* Volume 95, No. 3 (December 2008): 937–940.

Krebs, Albin. "Irving Stone, Author of 'Lust for Life,' Dies at 86." *New York Times,* August 28, 1989.

Liberty's Kids. Episode 103, "United We Stand." Directed by Judith Reilly. Accessed on YouTube, August 5, 2021. https://www.youtube.com/watch?v=oAbMPt1vXpU&list=PLHeaIWvdbER3Ic90BzhPsH2aJ5KI3UtmM&index=3.

_____. Episode 131, "Bostonians." Directed by Judith Reilly. Accessed on YouTube, August 5, 2021. https://www.youtube.com/watch?v=eqJ9PLGzvLc.

Library of Congress. "Finding Aid." *Catherine Drinker Bowen Papers.* Accessed June 24, 2021. https://findingaids.loc.gov/db/search/xq/searchMfer02.xq?_id=loc.mss.eadmss.ms011156&_faSection=overview&_faSubsection=scopecontent&_dmdid=d8949e19#ref1.

_____. *Journals of the Continental Congress, 1774-1789,* Edited from the Original Records in the Library of Congress by Worthington Chauncy Ford. Vol. 5, 1776, June 5-October 8th. Washington: Government Printing Office, 1909. Digitized by Google. Accessed June 29, 2019. https://babel.hathitrust.org/cgi/pt?id=mdp.39015068528697&view=1up&seq=96.

Lieberman, Paul. "Paul Giamatti is So Imperfect for the Role." *Los Angeles Times,* April 13, 2008.

Maier, Pauline. "Plain Speaking: In David McCullough's Telling, the Second

President Is Reminiscent of the 33rd (Harry Truman)." *New York Times,* May 27, 2001.

Marsh, Alec. *Ezra Pound.* London: Reaktion Books, 2011.

Massachusetts Court System. "Guide to John Adams and the Massachusetts Constitution." Mass.Gov. Accessed October 15, 2021. https://www.mass.gov/guides/john-adams-the-massachusetts-constitution.

Massachusetts Historical Society. "Adams Family Correspondence." *Adams Papers,* Digital Edition. Last Accessed June 28, 2022. https://www.masshist.org/publications/adams-papers/.

————. *Adams Family Papers: An Electronic Archive.* Accessed October 19, 2021. https://www.masshist.org/digital adams/archive/.

————. *Collections Online.* Accessed October 19, 2021. https://www.masshist.org/database/viewer.php?item_id=1746&pid=36.

Matthews, J.V. "'Whig History': The New England Whigs and a Usable Past." *The New England Quarterly,* Volume 51, No. 2. June, 1978: 193–208.

McCoy, Samuel. *This Man Adams: The Man Who Never Died.* New York: Brentano's, 1928.

McCullough, David. *John Adams.* New York: Simon & Schuster, 2001.

McGlone, Robert E. "Deciphering Memory: John Adams and the Authorship of the Declaration of Independence." *The Journal of American History,* Volume 85, No. 2 (September 1998): 411–438.

McNamara, Mary. "Never let Facts Get in the Way: 'Sons' Miniseries Takes Too Many Liberties on History about the American Revolution." *The Los Angeles Times,* January 24, 2015.

Middlekauff, Robert. "*John Adams* by David McCullough." *The New England Quarterly,* Volume 75, No. 1 (March 2002): 139–141.

Morgan, Edmund S. *Benjamin Franklin.* New Haven: Yale University Press, 2002.

————. "John Adams and the Puritan Tradition." *The New England Quarterly,* Volume 34, No. 4 (December 1961): 518–529.

Nagel, Paul C. *Descent from Glory: Four Generations of the John Adams Family.*

New York, Oxford: Oxford University Press, 1983.

National Archives. *Founders Online.* Last Accessed December 15, 2021. https://founders.archives.gov/.

National Park Planner. "Adams National Historical Park: Park at a Glance." Park Overview. Last modified June 1, 2020. Accessed October 22, 2021. https://np plan.com/parks-by-state/massachu setts-national-parks/adams-national-historical-park-park-at-a-glance/.

Nicolson, Colin and Edwards, Owen Dudley. *Imaginary Friendship in the American Revolution: John Adams and Jonathan Sewall.* New York: Routledge, 2019.

Nobles, Gregory H. "Historians Extend the Reach of the American Revolution." In Whose *American Revolution Was It? Historians Interpret the Founding,* edited by Alfred F. Young and Gregory H. Nobles, 135–255. New York: New York University Press, 2011.

O'Connor, John. "'The Adams Chronicles': American Television at Its Best." *New York Times.* January 20, 1976.

"Opening Season of Fall Treats." *Muncie Evening Press* (Muncie, Indiana). September 18, 1976.

Ourdocuments.gov. "The Sedition Act: Transcript of the Alien and Sedition Acts, 1798." Accessed July 10, 2020. https://www.ourdocuments.gov/doc.php?flash=false&doc=16&page=transcript #no-3.

Owens, Ken. "Historians and Hamilton: Founders Chic and the Cult of Personality." *The Junto: A Group Blog on The American Revolution.* April 21, 2016. Accessed December 11, 2021. https://earlyamericanists.com/2016/04/21/historians-and-hamilton-founders-chic-and-the-cult-of-personality/.

Parker, Theodore. *Historic Americans.* Boston: H.B. Fuller, 1871.

PBS NewsHour. "David McCullough discusses His Biography, *John Adams,* the Story of the Nation's Second President who Died on July 4, 1826." Public Broadcasting, July 4, 2002. Accessed June 25, 2019. https://www.pbs.org/newshour/show/david-mccullough-discusses-his-book-john-adams.

Peak, Marianne. "The Presidency: Presidential Libraries Symposium." C-Span,

February 28, 2011. 2:13:39. Time Stamp 2:06:55. Accessed November 17, 2021. https://www.c-span.org/video/?298234-1/presidential-libraries-symposium.

Piston, William Garrett. *Lee's Tarnished Lieutenant: James Longstreet and His Place in Southern History.* Athens: University of Georgia Press, 1987.

Pound, Ezra. *The Cantos of Ezra Pound.* New York: A New Directions Book, 1934–1972.

"Private Thoughts of a Founding Father." *Life.* June 30,1961.

Profiles in Courage. Episode 22. "John Quincy Adams." DVD. Directed by Michael Ritchie. Robert Saudek Associates, 1965. Converted to DVD by Thomas Film Classics, 2021.

———. Episode seven. "John Adams." DVD. Directed by Robert Stevens. Robert Saudek Associates, 1964. Converted to DVD by Thomas Film Classics, 2021.

Quincy Access Television. "John Adams Presidential Wreath Laying Ceremony, October 29, 2021." YouTube. Accessed November 16, 2021. https://www.youtube.com/watch?v=P12fVbRWHLw&list=PL6LRlnIInytB0a6L49RArSiLN3NMVLbNt&index=5&t=773s.

Quincy Historical Society. "Quincy's Historic Hancock Cemetery: An Introduction and Guide." Quincy Historical Society, Massachusetts Cultural Council, and the Quincy Arts Council, 2002.

The Quincy Patriot Ledger. "John Adams Statue to be Unveiled Sunday in Freedom Park." October 7, 1977.

The Quincy Sun. "Gov. Baker, Historian McCullough Keynote Hancock-Adams Common Dedication." *Historic Quincy: 2019 Visitor Guide,* Thursday, May 16, 2019.

———. "John Adams Statue to be Unveiled Sunday in Freedom Park." October 13, 1977.

Rakove, Jack. "The Patriot Who Refused to Sign the Declaration of Independence." History Net. Accessed September 9, 2019. https://www.historynet.com/the-patriot-who-refused-to-sign-the-declaration-of-independence.htm.

Rapid City, South Dakota. "John Adams." Visit Rapid City. Accessed November 19, 2021. https://www.visitrapidcity.com/things-to-do/all-things/attractions/city-presidents/john-adams.

The Rebels. DVD. Directed by Russ Mayberry. Universal Studios, 2019.

Reddy, John. "*1776:* The Idea That Would Not Let Go." *Reader's Digest* (February 1970): 199–204.

Revolution 250. "Revolution 250 Podcast: Adams National Historical Park." Host: Bob Allison speaking with Kelly Cobble, August 10, 2021. Accessed August 10, 2021. https://www.youtube.com/watch?v=WdRb8eDtwQ8.

Rollins, Peter C., Ed. *Hollywood as Historian: American Film in a Cultural Context,* Revised Edition. Lexington, Kentucky: The University of Kentucky Press, 1983.

Rollins, Richard. "Review of *The Adams Chronicles: Four Generations of Greatness* by Jack Shepard; *The World of the Adams Chronicles: Forging Our Nation,* edited by David J. Rothman; *The Adams Chronicles: A Student Guide* by Regina Janes." *The History Teacher,* Volume 10, No. 3 (May 1977): 453–455.

Rosenstone, Robert. *History on Film/Film on History.* New York: Pearson Education, 2006.

Rossiter, Clinton. "The Legacy of John Adams." *The Yale Review,* Volume 46 (1957): 528–550.

Russell, Francis. *Adams: An American Dynasty.* New York: American Heritage Publishing Co., Inc., Book Trade distribution by McGraw-Hill Book Company, 1976.

Sanders, Frederick K. *John Adams Speaking: Pound's Sources for the Adams Cantos.* Orono, Maine: University of Maine Press, 1975.

Sankovitch, Nina. *American Rebels: How the Hancock, Adams, and Quincy Families Fanned the Flames of Revolution.* New York: St. Martin's Press, 2020.

Scherr, Arthur. "John Adams, Political Moderation, and the 1820 Massachusetts Constitutional Convention: A Reappraisal." *Historical Journal of Massachusetts,* Volume 46, No. 1 (Winter 2018): 114–159.

———. *John Adams, Slavery, and Race: Ideas, Politics, and Diplomacy in an Age of Crisis.* Santa Barbara, California: Praeger, 2018.

Schocket, Andrew M. *Fighting Over the Founders: How We Remember the American Revolution.* New York: New York University Press, 2015.

_____. "The Founders Chic of Hamilton." *NYU Press Blog,* October 9, 2015. Accessed December 11, 2021. https://www.fromthesquare.org/the-founders-chic-of-hamilton/.

_____. "Little Founders on the Small Screen: Interpreting a Multicultural American Revolution for Children's Television." *Journal of American Studies,* Volume 45, No. 1. (February 2011): 145–163.

Seiler, Cotton. "The American Revolution." *The Columbia Companion to American History on Film: How the Movies Have Portrayed the American Past,* edited by Peter C. Rollins. New York: Columbia University Press, 2003.

1776: The Director's Cut. Blue-Ray. Directed by Peter Hunt. Columbia Pictures, 1972. Blue-Ray distributed by Sony Pictures Home Entertainment, 2007.

Shaner, Richard. Informal Interview with the Author. Peacefield Carriage House, Adams National Historical Park, Quincy, MA, October 28, 2021.

Sharbutt, Jay. "'Adams Chronicles' A $6.7 Million Series." *Lincoln Journal Star* (Lincoln, Nebraska). January 25, 1976.

Shaw, John A. *Eulogy on John Adams and Thomas Jefferson, Delivered August 2, 1826 by Request of the Inhabitants of Bridgewater.* Taunton, MA.: S.W. Mortimer, 1826.

Shaw, Peter. *The Character of John Adams.* Chapel Hill: The University of North Carolina Press, Published for the Institute of Early American History and Culture, Williamsburg, Virginia, 1976.

Shepherd, Jack. *The Adams Chronicles: Four Generations of Greatness.* Companion book to the series. Introduction by Daniel J. Boorstin. Boston: Little, Brown, and Company, 1975.

Shippy, Dick. "A Revolutionary winter for Doug McClure." *The Akron Beacon Journal* (Akron, Ohio, May 13, 1979).

Simon and Schuster.com. Accessed June 29, 2019. https://www.simonandschuster.com/books/John-Adams/David-McCullough/9780743223133.

Slaughter, Thomas P. *Independence: The Tangled Roots of the American Revolution.* New York: Hill and Wang: A Division of Farrar, Straus and Giroux, 2014.

Smith, Jean Edward. "*John Adams* by David McCullough." *Political Science Quarterly,* Volume 117, No. 1 (Spring 2002): 130–132.

Smith, Page. *John Adams,* 2 Volumes, Collector's Edition. Norwalk, CT: The Easton Press, 1962 and 1963.

Smith, Richard W. "Educational Television Is Not Educating." *Change,* Volume 10, No. 11 (Dec. 1978-Jan. 1979): 62–63, 78.

Sommer, Elyse. "Review of *American Primitive (Abigail and John)* produced by the Berkshire Theatre Festival's Unicorn Theatre, directed by Gary English." *CurtainUp: The Internet Theater Magazine of Reviews, Features, Annotated Listings.* May 2003. Accessed June 15, 2021. http://www.curtainup.com/americanprimitive.

Sons of Liberty. Blu-Ray. Directed by Kari Skogland. Lionsgate Films, History, 2015.

Sorkin, Aaron and Caddell, Patrick. "The West Wing," Season 2, Episode 8, "Shibboleth." DVD. Directed by Laura Innes. 2007.

Stanley, Alessandra. "Ale and Muskets Frame Revolt." *New York Times,* January 23, 2015.

_____. "Blowhard, Patriot, President." *New York Times,* March 14, 2008.

Stern, Jeremy. "What's Wrong with HBO's Dramatization of John Adams's Story." *History News Network,* Columbia School of Arts and Sciences, The George Washington University, no date given. Accessed June 30, 2019. https://historynewsnetwork.org/article/56155.

Stewart, Donald H. and Clark, George P. "Misanthrope or Humanitarian? John Adams in Retirement." *The New England Quarterly,* Volume 28, No. 2 (June, 1955): 216–236.

Stone, Irving. *Those Who Love: A Biographical Novel of Abigail and John Adams.* Garden City, NY: Doubleday, 1965.

Stone, Peter and Edwards, Sherman. *1776: A Musical Play.* New York: The Penguin Group, 1976.

Ten Eyck, David. *Ezra Pound's Adams Cantos.* London: Bloomsbury, 2012.

Thomas, Evan. "Founders Chic: Live from Philadelphia." *Newsweek,* July 9, 2001.

Topel, Fred. "Paul Giamatti Plays Really Weird John Adams." *Rotten Tomatoes,* August 24, 2007. Accessed June 29, 2019.

https://editorial.rottentomatoes.com/article/paul-giamatti-plays-really-weird-john-adams/.

Tully-McManus, Katherine. "House Backs Plan for John Adams Memorial." *Roll Call,* July 23, 2018, Accessed July 15, 2021. https://rollcall.com/2018/07/23/house-backs-plan-for-john-adams-memorial/.

United First Parish Church. "Visitor's Program." Last Modified 2020. Accessed October 22, 2021. https://ufpc.org/visitors-program-1.

United States Congress. *Adams National Historical Park Act of 1998.* Public Law 105–342, 105th Congress, 1998.

_____. *Authorizing the Secretary of the Interior to Accept the Conveyance of the United First Parish Church in Quincy, Massachusetts, and Authorizing the Secretary to Administer the United First Parish Church as a National Historic Site, and for other Purposes.* Public Law 96–435. 96th Congress, October 10, 1980.

_____. *National Park and Recreation Act of 1978.* Public Law 95–625, Section 312. 95th Congress, 1978.

U.S. Department of the Interior. National Park Service, *Foundation Document Overview, Adams National Historical Park, Massachusetts.* Washington, D.C., Department of the Interior, no date given.

Utterback, Betty. "George Grizzard: Living, Dying in PBS Series." *Democrat and Chronicle* (Rochester, New York). January 18, 1976.

Webster, Daniel. *A Discourse in Commemoration of the Lives and Services of John Adams and Thomas Jefferson, Delivered in Faneuil Hall, Boston, August 2, 1826.* In *Selection of Eulogies: Pronounced in the Several States in Honor of Those Illustrious Patriots and Statesmen, John Adams and Thomas Jefferson.* Kindle. Hartford, Connecticut: D.F. Robinson & Co., 1826. HardPress, 2018.

Weinstock, Matt. "The Legacy of *1776*: A Conversation with William Daniels and Lin-Manuel Miranda." *Playbill,* March, 2016.

Wendel, Thomas. "*The Character of John Adams* by Peter Shaw." *The American Historical Review,* Volume 84, No. 2 (April 1979): 541–542.

Westland, Bill. "Adams Temple and School Fund." Visitor Program Vignette. Sent to the author, November 2, 2021.

_____. "Church Building Dedication." Visitor Program Vignette. Sent to the author, November 10, 2021.

_____. "History of the Visitor's Program." Visitor Program Vignette. Sent to the author November 4, 2021.

_____. "Three Hundred and Eighty-One Years." Visitor Program Vignette. Sent to the author, October 7, 2020.

_____. "Wreath Laying." Visitor Program Vignette. Sent to the author, September 21, 2021.

White House Historical Association. "State Dining Room." *Whitehousehistory.org.* Accessed October 19, 2021. https://www.whitehousehistory.org/white-house-tour/state-dining-room.

Whitfill, Mary. "Boston Library Board Discusses Quincy Request for John Adams Collection." *The Patriot Ledger,* September 30, 2020.

_____. "'The most important woman of her generation': Abigail Adams to get downtown Quincy statue." *The Patriot Ledger,* April 14, 2022. Accessed April 18, 2022. https://www.patriotledger.com/story/news/2022/04/14/abigail-adams-get-downtown-quincy-statue-section-hancock-adams-common/7311895001/.

_____. "Quincy Takes First Step Toward Potential John Adams Presidential Library." *The Patriot Ledger,* August 14, 2020.

Wilentz, Sean. "America Made Easy: McCullough, Adams, and the Decline of Popular History." *The New Republic.* Online. July 2, 2001. Accessed June 30, 2019. https://newrepublic.com/article/62368/tnrs-founding-fathers-spectacular.

Wilson, Benji. "Laura Linney in *John Adams*: Closest to Tears When She is Smiling." *The Telegraph,* December 8, 2008.

Windsor, Daniel. "Hancock Adams Common: Quincy's Vision Four Decades in the Making." Last modified in 2021. Accessed November 22, 2021. https://www.woodardcurran.com/blog/hancock-adams-common.

Wood, Gordon S. *The Creation of the American Republic, 1776-1787.* Chapel Hill and London: Published for the Omohundro Institute of Early American History and Culture at Williamsburg,

Virginia by The University of North Carolina Press, 1969.

_____. *Friends Divided: John Adams and Thomas Jefferson.* New York: Penguin Press, 2017.

_____. "In the American Grain." *The New York Review of Books,* June 1, 2001. Accessed June 30, 2019. https://www.nybooks.com/articles/2001/06/21/in-the-american-grain/.

Young, Alfred F. *The Shoemaker and The Tea Party: Memory and the American Revolution.* Boston: Beacon Press, 1999.

Youngquist, Lorraine. "Life: For 'Those Who Love.'" *The Marysville Advocate* (Marysville, Kansas). February 19, 1976.

Zabin, Serena. *The Boston Massacre: A Family History.* Boston: Houghton Mifflin Harcourt, 2020.

Index